CW00555964

25|9

VOLKSWAGEN
BUS · CAMPER · VAN
PERFORMANCE PORTFOLIO
1968-1979

Compiled by R M Clarke

ISBN 1 85520 5025

BROOKLANDS BOOKS LTD.
P.O. BOX 146, COBHAM,
SURREY, KT11 1LG. UK

Printed in Hong Kong

ACKNOWLEDGEMENTS

Volkswagen products remain a firm favourite with motoring enthusiasts and this book replaces an earlier 100-page Brooklands Road Test volume which is now out of print. It includes a large selection of new material which we have found in our archives, and we are pleased to add it to our list of other titles covering the Volkswagen range.

As with all the anthologies in this series, we have relied on the generous help of the major motoring magazine publishers. Our sincere thanks in this case go to the managements of *Bushdriver, Car South Africa, Car and Driver, Complete Volkswagen Book, Foreign Car Guide, Motor, Motor Trend, Overlander, Popular Imported Cars, PV4, Road & Track, Road & Track Specials, Safer VW Motoring, Technicar* and the *World Car Guide*.

R.M. Clarke

The original VW commercial, which also formed the basis of the ever-popular camper, was launched as the Type 2 in 1950. The first models had an 1131cc engine with just 25bhp, which made them slow and noisy, but they were immensely practical as pick-ups and light commercials. These very early examples were distinguished by a split windscreen and a large engine cover, often described as the "barn door" type. A later upgrade to 30bhp made a welcome improvement.

The Microbus followed in 1955, initially with the 1192cc engine and no fewer than 23 separate panes of glass in the body! Like the first commercials, these models had a split windscreen at first, and this remained a characteristic right the way through to 1967. Meanwhile, 1960 had brought another significant change in the configuration, when the tailgate window was enlarged and the two rear quarter-windows disappeared. The factory camper conversion was called the Westfalia, but in the UK at least there were also well-respected aftermarket conversions from Danbury and Devon. Becoming available on the used-car market towards the middle and end of the 1960s, it is no surprise that these affordable and likeable machines swiftly became associated with the hippie movement of the times.

From 1967, a re-style retained the essential lines of the original and was readily recognisable by its single-piece windscreen. Power increases helped the models to remain abreast of the times but by the end of the 1970s there was no disguising the age of their basic design. So in 1979, the Type 2 went out of production and was replaced by a much less appealing range of models with squarer, almost characterless lines.

These VWs are characteristic of an era which has now passed, but many of them still remain in use as practical and affordable vehicles. Others are cherished by enthusiasts and see only occasional use. Their original designers would nevertheless be both pleased and amazed to see how enduring their creations have been.

James Taylor

Brooklands Books

CONTENTS

ROYAL AUTOMOBILE CLUB'S INTERNATIONAL RALLY OF GREAT BRITAIN

Peter Noad and Brian Coe, with cameras, films and flashguns, reporting from:

THE VW CARAVAN THAT 'JOINED IN' THE RAC RALLY

Vic Elford's Porsche 911 T is flagged away from the starting ramp at the Centre Airport Hotel, near London Airport, by Transport Minister Richard Marsh, at the start of the 2,500-mile 1968 RAC Rally

Timo Makinen—who fought for the lead for much of the rally with Lampinen's Saab—waits for the "Off" on the special stage at Craik, in Southern Scotland, in a very fast twin cam Ford Escort.

Ex-VW star driver Harry Kallstrom, this year driving a works Lancia Fulvia, who took over the lead at one stage but retired on the last night in thick fog.

Simo Lampinen's eventually triumphant overall Saab V4, starting down the mountainside on the Ardgarten special stage, Argyllshire. Lampinen's 1969 model Saab was fitted with four Cibie auxiliary QI spotlamps.

IN order to see as much as possible of the RAC International Rally—a 2500 mile route through most of the forest and mountain areas of England, Wales and Scotland, to be covered in four days—I borrowed a VW Clipper, fitted with **Richard Holdsworth's** caravan conversion.

This really proved to be the ideal vehicle, and enabled **Brian Coe** and myself to eat and sleep anywhere and at any time, to fit in with the rally schedule.

Our plan was to see the competitors through about three special stages each day, and then when it became too dark for taking photographs we leap-frogged ahead of the rally, snatched as much sleep as possible, and were ready to see the competitors again at daybreak the next morning.

The Richard Holdsworth conversion—which is unique in being available as a do-it-yourself kit for the remarkably low price of £125—consists of a complete kitchen unit at the side of the rear seat, a double bed, plus a third bed for two children, table, storage compartments, water tank, floor covering, etc.

A particularly cheap way of producing a caravan is to start with a delivery van, and fit Richard Holdsworth's window conversion, plus the caravan interior kit.

The cooker has two burners and a griller, and is supplied from a **Gaz** cylinder fitted in a cupboard beneath. The 6-gallon water tank is under the rear bench seat, and there is a foot operated pump supplying water to the washing bowl next to the cooker.

Two separate 3-gallon containers of drinking water are also carried behind the rear seat.

We found that it was perfectly feasible to cook and wash whilst driving along a motorway or similar road!

The navigator could walk through to the back, and we took it in turns to drive, navigate, and do the kitchen work.

Sleeping on the move was not possible because we had rather more special equipment on board, and some of this had to be transferred to the driving cab in order to make room for the bed.

For better grip on mountain roads I fitted **Pirelli** Cinturato tyres on the front and **Dunlop** SP 44 radial tyres on the back.

Although these were 15-inch tyres (on **Porsche** offset wheels), due to the lower profile of the radials, compared with the standard 14-inch cross plies, the circumference was slightly smaller—giving lower gearing (an advantage in the mountains).

In addition to the standard tool kit I carried my full toolbox, and extra spares such as bulbs, fuses, plugs, etc., also a 2-gallon can of petrol and a footpump—none of which was needed, but I'm sure they would have been if I hadn't taken them!

Also taken, but fortunately not required, were the **Pyrene** fire extinguisher, Compact temporary windscreen, and **Johnson's** first-aid kit.

A shovel, wellington boots, de-icer and tow rope were added to the equipment, plus two torches, and a chamois leather.

In addition to the normal complement of clothes, food and eating utensils, we took extra coats, umbrellas, thermos flasks (for soup) and walking shoes, so that we could survive the November weather outside the caravan.

Two alarm clocks (to wake us up) and a portable radio (to keep us awake) were essential extras.

Then there were our two **Pentax** cameras with telephoto and wide angle lenses and flashguns, and a large box of films, so you can see that the Clipper was fully loaded!

LEFT: End of the rally—Lampinen and co-driver John Daven arrive back at London Airport in their winning Saab and are interview by television newsmen.

RIGHT: Saab service wag —fully laden with spare wheels, pet tools and food to the Saab rally car and crews in first-order throughout the rally.

Brian Coe driving, the Richard Holdsworth VW Clipper caravan, in which this rally report was written, on the forest track leading to the Clocaenog special stage.

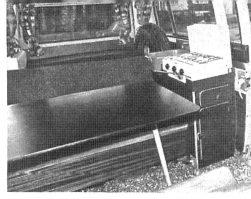

CARAVAN COMFORT (1): Black plastic covered table in position, with 3-burner cooker conveniently sited beside the bench seat, with washing bowl—supplied with pumped water—next to it.

THE rally, sponsored by the *Sun* newspaper, started near London Airport, and after seeing all the leading cars start we headed straight to Savernake Forest—stopping on the way at **Central Newbury Motors** to pump up the screen washer, which I had previously forgotten to do.

The special stage at Savernake was mainly on a smooth road, but very narrow between trees, and about five miles long. **Bjorn Waldegard**, who had previously competed in a VW 1600 TL, held the lead in his **Porsche** 911 T, and with **Tony Fall** and **Vic Elford** in works Porsches also going well we had high hopes for a Porsche win.

Rauno Aaltonen, driving a 1,584 c.c. works **Lancia** Fulvia, was overall fastest, but along with several other highly modified cars the Lancia was running in a separate class and was not eligible to win the main part of the rally.

The 1298 c.c. Lancia Fulvia driven by **Harry Kallstrom** (who drove a VW 1500 S to second place overall in 1963) was competing in the main rally, however, and took the lead on the first night after Waldegard's Porsche retired with gearbox trouble.

We went from Savernake to King Alfred's Tower, on the Wiltshire-Dorset border, and then did our first long night drive to North Wales via the Severn Bridge. The weather was fine, but I still appreciated the grip of the Cinturatos and the remarkably good light from the standard headlamps.

It may be due to the higher positioning of the lamps but, intentionally or otherwise, VW seem to have given their "commercials" better lighting than the cars.

We took the mountain road (1700ft.)

from Llanidloes to Machynlleth and went on to Dovey Forest, arriving about midnight.

The rally competitors were due to start arriving about 9 a.m. but when we awoke there were hordes of spectators and no signs of rally organisation. It transpired that the stage had been deleted, so we rapidly headed the VW northwards to Coed-y-Brennin, two stages further along the route.

Coed-y-Brennin provided great drama when a marshal overturned his Beetle.

He was supposed to be checking that the course was clear—but seemed to be trying for fastest time of the day!—and this happened just seconds before **Simo Lampinen** arrived in his **Saab**.

Spectators lifted the Beetle out of the trees and the marshal drove on with flattened roof and buckled wheels, and crossed the finish line at the same time as the Saab!

Källström's Lancia was delayed by electrical trouble and it now looked as though Lampinen in the Saab was fighting for the lead with **Timo Makinen**, in a much lighter and higher powered **Ford Escort Twin Cam**.

Porsche hopes were not so good with only Elford's car still running —and that had a damaged sump guard and suspension.

Everyone was impressed by the East German **Wartburgs** — all four coming through on schedule and going surprisingly quickly for 992 c.c. two-strokes.

Our next stage was Clocaenog, in

● Continued on next page

CARAVAN COMFORT (2): Fair-sized wardrobe behind the front passenger's seat and, behind the driver's seat, a food storage compartment covered with cushions as an extra seat.

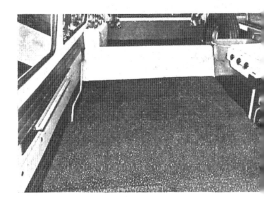

CARAVAN COMFORT (3): Double bed is formed by rearranging the seat cushions on a base formed by the table and wooden flap opening from the lid of the food compartment.

NON-STANDARD: For extra grip on the Welsh and Scottish mountain roads Peter Noad fitted Dunlop SP 44 radials on the rear wheels of the caravan, and Pirelli Cinturatos on the front wheels

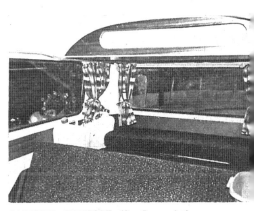

CARAVAN COMFORT (4): Rear platform above the engine can be used as the base for an extra bed for two children, or for one not-too-tall adult—if the water containers and spare wheel are moved.

● **Continued from previous page**

Denbighshire, another typical loose-surfaced forest route.

The Minis, on their tiny wheels, thumped, crashed and scraped along, in contrast to the **Rover** 3500 and **BMW** 2002 which gave their occupants a completely smooth ride.

From Clocaenog in Wales, to Ardgarten in Scotland (west of Loch Lomond) was our longest night drive—about 300 miles.

The VW caravan maintained a fairly steady 70 mph on the M6 motorway, dropping to 60 or even 55 on some of the steeper gradients, and we actually prepared a meal on route.

Including the stop for eating this trip took only eight hours.

On this second night we were a little quicker at getting the bed made up—it has to be supported on the table and an extra piece of wood, and does not leave much floor area.

We ran out of washing water and found refilling the tank a rather slow job, but I understand from Richard Holdsworth that this will be modified for future conversions.

The Ardgarten stage was used twice on the rally and had a steep climb and descent, with long drops off the edge in places.

One of the Wartburgs appeared to have been taken out of the rally and delegated to act as service car, but the leading Wartburg was still well up on time and going strongly, driven by **Gunther Ruttinger**.

Already a high proportion of the 112 cars that started were missing, and it seemed that a lot of the remaining crews were just plodding on slowly to finish and not trying hard at all.

The Lancias were still trying very hard, but needed numerous repairs.

Devilla, a 3-mile section near Dunfermline, was the last test before the competitors had their first rest overnight at Edinburgh, and it was hard to say which looked the more tired—the cars or the drivers.

We took our caravan over the high Forth Bridge—the radial tyres and special wheels certainly made it much safer in cross winds—and motored south to camp at Cardrona Forest, which was the third stage, the following morning.

I heard that on Ingliston racing circuit the Porsche had made fastest time, but second fastest was the incredible Saab of Simo Lampinen.

I would expect the Saabs to do well in mud or snow or rough going, but am amazed that enough power can be extracted from the V4 engine to keep up with the Escort Twin Cams on tarmac.

Timo Makinen's Escort (not a works car, but entered by Ford dealers **Clarke and Simpson Ltd.**) had broken its steering column mounting and its rear axle, and no doubt Saab supporters were hoping that it would not finish!

Both Lampinen and **Carl Orrenius**, in the second works Saab, were holding a lead over Elford's Porsche and Kallstrom's Lancia.

Leapfrogging ahead again we saw the leaders on the very bleak moorland section at Craik, then continued to Kielder, just over the border in Northumberland.

This was one of the longest stages —nearly 12 miles—and the part we saw was a narrow rocky track built up on a ridge.

The Porsche was running very late, and there was no sign of the Escort.

From Kielder we motored down the A1 all the way to Sherwood Forest. The radio announced fog warnings and it was certainly getting quite thick.

The rally cars had another 18 stages to do in Northumberland and Yorkshire that night, and the fog put an end to many of the remaining competitors, including the Porsche and all the Lancias.

Drivers who had stopped for lengthy service and repairs, expecting to regain time on the modest 30 mph average between special stages, couldn't make it because of the fog.

The Saabs, which required very little service apart from refuelling—carried out from cans in the heavily laden Saab station wagon service cars, rather than relying on garages—remained on schedule, and could even afford to ease up.

Lampinen had a lead of six minutes over team mate Orrenius, who was nearly 50 minutes ahead of the third place Ford Escort Twin Cam driven by **Jim Bullough**.

And that was how they finished—the remaining tests, including the speed events at Silverstone and Mallory Park, could hardly have affected the overall position.

Fourth was a Mini Cooper S, fifth another Escort Twin Cam, sixth a **Peugeot** 204, and seventh the remaining Wartburg —which must have enhanced the East German firm's reputation in Britain.

Altogether there were 35 finishers.

It really was a great pity that no VWs took part—I am sure that this year, with so many cars suffering mechanical failures, a VW could have been extremely well placed.

Prestigewise it would have been a very welcome sales boost.

After washing the mud off our VW caravan I returned it to Richard Holdsworth with an extra 1400 miles on the clock—it had averaged about 23 mpg and used half a pint of oil.

We couldn't have wished for a more suitable vehicle.

Gunther Ruttinger, in one of the surprising quick works entered East German Wartburgs-992 cc two-stroke engine, with front-wheel-driv —cornering at Cardrona Forest, near Peeble Scotland. Ruttinger finished seventh overal

Epic Accessories, suppliers of the Herme aerofoil, the "Variwipe" and other useful extr previously described in *Safer Motoring*, sponsore this Singer Chamois driven by Richard Iliff

Carl Orrenius, in the second place Saab, sta close to the rocks at Coed-y-Brennin, Nor Wales. This works Saab is a 1969 model wi rectangular headlamps and a row of four Bos spot and fog lamps.

CRASHED BEETLE, or what can happen whe a marshal tries to emulate the rally competitor The Beetle overturned and landed in among th trees as the official went a shade too quick when checking that the course was clear.

ALL NEW THIS YEAR INSIDE AND OUT!

Rounded corners, wraparound windshield, "picture windows" and sliding side door contribute to station wagon's new look.

1968 VW STATION WAGON

Interior features include safety-padded dashboard, added foot and leg-room in front

■ While safety and smog occupy much of the 1968 automotive head-line news, appearance, comfort, convenience, handling, ride and utility are additional nouns you can use to describe the new Volkswagen "boxes," the beetle's harder working cousin.

Taking the obvious first, let's discuss the body. While VW's Type 2 vehicles, known to the public as station wagons and trucks, have never been glamour wagons, you'll have to decide for yourself this year if the term applies! Their all-new, longer, sleek bodies start with a 27% larger, one piece, wrap-

New front axle and double-jointed rear axles give all new trucks passenger car road-holding ability. Payload is 2,205 pounds.

Trucks and wagons are higher, wider and longer this year.

Warranty period is now 24 months or 24,000 miles

1968 VOLKSWAGEN SUGGESTED RETAIL PRICES

PASSENGER CARS	East	West	Hawaii
De Luxe Sedan	$1,695	$1,773	$1,946
De Luxe Sunroof Sedan	1,785	1,863	2,036
Karmann Ghia Convertible	2,445	2,542	2,755
Karmann Ghia Coupe	2,250	2,347	2,560
VW Convertible	2,095	2,173	2,346
Fastback Sedan	2,175	2,275	2,453
Fastback Sedan with Sunroof	2,295	2,395	2,573
Squareback Sedan	2,345	2,445	2,623
Squareback Sedan with Sunroof	2,465	2,565	2,743
STATION WAGONS			
Station Wagon 7-Seater	2,495	2,612	2,833
Station Wagon 9-Seater	2,517	2,634	2,855
Kombi with Center & Rear Bench	2,265	2,382	2,588
Kombi with Center Bench only	2,221	2,338	2,544
Kombi with Rear Bench only	2,211	2,328	2,534
Basic Campmobile	2,110	2,227	2,433
TRUCKS			
Panel Truck, Double Door Right	2,295	2,395	2,597
Panel Truck, Double Door Both Sides	2,395	2,495	2,697
Pick-Up Truck	2,295	2,395	2,597
Pick-Up Truck w. Tarpaulin	2,395	2,495	2,697
Double Cab Pick-Up Truck	2,385	2,495	2,697
Dbl. Cab Pick-Up Truck w. Tarpaulin	2,455	2,565	2,767

Optional Equip. for Cars	All U.S.
Two Tone Paint, KG	$19.70
Leatherette Upholstery, VW & 1600 Series	30.00
Opening Rear Side Windows, VW	24.00
White Wall Tires—All	29.50

Optional Equipment for Station Wagons & Trucks

Lockable Comp. Lids Both Sides	$17.40
White Wall Tires	29.50
Vent Windows in Driver's Compartment	15.00
3rd Vent Window in Passenger Comp.	11.00
Camping Equipment	$ 655.00
Camping Equipment w. Pop-Up Roof	935.00
Camping Equipment w. Pop-Up Roof & Tent	1,075.00

NB—All prices are Port of Entry, excluding inland transportation and make-ready charges.

round, double thickness interlayer windshield some 2 inches higher and 9 inches wider. It is wiped by a two-speed wiper having longer blades powered by a stronger motor.

Three long large windows on each side replace the many small windows we all know, which when combined with the five inch increase in length, produce a long, modern appearance.

On the right, a 41.7 inch wide sliding door replaces the familiar double doors. The door slides in three tracks, top, bottom and middle. Turn the handle and the back of the door pops outward; a touch of the handle more and the door slides back easily into a locked-open position. A light push, and the door closes and locks, and an additional turn of the handle pulls the back of the door in flush and secures it tightly shut. The door is 48.2 inches high, plenty big for the largest goods a home owner is likely to want to move. The door can be locked on the inside by a button or outside by key.

There is a vent wing window in the sliding door and another in the left rear window; a third vent wing is optional opposite the sliding door.

Double-jointed rear axles, more rear suspension links, softer springing are new.

The higher, stronger, larger, one piece bumpers wrap around to the sides, the ends of the front bumper being flattened and rubber-covered to form steps to enter the front doors. The doors are about 2½ inches wider and contain larger, roll-down windows. Stationary glass fills out in front of the roll-down windows, but vent wings are optionally available.

Just below the windshield is a large horizontal air intake grille for the ventilation system. The glass covers for the headlights have been dropped providing better light output and the parking lights have been moved into the front turn signal housings via dual filament bulbs. The turn signals are mounted below the headlights and wrap around for visability from the sides. Amber reflectors are attached to the sides of the body just below the front doors, red reflectors at the rear. Two large outside mirrors are mounted on the doors to provide excellent driver visibility. For

A Universal joint at end of each rear half-axle allows rear wheels to move up and down with a minimum of camber change

1968 VW STATION WAGON

safety, they fold backward or forward upon impact. Door hinges are hidden in the jams to smooth the outside skin and reduce maintenance. The air intakes for the engine have been moved high on the sides of the body in the form of scoops, where they will draw in less dust. All of the models come with white roofs and a variety of body colors, except black. While the vehicles are fractionally wider and higher, they are up to 5 inches longer. So that everyone will still recognize the make of vehicle, the circled VW insignia remains at the front.

The inside of the vehicle now has what can be called decor. While the law specified a certain amount of padding for each passenger, it wasn't just pasted on. Thorough planning went into the integration of the new vinyl upholstery and the padding to produce a beautiful modern interior. The entire dashboard is padded, and the padding is shaped into a thick hood across the entire width of the dashboard; the instruments are also recessed to prevent windshield reflection. There's also padding on the sun visors, all six armrests and ashtrays, and the partitions behind the front seats and upper edges of center seat. The rest of the inside is covered with tasteful vinyl upholstery and headlining, and rubber floor mats.

The dashboard is all new. Three round dials face the driver. The left contains a new electric gas gauge in the top half, and warning lights for generator, oil pressure, high beams, parking lights and turn signals occupy the lower half. The speedometer is centered and the right dial is a dummy for installation of a clock.

All dashboard knobs are large, flat, rubber-covered and identified with symbols. They are arranged below the dials for convenience of the driver. To the right of the dials are four knobbed levers for control of heater and ventilation systems. Centered on the dash is a dummy for the radio. Below it is a padded, draw-type ashtray with a flipper that pops up to protect the dashboard from smoke. Below the ashtray is a padded pull-twist type handbrake handle. It attaches to the same type long handbrake lever behind the dash to provide the usual excellent positive handbrake action. On the right is a conventional glove compartment with padded, top-hinged door. An over-center hinge action holds the door open for access. Above the door is a padded "chicken" handle.

The two-spoke steering wheel is now deep-dished and the steering column is angled downward toward the driver more than previously. The ignition key lock is mounted in the steering column where it is out of the way for safety, and the lock is angled upward for convenience. Only one key is needed for ignition and doors. The dimmer switch is the turn signal lever, actuated by pulling it upwards. The fuse box under the dash now has a total of ten fuses to spread the circuits out, and the cover is marked with sym-

SAFETY FEATURES FOR 1968

* Deep dish steering wheel

* Improved headlights

* Larger windshield, double thickness interlayer

* Padded dashboard, visors, armrests, seat tops and handbrake

* Sliding side door

* Plastic encased rearview mirror

* Two large outside mirrors that fold upon impact

* Defogging system

* Soft, flat, rubber covered knobs on dash, vent windows, window winders

* Angled ignition key

* Hooded dashboard with recesses dials

* Brake warning light

* Dual brake system (as in 1967)

* Front seat backrest locks

* Seat belts for each seat; anchor points for lap/shoulder belts for

those seats equipped with lap belts on outboard seats

* Improved wiper system
* Larger windshield washer reservoir

* Non reflecting interior surfaces

* Eight ply rating tires on trucks

* Dashboard knobs labeled

* Shift pattern decal on windshield

* Rotating vent wing locks for theft protection

* Integrated back-up lights (as in 1967)

* Flattened outer door handles

* Wraparound front turn signal/parking light

* Front and rear bumpers deeply wrapped around

* Front and rear side reflectors

* Non-override inside door handles

* Grab handles for rear seat passengers

LEFT AND ABOVE: VW's all-new panel truck features more driver room, greatly improved handling characteristics plus sliding side door. Gas tank hold 16 gallons

bols to identify each one.

Doors are neatly upholstered in leatherette, the armrests padded, and window winder and vent wing knobs, large, flat and rubber-covered. The inside door handles are the small, flush, pull type used in the sedans, while a plastic door pull permits closing. At the rear of the window sill of each door is a plunger for locking the door from the inside. Doors can be locked from the outside with or without a key. The vent wing catch is an unusual one with a knob that must be rotated forward before the whole catch can be pushed forward to open the window. This type lock adds an extra measure of theftproofing. On the wagons, the armrest is formed on top of a box section channel running the width of the door and used to conduct fresh air from under the dashboard to the outlets behind the front seat partitions.

There are two model station wagons available, named appropriately enough, from their chief distinctions, their seating arrangements. The nine-seater has a separate driver's seat and double passenger seat in front, a three passenger center seat and a three passenger rear seat. With this configuration, the driver's seat slides separately into 8 different positions through five inches of travel, front to rear, via a lever at the front of the seat, and the backrest adjusts by turning a wheel next to the lever. The passenger seat adjusts to two positions by moving the whole seat into one of two mounting notches on the seat bottom section. The backrests of both seats hook firmly to the partition behind them for safety. The right hand seat on the center bench has a folding backrest that locks in the upright position for safety. The release is incorporated into the backrest high up on the side.

In the seven-seater, the driver's seat and front passenger's seat are separated by a wide aisle, and the center bench seats two passengers. As noted in VW advertising, this arrangement makes it convenient to swat the children seated in the rear without having to stop the car!

In either model, the center and rear seats can b quickly unbolted for removal to carry 177 cubic feet of almost anything. There are grab handles on the back of the partition for the front passenger seat and behind the center seat.

The all new heating and ventilating systems are an interesting surprise, and both seem to perform more than adequately. There are two defroster slots toward the center of the windshield, two heater vents under the dash, another in the back of the small step between the front seats and two more under the rearmost seat. Two red knobbed levers on the dash control the heat, individually on the left and right sides. Depressing one or both releases heat from the defrosters. Some of this heat can be tapped for the underdash vents by throwing the lever near the vents upward. More of the heat can be taken off for the vent in front of the center seat by a pull knob under the front of the driver's seat where the twist type heater control used to be. The two vents under the rear seat bench are controlled by levers on the vents themselves. The whole system is fast and easy to use, provides more heat, and an even distribution, with individual control front to back and left to right. At highway speed, on a cool day, it pushed enough heat to the

SPECIFICATION COMPARISON

BODY CHASSIS	1968	1967
Overall Length, Inches	174.0	168.5-169.3*
Overall Width, Inches	69.5	68.9- 70.9*
Overall Height, Inches	76.4-77.0*	75.2- 75.8*
Front Overhang, Inches	42.3	39.8
Rear Overhang, Inches	37.2	34.3- 35.0*
Turning Circle, Feet, Approx.	40	39
Wheelbase, Inches	94.5	94.5
Front Track, Inches	54.5	54.1
Rear Track, Inches	56.1	53.5
Ground Clearance, Inches	7.3	7.9
Interior Capacity, Cu. Ft.	176.6	169.5
Area Behind Front Seat, Inches		
Length	110.2	106.3
Width	61.8	61.8
Height	55.1	53.1
Gas Tank Capacity, Gallons	15.8	10.6

WEIGHTS		
Station Wagon, 7-9 Seater		
Curb	2723	2502
Payload	1962	2062
GVW	4685	4564
Kombi, w/o center seat		
Curb	2557	2448
Payload	2238	2116
GVW	4795	4564
Panel Truck		
Curb	2425	2359
Payload	2370	2205
GVW	4795	4564
Pickup Truck		
Curb	2425	2392
Payload	2370	2172
GVW	4795	4564

Wheels & Tires		
Wheels	5 JK x 14	5 JK x 14
Tires (Tubeless)	7.00 x 14	7.00 x 14
	Wagons 6PR; Trucks 8PR	6PR
Tire Pressure		
Front	28	28
Rear ¾ Load	36	33
Rear Full Load	41	40
High Speed Driving	add 3psi,fr.&rr.	N.A.

Engine		
Displacement, cc	1584	1493
Displacement, Cu. In.	96.6	91.1
Horsepower	57 @ 4400rpm	53 @ 4200rpm
Torque, Ft. Lbs.	81.7 @ 3000rpm	78.1 @ 2600rpm
Bore, Inches	3.36	3.27
Stroke, Inches	2.72	2.72
Compression Ratio	7.7:1	7.5:1
Carburetor	30 PICT-1	30 PICT-2
Gas Mileage, Approx.	23mpg	23mpg
Max. Speed, mph	65	65
Valve Gap, Int. & Ex., Cold	.004"	.004"
Initial Ignition Timing	0 degrees (TDC)	10 BTDC
Idle RPM	850 ± 50	—

Transmission		
Gear Ratios		
1st	3.80	3.80
2nd	2.06	2.06
3rd	1.26	1.26
4th	.82	.82
Rear Axle	5.375	4.375
Reduction	—	1.26
Overall Gear Ratio, 4th gear	4.407	4.519
Reverse	3.61	3.88

Electrical System		
Voltage	12	12
Battery, AH	45	45
Generator, Watts (low cut in)	360	360

* Varies according to model

defroster vents to make it impossible to hold a hand on the vent! The larger engine and better insulation is responsible.

The ventilation system has two slots under the windshield for defogging, two air-conditioner-type rotating louvered outlets on the extreme ends of the dashboards and two more on the backs of the front seat partitions. Depressing one or both of the blue-knobbed levers on the dash turns it on left to right, and individual levers on the four round outlets permit turning each outlet off by itself.

The windshield washer, activated by a push of the button in the center of the wiper knob has a capped plastic container mounted in the kick panel in front of the front seat passenger. Pulling the black cap off permits access to the 1½ quart container. A hose with a tire valve on it allows it to be pressurized easily.

Front and rear dome lights are mounted in the center of the headlining; the rear light is controlled from the dashboard, the front by a switch on the light itself.

The large inside rear view mirror and its stalk are covered in plastic for safety and provides excellent visibility when combined with the two generous outside mirrors. The visors swivel to the side or clip into their forward position.

The plastic brake fluid reservoir is mounted under the left side of the dashboard for ready accessibility, and is transluscent for checking the fluid level at a glance. It leads to dual circuit brakes designed to leave one circuit operating at all times if one of the two circuits fails. A brake warning light on the dash lights when the brake pedal is depressed if either front or rear wheel circuit should leak. Depressing the light bulb turns the bulb on as a check on the bulb and the electric circuit. The light is activated by a shuttle piston in a separate cylinder inside the housing for the brake master cylinder. The front hydraulic brake circuit pressurizes one side of the double headed piston, the rear the other ide. When the system is pressurized by stepping on the brake pedal, each of the opposing pistons is pressed upon equally and the piston doesn't move. A leak in either circuit reduces the pressure on one side forcing the piston to move; this in turn makes an electric contact in the cylinder, lighting the warning light. Building the cylinder and its hydraulic connections into the master brake cylinder housing minimizes the chance of leaks at the connections.

There's one seat belt for each seat. The two front outboard seats will have combination lap/shoulder belts, while all the other seats have lap belts. The combination belts will have retractors to keep the belts off the floor and handy, while all the belts are of the quick release type.

In the wagons and trucks with two separated front seats, the spare tire is mounted upright in a well in the left side of the luggage compartment behind the rearmost seat, and covered with a semi-rigid plastic hood that snaps to the floor; in the three-passenger seat models, the spare is under the front seat.

These vehicles now have the 1600 engine used in the Squareback and Fastback, but with the upright superstructure for the fan. Bore and stroke are 3.36 and 2.72 inches (1584cc capacity), raising the horsepower to 57 at 4400 rpm and torque to 81.7 ft. lbs. at 3000 rpm. The engine governor has been dropped and there's a new carburetor (Solex 30 PICT-2) which has a larger float bowl, different jets and a larger oil bath air cleaner. However, top speed remains at 65 mph and acceleration is substantially the same because of the heavier curb weight and heavier payload of the vehicle, and slightly slower turning engine. Compression ratio is raised to 7.7:1 but regular fuel is still used and delivers 23 miles per gallon.

The positive crankcase ventilation system is continued while the exhaust emission control system consists of a modified carburetor designed to more accurately deliver the fuel, a distributor with modified advance curve and 0 degree (Top Dead Center) initial timing, and a carburetor dashpot. The dashpot is vacuum controlled from the intake manifold and holds the throttle cracked lightly open during conditions of high vacuum such as deceleration, to provide enough fuel at all times for a more completely burned mixture. The 0 degree timing and an idle speed of 850 rpm control emission at idle. (The .004" valve gap still applies, as do all other tune-up specifications.)

The carburetor preheater is an interesting development. The underslung oil bath air cleaner has one air intake horn. Last year's weight loaded air valve is replaced by a valve controlled by cable running to the engine's thermostat. When the engine's cold, the thermostat closes the valve and all carburetor air comes via a large flexible hose from the area of the two right hand cylinders. This produces a warm air supply to better vaporize the fuel during warmup, regardless of engine speed. When the engine warms up, the valve opens, letting cooler engine compartment air into the carb. The whole system keeps the carburetor air temperature more in tune with engine temperature for smoother performance when the engine's cold.

The gas tank capacity has been increased to 15.8 gallons to provide a cruising range of more than 300 miles.

The sleeper for '68 is the new suspension and transmission. The four transmission ratios remain the same, but the reduction gears in the wheel housings have been dropped and this ratio incorporated into the ring and pinion ratio, which is now 5.375:1; this new ratio does not completely make up for the dropped reduction gear ratio however, and the engine now turns over slightly slower for a given road speed. Dropping the reduction gear housings from the wheels increases the sprung/unsprung weight ratio to improve the ride and better hold the wheels on the ground. The transmission is now a strongly ribbed three-piece job with a separable bell housing, one oil drain plug, and an oil capacity of 7.4 pints. The ring and pinion gearing is now hypoid with 10mm offset for quieter running and the differential housing is carried in tapered roller bearings.

Together with these changes is a double jointed rear axle having constant velocity universal joints at each end of each axle, each joint being capable of absorbing up to one inch of axial play. In addition to the usual trailing arms which absorb acceleration and deceleration thrust, there are now diagonal trailing links which absorb side thrust (the axle tubes have been dropped and the rear wheel bearings have self contained lubrication). The diagonal links are bracketed onto the torsion bar housings on each side of the forward transmission mount and swivel on rubber-bushed lateral axes. They then curve outward and attach to the rear axle at the wheels. The rear wheel track is also increased about 2½ inches.

The importance of this is the nega-

tive rear wheel camber achieved regardless of vehicle loading or body lean, and the minimized track, toe-in and camber changes during the full range of vehicle loading and body lean.

At the front, kingpins are replaced by ball joints which extend the lubrication period to 6,000 miles and reduce the number of grease nipples to four on the axle tubes and one for the swing lever shaft. The trailing arms have been lengthened about an inch, having the effect of softening the front torsion bars. The front stabilizer is continued and the **front track** increased .4 inch. The **steering shaft** now has the flexible coupling **used** in the sedans, and the steering ratio has been speeded up slightly to 14.7:1.

The 6 ply rating tires are continued for the wagons, while the trucks get 8 PR shoes; both vehicles have slightly increased tire pressures.

The final result of these suspension changes is passenger car like ride and handling that has to be tried to be believed. The road for this vehicle has been almost miraculously smoothed and even hard bumps are easily taken at speed. The handling properties are neutral up to all practical cornering speeds and body lean negligible. Heavy side winds can still be felt, but the resulting vehicle movements are largely self correcting.

The new heavier engine is no longer canti-lever mounted to the transmission. It now has a "crossmember type" two point mount of its own at the very rear, similar to that used in the Fastback and Squareback. A new single mount at the front of the transmission completes the three-point engine/transmission mounting system, designed to provide better engine support, torque resistance and vibration absorption.

With only minor changes, the maintenance service for these vehicles remains substantially the same. The maintenance interval stays at 6,000 miles, and the oil change at 3,000; the lubrication period has been increased from 3,000 to 6,000 miles. There is still a free initial maintenance service, now given at 600 miles instead of 300.

The warranty period for all 1968 Volkswagen vehicles has been increased from 6/6 plus goodwill policy, to 24 months or 24,000 miles whichever comes first.

All in all, the VW "boxes" have been considerably improved in all the important areas. We leave it to you to decide if beautiful is the word to describe them, but they have got to be driven to be believed.

Volkswagen Dormobile

with elevating roof

THE VW Microbus was replaced last autumn by the Clipper and Kombi, vehicles of similar shape but a few inches longer. Revised front-end styling includes a one-piece windscreen; rearwards of the cab the side door now slides backwards (previously it opened outwards in halves); there is now walk-through from the cab to the interior; the engine has been increased in capacity to 1,584 c.c.; and there is trailing arm rear suspension.

This is the basis of the Martin Walter Dormobile conversion which we tested in elevating roof form,—with four berths and an optional extra fifth for a child. Without an elevating roof the price drops by £85 and there are, of course, no roof bunks.

The vehicle was notable for being light to drive, for having a simple and neat arrangement for sleeping, ingenious "kitchen" location and good living space for a van of this size.

On the road

Driver and passenger have comfortable individual seats with a small range of fore-and-aft movement and an even smaller range of adjustment for the back-rest angle; in general the comfort and furnishing of the cab are up to the standard of many private cars.

The foot controls are light, especially the clutch, and the centrally placed pull-out handbrake is light and powerful; the large, near-horizontal steering wheel is comfortable to use; the stalk below it controls winkers, flashers and headlamps. The heating was poor but we later tried a similar vehicle and from that we had plenty of warmth.

The VW Dormobile is reasonably quick off the mark and could probably be cruised at its top speed of around 65 m.p.h. In practice we found it preferable to keep below 60 (or 40 m.p.h. in third) because at these points a resonant beat came in which proved slightly annoying to those in the cab and uncomfortable for passengers in the rear. There is, in fact, much more noise in the back of the van than the driver thinks. The stowed cooker was a source of rattle but Martin Walter state that this is being rectified.

We made some fairly long journeys on wet roads and found the VW stable and safe, except in strong cross-winds. Rough roads are taken in a restrained float and pitch is damped out quickly.

All round vision from the driver's seat is good and even without the external rear-view mirrors there are no notable blind spots.

The rear-mounted engine is reached through a low-mounted flap and is thus not easy to work on; even checking the dipstick is awkward in poor light.

Seating and sleeping

Normally there are four forward-facing seats —two in the cab and two on the bench seat at the rear of the living space. The Dormobile we tried had the optional extra and removable rearward-facing single seat located to the rear of the gap between the front ones.

With the roof raised to give over 8ft. of headroom two stretcher bunks are quickly erected from their stowed positions at the sides of the roof and the "ground floor" double bed is formed in two easy movements by pulling a loop at the rear of the bench seat which raises it and the back rest into the horizontal position from where they are slid easily to the offside of the van.

In usual Martin Walter fashion, the cushion at the forward end is raised slightly to act as a low pillow. The table, aided by additional screw-in legs, supports the overhanging section of the double bed. The most difficult bunk to erect is the optional child's stretcher berth over the driver's compartment where the space is somewhat confined for manoeuvring it into position on its supports.

Storage

There is adequate drawer and cupboard space for crockery and pots and pans in the region of the sink although the largest of the cupboards is occupied by three 3-gal. water containers. Behind the front passenger's seat there is a small hanging wardrobe tall enough to take a suit on a hanger, and there is space for bedding and other bulky objects beneath the bench seat in the body of van and beneath the permanently positioned rear portion of the mattress. Space beneath the bench seat would normally be the housing for the optional extra awning when not in use. The gas bottle takes up no interior space being carried in the nearside of the engine compartment.

Living in it

The gas stove (two burners and grill) folds away between the back of the front passenger seat and the wardrobe; when erected it causes no obstruction. The cook would normally sit on the driver's seat to work; she could stand outside with the passenger's door open but would then find the gas taps difficult to reach.

Four people can sit down comfortably to eat at the table making use of the two steel-framed folding chairs supplied. Alternatively the optional extra rearward facing seat can be used. On each side of the sink (fed by a foot pump) there is plenty of Melamine covered space for laying out dishes.

We found the main double berth quick to erect and comfortable to use but in mid winter the interior of the van suffered considerable heat loss with the elevating roof raised; to prevent a quick drop in temperature it was best to sleep with the roof down with only two people in the van. The optional extra Solarsol gas heater was very effective and raised the interior temperature quickly.

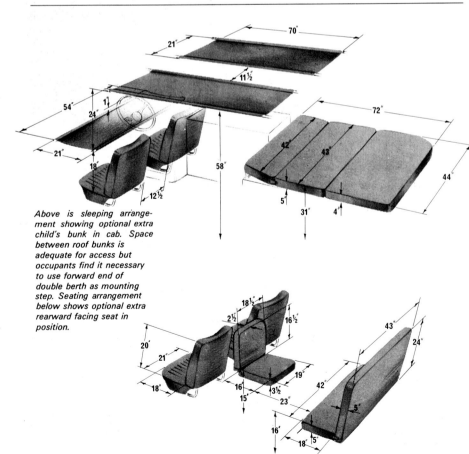

Above is sleeping arrangement showing optional extra child's bunk in cab. Space between roof bunks is adequate for access but occupants find it necessary to use forward end of double berth as mounting step. Seating arrangement below shows optional extra rearward facing seat in position.

New VW Kombi has one-piece windscreen and easy-action slide-back side door. Side sun awning is offered at £14. 2s. Interior (below) provides reasonable day-time space; table is easily removable and can be slid forwards and backwards (in rearward position it provides support, with the aid of screw-in legs, for forward end of double bunk). Folding chairs are steel framed and are supplied as standard. On left of picture is wardrobe; ice-box is in cabinet beside bench seat.

Easy to use conversion on new VW 1584 c.c. Kombi. Four berths (two in elevating roof); optional fifth bunk for child. Costs £1,213. 10s. (£1,255. 6s. 5d. as tested). Made by Martin Walter Ltd., Dormobile Works, Folkestone, Kent.
Length of test — 400 miles.

Below: Off-side stretcher bunk ready for use at base of elevating roof. Seating and sleeping diagrams on facing page show the relative positions of the berths. In daytime the roof bunks fold away completely.

Top: Cooker can be folded out when front passenger's seat is tipped forward; cook is sitting on driver's seat. Splash/draught guard (not shown) fits round three sides of cooker. Above: Upward-opening rear gives access to store space beneath rear of double-bed mattress; optional occasional seat can be seen stowed on left. Hatch above bumper (just visible) gives access to engine and to storage for 6 lb. gas cylinder.

Performance

(Load equivalent to driver and two passengers).

Comfortable cruising speed:
55-60 m.p.h.
Top speed (banked circuit):
65·2 m.p.h.
Acceleration, 0-50 through gears:
23·0 sec.
Standing ¼ mile: 26·5 sec.
30-50 in top: 22·0 sec.
Hill starting: 1 in 3 gradient. Handbrake held, restart accomplished with clutch slip. (**Note:** Facing forward on 1 in 3 down grade, van slid down with back-wheels locked). **Fuel consumption on tour:** 21·4 m.p.g. (2-star petrol). **Speedometer:** At 60 m.p.h., 1% fast; at 30 m.p.h. 6% fast. Mileage recorder 2% slow.

Specification

Length: 14 ft. 6 in. **Width:** 5 ft. 9 in.
Height: 6 ft. 9 in.
Ground clearance: 7¼ in.
Turning circle: 40 ft.
Fuel capacity 13·0 gal.
Engine: 1584 cc, air-cooled flat four; 57 b.h.p. (gross).
Transmission: Four speed (all synchromesh).
Tyres: 7·00 × 14
Extras offered: Roof rack*: £5. 5s. Child's Bunk*: £9. 18s. Occasional seat*: £9. 10s. Solarsol gas heater*: £10. 0s. 9d. Gas cylinder (6 lb.), tap and regulator*: £7. 2s. 8d. Also embellishments for exterior, crockery, cutlery and many other items.
*Fitted to test van.

VOLKSWAGEN CAMPMOBILE

◆ Volkswagen's Campmobile for 1968 rates as one of the world's fastest quick-change artists—mountain cabin, hunting lodge, fishing camp, seaside cottage or practically any type of resort a vacationing or week-ending family could want.

About all it takes to work the Campmobile's own sort of magic is a map and the time needed for wander-lusters to drive to their favorite spots. Once at a camp site—either a state or national park or secluded hideaway "miles from nowhere"—the Campmobile settles down to carefree use.

By turns it is a dressing room, kitchen, dinette and living room and then switches into sleeping quarters at night.

Basis for the 1968 Campmobile is VW's bus-type station wagon which teams attractive new looks this year with a number of major mechanical improvements. They all contribute to easier handling, sedan-like road-

CONTINUED ON PAGE 132

The new Campmobile priced from $2,765. to $3,185. The $3,045 mo[del] shown includes "Pop top" that provides roof top sleeping accommo[da]tion for a child and includes built-in luggage area in the rear of eleva[ted] section. Included also is icebox.

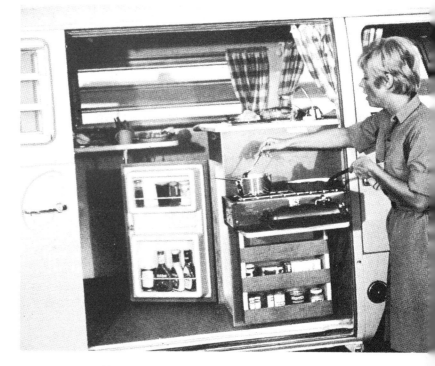

LEFT: Club Car Comfort — Center "picture windows" are louvered and screened on the inside for rain-proof and insect-free ventilation. All windows are equipped with curtains for full night-time privacy when the inside changes into a bedroom. Center compartment seats four with two more people up front.

BELOW: Free-standing tent and other features are included in $3,185 model. Tent adds a separate and extra room alongside Campmobile. It can be left behind as vacationers drive off from their camp site for a day of sightseeing to the nearest town.

RIGHT: In the city after a camping or vacation jaunt. It serves as a six-passenger station wagon. Side door slides to the rear as it opens. Note storage lockers alongside door and under rear seat.

LEFT: Campmobile even includes a kitchen sink—recessed into the top of the icebox cabinet which also houses a 4½ gal. water supply. The cover for a three-shelf pantry built onto the side of the icebox cabinet lifts up to form a utility work surface, used in the picture LEFT to hold optional portable gas stove.

VW SPORTSMOBILE

Accessory penthouse gives 7-foot headroom inside the Sportsmobile when extended (left), but folds almost completely out of sight for road use. The accessory luggage carrier is designed for carrying the tent.

Tent sold as an option is 10-feet square, may be backed up against camper for water-proofing passage between them or used separately.

Sleeping arrangements permit children to be stashed away early and in privacy when curtain is lowered. Two more children can be slept in the driver's compartment or the upper bunk, with an extension, could be used for adults.

Factory or kit conversion sleeps six for less cost than many travel trailers.

We know from surveys and correspondence that hundreds of WCG readers own VW panels, Kombis and wagons that have been converted in varying degrees of completeness and ingenuity to campers. We also know that a majority of these conversions have been designed and fabricated from scratch, in many instances, by the owners themselves.

There's no denying the satisfaction to be derived from doing all your own work but handicraft, particularly as complex as this, is not everyone's cup of tea. For example, only a relative few boating enthusiasts start with a kit or even a bare boat. They buy their craft as complete as budget will allow and as time and pocketbook permits, accessories are added that are specifically designed for that installation.

With this thought in mind, we plan to present from time to time on these

Tables, seats and the combined stove-refrigerator may be readily removed for use on the campsite, or between trips these may be taken out to clear a cargo area.

When in traveling position, equipment is well located and there is an unusual amount of storage space available. No metal shows in the interior after a factory conversion.

pages outstanding camper conversions, whether they be homemade or available commercially. In either case, a prospective builder of his own unit can get ideas that might save him a lot of time, money and frustration.

One commercially available unit that we consider to be outstanding is the Sportsmobile which may be ordered either in kit form, or complete through some participating VW dealers or, you can bring your new or used vehicle to their factory in Andrews, Indiana and have the job done in a day. Price for their deluxe kit including factory installation ranges from $782.00 for a panel to $529.60 for the station wagon. The difference mainly represents the cost of window installation in the panel but despite this, when you add up the total cost of the vehicle and conversion one body style offers no significant advantage over another. A disadvantage of converting a wagon is that you end up with a lot of unneeded parts that come with the original car. The Sportsmobile may be readily stripped for temporary cargo carrying, but you can't turn it back into a station wagon on the spur of the moment.

Major accessories not included in the kit but shown in our photographs include the "penthouse" top at $453.75, a portable (40-lb.) 10-foot square tent at $159.80 and a refrigerator which can be exchanged for the standard ice chest at time of installation for $174.10. All

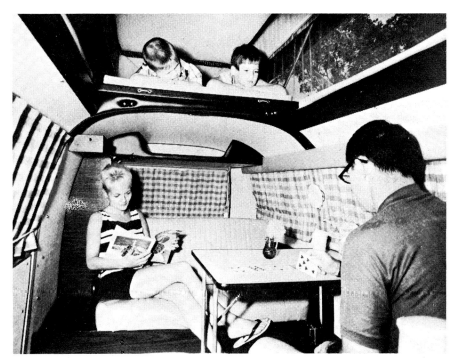

Interior from another angle shows the adequate lounging space provided. This converts at will to the adult sleeping area.

of these prices include conversion labor. You'll note that when everything is added in, the total is still considerably less than what you'd pay for a large American wagon such as a Mercury or Chrysler, not to mention future savings in motel and restaurant bills.

With penthouse, the Sportsmobile will sleep a maximum of four adults and two children in adequate if cozy comfort. The tent is not so much to add capacity (you can't seat the extra

people) as to reduce crowding and to free the vehicle for sightseeing without losing rights to the base camp. With penthouse erected, there is 7-foot standing room but when folded down, overall vehicle height outside is only 83-inches, permitting it to be stored in the average garage. A complete catalog plus information on conversion arrangements may be had by writing to Mr. Charles L. Borskey, Sportsmobile, Andrews, Inc. 46702. Please say WCG motivated you.●

Kombi

* This blend of wagon and caravan is a compromise, and an interesting pointer towards future trends ...

A CAR ROAD TEST

A VEHICLE unique in South African production is announced by Volkswagen of South Africa this month: the VW Kampmobile, a 4½-berth mobile camper based on the popular Kombi, but with a more powerful engine.

The VW Kampmobile (this name is tentative) is known in Europe as the Campmobile. It is going into assembly at the VWSA plant at Uitenhage, and will be released at mid-October. Price had not been announced, but to cover the amount of special equipment and fittings, we expect that it will be considerably higher than that of the standard Kombi 10-seater.

The Kampmobile is very much of a compromise: it is a camper, yet it retains an eight-seater passenger car capacity to make it usable as a weekday "runabout".

TREMENDOUS INTEREST

There has been tremendous public interest in this type of vehicle, VWSA reports, and the company had received many inquiries about the introduction of a camping model.

The principle of a mobile camper is sound, particularly in a country like South Africa with its great distances, wealth of outdoor living facilities and good climate.

The Kampmobile represents the accumulation of many years' experience in quality design and manufacture. It sleeps three adults and two children in comfort and provides seating for a driver and seven passengers when travelling. A freestanding tent, which can be bought as an accessory, provides extra room for living accommodation.

KAMPMOBILE

HIGH-COMPRESSION ENGINE

The unit is powered by a 1,600 c.c. engine which differs from the normal VW 1600 engine in that it has a higher compression ratio of 7·7 : 1, as against the conventional 6·6 : 1 of the standard Kombi. The higher compression ratio results in an improved S.A.E. 57 b.h.p. — 4 b.h.p. more than in the conventional engine — and an increase in torque from 77 lb./ft. to 82 lb./ft.

The roof of the Kampmobile is made of fibreglass with reinforced polyester. The major part of the roof is a pop-up unit enabling an adult to stand up straight with still plenty of headroom to spare in the living compartment. The sides of the pop-up unit are made of canvas and the rear and side walls have zip-operated vents covered with mosquito netting, giving ample ventilation in warm weather.

To the rear of the pop-up roof a luggage rack is provided for any bulky luggage. This rack is styled into the fibre-glass roof assembly of the vehicle.

DOUBLE BED

In the passenger compartment the rear bench seat is designed to fold out level with the rear of the compartment to form a double bed 74 in. long by 47 in. wide. The polyester foam seat cushions form a comfortable mattress and can sleep two adults.

A child's hammock fits in the driver's compartment, while a stretcher opens up in the pop-up roof section of the vehicle.

DRAINED ICEBOX

Behind the front passenger seat there is a 2·6 cu. ft. icebox which operates with ice or dry ice. Water from the melting ice is collected in a drip tray and drained off outside the vehicle.

In the rear of the cabinet is a 6·6 gallon water tank above which is

situated a sink. The water tap next to this is operated with a hand pump. A drawer for cutlery is located next to the sink, as well as two "flap-up" table-tops for extra "kitchen" working space.

A dinette table is located between the two bench seats in the rear compartment. The table can be folded down and is maintained in position by a snap lock.

STORAGE SPACE

Storage space is provided under both bench seats in the living compartment, as well as having a net slung from the roof in the rear of the vehicle. A wardrobe with mirror and linen closet also provide further storage space.

The floor covering in the living compartment consists of flat PVC, and the interior panelling of the compartment is of birchwood. There is a thick layer of insulating material between the body shell and the interior lining.

A clip-on mosquito net is provided for the rear door when kept open and the two louvred side windows are also mosquito-proof, to provide good ventilation while keeping insects out of the living accommodation.

CURTAINED WINDOWS

All the windows, including the front windscreen, are provided with curtains which can be drawn across the entire glass area and closed tight with snaps.

A ceiling lamp with three bulbs supplies light inside the vehicle. One, two or all three of the bulbs can be used as preferred.

The driver's compartment is similar to that of the Microbus, except that there is a double co-driver's seat so that three people can be accommodated up front. The spare wheel is housed under the co-driver's seat.

PERFORMANCE

The Kampmobile is heavier than

MAKE AND MODEL:

Make . . . . Volkswagen
Model . . . . . 1600 Kampmobile

PERFORMANCE FACTORS:

Power/weight (lb./b.h.p.) . . . 60·2
Frontal area (sq. ft.) . . . . 39·4
Drag at 60 m.p.h. (lb.) . . . . 177·2
M.p.h./1,000 r.p.m. (top) . . . 17·2
(Calculated on licensing weight, gross
frontal area, gearing and net b.h.p.)

INTERIOR NOISE LEVELS:

	Min.	Wind	Road
Idling . . .	57·5	—	—
30 m.p.h. . .	72·5	74·0	80·0
45 m.p.h. . .	78·5	80·0	84·0
60 m.p.h. . .	84·5	86·0	88·0
Full throttle	See graph		
Average dBA at 60	86·2		

(Measured in decibels, "A" weighting,
averaging runs both ways on a level road;
"Minimum" with car closed; "Wind" with
one window fully open; "Road" on a coarse
gravel surface.)

ACCELERATION FROM REST:

0–30 . . . . 7·1
0–40 . . . . 13·0
0–65 . . . . 23·4
0–60 . . . . 55·4
¼ Mile . . . . 24·5

OVERTAKING ACCELERATION:

	3rd	Top
20–40	11·2	19·1
30–50	18·3	22·3
40–60	—	42·6

(Measured in seconds, to true speeds,
averaging runs both ways on a level road,
car carrying test crew of two and standard
test equipment.)

MAXIMUM SPEED:

True speed . . . . 63·6
Speedo reading 68
Calibration:

Indicated	20	30	40	50	60
True speed	19	28	37·5	47	56

FUEL CONSUMPTION:

30 m.p.h. . . . . 37·1
45 m.p.h. . . . . 28·6
60 m.p.h. . . . . 20·2
Full throttle . . . . . . See graph
(Measured in miles per Imp. gallon,
averaging runs both ways on a level road.)

BRAKING TEST:

From 50 m.p.h.:
First stop . . . . 3·3
Tenth stop . . . . 4·1
Average . . . . 3·63
(Measured in sec., with stops from true
speeds at 30-sec. intervals on a good bitu-
minised surface.)

GRADIENTS IN GEARS:

Low gear . . . . 1 in 3·7
2nd gear . . . . 1 in 5·1
3rd gear . . . . 1 in 8·0
Top gear . . . . 1 in 15·4
(Tabulated from Tapley g. readings, car
carrying test crew of two and standard test
equipment.)

GEARED SPEEDS:

Low gear . . . . 15·2
2nd gear . . . . 30·2
3rd gear . . . . 44·3
Top gear . . . . 68·7
(Calculated to true speeds, at engine
peak r.p.m. — 4,000.)

TEST CONDITIONS:

Altitude . . . . At sea level
Weather . . . . Fine and mild
Barometric reading . . . . 30·04
Fuel used 93-octane
Test car's mileage 980

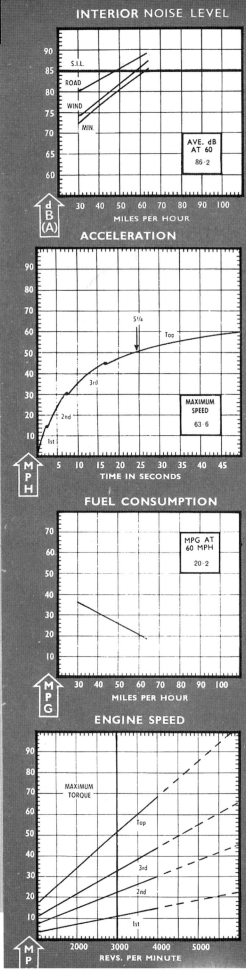

INTERIOR NOISE LEVEL

dB(A) — MILES PER HOUR

S.I.L.
ROAD
WIND
MIN.

AVE. dB AT 60
86·2

ACCELERATION

M.P.H. — TIME IN SECONDS

S¼
Top
3rd
2nd
1st

MAXIMUM SPEED
63·6

FUEL CONSUMPTION

M.P.G. — MILES PER HOUR

MPG AT 60 MPH
20·2

ENGINE SPEED

M.P. — REVS. PER MINUTE

MAXIMUM TORQUE
Top
3rd
2nd
1st

ENGINE:

Cylinders . . Opposed 4, rear-mount
Carburettors . . Single Solex 30 PICT
Bore . . . . . 3·36 in. (85·5 mm
Stroke . . . . 2·72 in. (69·0 mm
Cubic capacity . 96·6 cu. in. (1,584 c.
Compression ratio . . . . 7·7 t
Valve gear . . . O.h.v., pushr
Main bearings . . . . . . Thr
Aircleaner . . . . . . Oil ba
Fuel rating . . . . . . Premi
Cooling . . Air, thermostat-controll
Electrics . . . . . . 12-volt D

ENGINE OUTPUT:

Max. b.h.p. S.A.E. 5
Max. b.h.p. net 4
Peak r.p.m. 4,0
Max. torque/r.p.m. . . 81·7/3,0

TRANSMISSION:

Forward seats . . . . . . F
Synchromesh . . . . . .
Gearshift . . . . . . Fl
Low gear . . . . . . 3·80 t
2nd gear . . . . . . 2·06 t
3rd gear . . . . . . 1·26 t
Top gear . . . . . . 0·82 t
Reverse gear . . . . . 3·61 t
Final drive . . . . 5·375 t
Drive wheels . . . . . R
Tyre size . . . . . 7·00 x

BRAKES:

Front . . . . Dru
Rear . . . . Dru
Total lining area . . . . . N
Boosting . . . .
Handbrake position . . Under da

STEERING:

Type . . . . . Ross, worm and p
Lock to lock . . . . . 2·8 tur
Turning circle . . . . . 36·9

MEASUREMENTS:

Length overall . . . . . 175·0
Width overall . . . . . 71·5
Height overall . . . . . 80·0
Wheelbase . . . . . . 94·5
Front track . . . . . . 54·5
Rear track . . . . . . 56·1
Ground clearance . . . . 10·0
Licensing weight . . 2,920 lb. appr

SUSPENSION:

Front . . . . Independe
Type . . . . Torsion b
Rear . . . . Independe
Type . . . . . Dual-joint half-axl

CAPACITIES:

Seating . . . . Eig
Fuel tank . . . . . . 13·0 g
Luggage space . . . . 35·3 cu.
Utility space . . . 177·0 cu. ft. gro

SERVICE DATA:

Sump capacity . . . . 4·4 pir
Change interval . . . . 3,000 mi
Gearbox diff. capacity . . 6·1 pi
Change interval . . . . .
Greasing points . . . . .
Greasing interval . . . 30,000 mi
(These basic service recommendatio
are given for guidance only, and may va
according to operating conditions. Inquir
should be addressed to authorised deal
ships.)

TYRE PRESSURES:

Crossply: Front . . . . . 28 to 34
Rear . . . . . 28 to 36

WARRANTY:

Six months or 6,000 miles.

BASIC PRICES:

Not announced.

PROVIDED TEST CAR:

Volkswagen of South Africa, Uitenha
Cape.

the standard Kombi by about 200 lb., but the extra 4 horse-power exactly makes up for this. Its weight-power ratio is 60·2 lb./b.h.p. net, the same as that of the Kombi Clipper which we tested in June, 1968.

(In the Test of the Clipper the overseas specifications were inadvertently given: in fact, the South African Kombi Clipper and 10-seater models were kept to a 6·6 to 1 compression ratio, not the 7·7 to 1 used overseas, so that regular-grade fuel could be used. This gives the local models 53 b.h.p. S.A.E., and torque of 77 lb./ft., while the Karavette develops 57 b.h.p. S.A.E. and 82 lb./ft. of torque.)

So in spite of a small increase in frontal area and weight, the more powerful Kampmobile exceeds the performance of the Kombi Clipper by a fair margin, both in acceleration and maximum speed. A short comparison:

		Clipper	**Kampmobile**
0–30	.. ..	7·9	**7·1**
0–50	.. ..	25·9	**23·4**
¼ Mile	..	25·5	**24·5**
Speed	..	61·8	**63·6**

The Kampmobile is capable of sustained 60-m.p.h. cruising, with quite reasonable gradient ability. When a long hill is faced, it has to drop back into the 44-m.p.h. third gear.

ECONOMY, NOISE, BRAKING

With high-compression engine (by VW standards) the Kampmobile also shows improved fuel economy, and should be capable of 20 m.p.g. or just over, in cruising.

The mechanical noise level is much the same as that of the Kombi, but rising slightly at higher speed. The abundant cool air ventilation system makes it unnecessary to open windows, though wind noise is not severe. Road noise is high, as with most wagon-type vehicles.

Braking is sound, but with more of an inclination for the body to pitch forward, because of the extra rooftop weight.

HANDLING AND LOAD

Driving a forward-control vehicle is delightfully easy. The steep angle of the steering column allows variation of arm reach, and the driver has unrestricted forward vision. Supplementing this is the smooth VW gear shift and light clutch and brake controls: the vehicle seems big, but handles effortlessly and is very manoeuvrable.

The all-independent suspension is a

CAMPING SPECIFICATIONS

ACCOMMODATION:
Double berths	One
Single berths	One, half-size
Hammocks	Two
Total	4½

VENTILATION:
Opening rooflights	One
Opening windows	Six

FURNITURE:
Tables	Three
Cupboards	Three
Lockers	Two
Electric lights	One, triple-unit
Doors	Four
Wash-up	One, with 6-gallon tank
Refrigerator	One ice-box type

OPTIONAL FEATURES:
Side tent (price not stated).

sterling feature, particularly on the new Kombi models with their wider track and fixed-camber rear wheel layout, which makes them safe and stable at speed.

The Kampmobile has extra high-up weight in the form of the glass fibre double roof, so it cannot be cornered with quite the verve of the Kombi, but it proved quite vice-free in normal driving.

EXTRA FITTINGS

We missed the walk-through ability from the front seat found on the Clipper—one of the failings in the Kampmobile compromise. The unit effectively sleeps only four (plus one minute berth which would suit a very small child), yet VW have gone to pains to provide eight seats!

The optional side tent would increase living and sleeping space (a couple of light folding stretchers could be used) but somehow the layout is not very practical.

For instance, the elaborate roof compartment provides only one narrow stretcher space, while adding considerably to the cost of conversion. To get into this high stretcher, a person has to climb on the furniture, and this sleeping position is cold in winter.

A better and more economical layout can have been planned to provide, say, four sleeping berths and five or six riding seats, without opening the roof — we are sure any competent caravan manufacturer could do a conversion of this sort with fewer frills and at reasonable cost. And headroom inside the vehicle is not that important.

There is also some lack of practicality in the rubber beading round the roof aperture, which came loose easily and is difficult to replace, and in the side curtain slides, which are

not robust enough for family camping purposes.

SUMMARY

The Kampmobile is a bit big for the elderly couple who want a two-berth camper, and a bit small for the kind of family that normally requires a Kombi.

Nevertheless, it is an attractive and enterprising vehicle, based on a much-loved family wagon and combining a good measure of the facilities of a car/caravan combination, while being much more mobile.

There is no doubt that there is a future for this type of camper in the Republic, and the VW Kampmobile will certainly set the ball rolling. ●

View through the side door of the dinette, with table folded down. Ice box/washup unit is on the left.

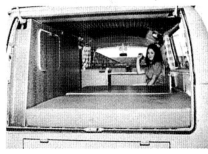

View through the tailgate of the 74-in. by 47-in. double berth, with thick, upholstered foam mattress. There is a roof storage net above it, and built-in linen closet at left.

The 1600 engine is that of the Kombi models, with 7·7 to 1 compression ratio giving extra horse-power and torque.

Road Test

1970 VW BUS... practical for 7

CAR AT A GLANCE: 22-mpg economy . . . 68-mph top and cruising speed . . . Fine attention to detail trim . . . Beefed-up frontal structure . . . Edwardian performance . . . Extremely comfortable ride.

by Don MacDonald   photos by Lester Nehamkin

Purposeful looking front of the VW bus boasts the world's largest "radiator" badge but it does not look out of place. Many owners mount the spare there which helps protect them and the painted bumper.

Optional sunroof is easy to manage and causes no unpleasant drafts. It's also handy when you're carrying cargo such as 7-foot Christmas tree.

If the Greenbrier, a slab-nosed, rear-engined equippage produced by Chevrolet in the early sixties were still around in modernized form, a tester would have at least some basis from which to take the measure of a Volkswagen Station Wagon. The Greenbrier was an imitator and follower but like VW, design emphasis favored passenger rather than commercial versions. The current crop of domestic front-engined boxcars are overly expensive, gussied-up trucks.

The VW bus, thus, stands in a class by itself. It's such a practical shape for carrying people and their recreational accoutrement that unfortunately, the tendency is to cram more into it than its engine will handle. The summer scene at our mountainous national parks anywhere is a long line of cars crawling up the slope, headed by a VW camper conversion, almost like a heavy freight train being pulled by its caboose. Even without the 700 pounds or so of stuff that makes a Campmobile, the bus still weighs 1,000 pounds more than a beetle and the same 57 horsepower engine is used in both.

Bus and Campmobile owners soon acquire downshifting skills, patience, and a talent for ignoring those behind them on the highway. And for some

reason the odds are at least even that the head of the bus-owning household will acquire or already has a beard. If you don't believe this, count them the next time you're out for a drive. The purchase of one of these vehicles is a form of escape or rebellion, if you will, from the hurly-burly, as much so as a farm in Vermont or a shanty on the desert, and perhaps that accounts for the beards.

The purchase is also an excellent investment. Well-used VW buses are threatening Detroit's traditional concept of the youth market. Again, escape via a bus is far less expensive and more promising in terms of birds and bees than being encumbered with a bucket-seated, thirsty-engined GTO or Scat-Pack Dodge. Admittedly, however, flower symbols and curtained windows seem to attract the police as readily as racing stripes.

Testing the bus in some meaningful way is a challenge in itself. We found that it will accelerate from zero to 60 mph in 37.11 seconds, a figure matched only by the diminutive Subaru 360 and the belt-driven Dutch Daf but then, who "accelerates" from zero to 60 in any of these cars? For much the same reasons, we didn't investigate whether the bus understeers or oversteers and when it

commenced to lean even slightly in a corner, we slowed down. We know, though, that both the cruising and top speed is 68 mph because the gas pedal must be floored most of the time unless you want to stay in the truck lane.

In the two weeks we lived with it, the bus did its job which was to take us wherever we wanted to go. The fact that it required twenty more minutes to make the run from Los Angeles to San Diego seemed quite unimportant when, the next day, we purchased the family Christmas tree and carried all seven feet of it upright, branches unbroken, with the top protruding through the sunroof. You can't do that in a Cadillac despite its 375 horsepower.

Looked at another way, the 375-horsepower Cadillac requires 245.5 inches and several tons of machinery to carry seven passengers. The VW bus does this within 170.0 inches and with only 2,833 pounds of machinery. It will make a U-turn in 40 feet; the Cadillac limousine requires 57.4 feet. Then, to end our analysis of the seven-passenger car market, the Cadillac costs $8,440 more, or the equivalent of three additional VW buses plus $1,200 in pocket money to run the fleet. It's rather surprising that America's undertakers haven't discovered this economic

Sliding passenger door on the right side is perhaps a portent of what will be required on all cars sold in the U.S. in the forseeable future.

A familiar scene greets you here, complete with a battery tucked away so that you have to first remove the air cleaner, then the battery itself, to check electrolyte level.

fact because relatives of the departed could be transported in equal dignity and with more legroom.

Though the bus is easy to drive, anybody who has owned one will admit to climbing a curb or two with the rear wheel the first few times a right turn is attempted. You've got to remember that the front wheels are behind you and not start a sharp turn until you protrude about half the vehicle's length into the intersection. If the corner happens to be adorned with an obstacle, such as the gatepost of a driveway, rather expensive alterations are made in the big sliding door on the right side. The novice driver will also feel that he's going to be scraped along the pavement

This view shows only one of the various places in which to stow luggage.

The middle seat unbolts in minutes and the lugs themselves slide right out to gain a flat loading floor for bulky cargo.

VOLKSWAGEN STATION WAGON
Specifications from the Manufacturer

ENGINE:

Type: Rear-mounted, rear-drive, overhead-valve, flat four, air-cooled
Bore and stroke: 3.36 x 2.72 ins.
Displacement: 96.7 cu. ins. (1,584 cc)
Horsepower: 57 @ 4,400 rpm
Torque: 81.7 lbs. ft. @ 3,000 rpm
Compression ratio: 7.5 to 1

TRANSMISSION:

Type: 4-speed manual, fully synchronized
Gear ratios: 1st-3.80, 2nd-2.06, 3rd-1.26, 4th-0.82, R-3.61
Axle ratio: 5.38

SUSPENSION: Torsion bar, front and rear, front stabilizer

STEERING: Ross-type with hydraulic dampener

WHEELS AND TIRES: Bolt-on steel disc with 7.00 x 14 bias-ply tires

BRAKES: 4-wheel drum

CAPACITIES:

Fuel: 15.9 U.S. gals.
Oil: 5.3 U.S. pts.
Transmission: 7.4 U.S. pts.

BODY AND FRAME: Unitized with reinforced side plates

DIMENSIONS AND WEIGHTS: Wheelbase 94.5 ins., Overall length 174.0 ins., Width 69.5 ins., Height 77.0 ins., Weight 2,833 lbs.

Instrumentation is mostly warning lights but it's obviously right in front of you. Steering position is comfortable, the wheel moves forward in an accident and there's new bracing of the front structure.

the first time he encounters a severe dip and as happened to us, we suggest that you keep your distance from cattle trucks immediately in front of you in traffic.

The gear shift lever on the new model is 1-3/4 inches longer and thus, 1-3/4 inches more vague in its relationship to the gears way back at the rear. Now that Hurst and others have introduced positive-action beetle shifters, we suggest that they devote their attention to the bus as finding reverse is kind of like the old party game of pinning a tail on the donkey. This criticism evaporates once you're in gear, however, as the clutch action in the bus is undoubtedly the sweetest ever to be put in a car. Captain Ahab could operate it with that peg leg of his, cut from the jawbone of a whale.

During the two weeks we had the bus, many persons who had never ridden in one before commented favorably on the comfortable, soft ride. The suspension is a carryover from the big redesign effort of 1968 and there is no need to change it. One guest likened it to a baby carriage but that is

CONTINUED ON PAGE 121

VW TYPE II STATION WAGON

Prime people mover with new, highly effective front disc brakes.

One of the latest automotive fads, particularly in trend-setting Southern California, is the use of a delivery van for personal transportation. You see all manners and types of vans, with curtained windows, rear shackles lengthened to hoist the rear end, fat rear tires, surfboards mounted on top or protruding from the rear door, and eight-track stereo blaring away. It makes lots of sense. You can carry a staggering volume of people and/or sports equipment in a van, people have been known to live in them and by adding a few seats, the utility of a station wagon is obtained at a lot less cost.

There is undoubtedly a substantial market for box-like vehicles seating seven or more in comfort in a large space which can be readily filled by a standard commercial van. Since Volkswagenwerk AG has been highly successful in sensing new market trends, one might wonder what new offering could be expected in 1971 from Wolfsburg to capitalize on this one. The answer is none. Their entry in the van-wagon-campmobile market was introduced to the U.S. in 1955. It is called the Type II, differentiating it from the Beetle (Type I), or the 1600 fastback (Type III). Instead of Volkswagen having to come up with a new vehicle for this sector of the automotive market, their Type II has probably helped more than any other to create it.

There are five two-tone color combinations available in the single body style, each sharing the pastel white top. Chianti Red will no doubt be favored by most customers. In addition there is a soft blue, green, beige and finally the color of our test car, Sierra Yellow, which is an exact duplicate of the color scheme recently adopted by General Telephone Com-

pany for its fleet of thousands of service vehicles. We were repeatedly asked when we had gone to work for the telephone company, so unless you are a career professional in the telephone communication field, pick another color.

Consistent with Volkswagen policy on model changes, the 1971 Type II is the result of evolutionary rather than revolutionary changes. The opposed four-cylinder engine now has 50% more displacement and twice as much horsepower than when it started life in 1951. The rounded edges found on the early wagons have been squared off so that no space is wasted. It appears Volkswagen has adopted the philosophy that if the blessed thing is going to be called a box, it might as well look like one.

There are comparatively few departures from conventional Volkswagen design in the 1971 station wagon. One of them is an increase from 57 to 60 horsepower, brought about by a change to a dual-port intake mani-

It takes a dusty road to get photographic evidence of acceleration from a VW bus. Actual times to 60 mph are in the low thirties.

Horizontal steering wheel is in the style of a truck or bus and very comfortable on long trips. Firm upright seat puts driver in position for good view of road ahead and to side.

fold and improved carburetion. Longer engine life will result from the use of a new magnesium alloy in the crankcase and also from improved cooling contributed by a new aluminum oil cooler and a larger fan. Among the changes needed to maintain engine emissions within 1971's more stringent levels are additional internal engine modifications, a new carburetor, and the evaporative control fuel system. We also noticed that the ignition timing has been retarded another five degrees, and is now at 5 degrees after top-dead-center.

The four-speed all-synchromesh manual transmission connected to the engine with a single plate dry clutch is the only one available on the Type II. Gear ratios are quite low, with a 5.375 final drive ratio. Although this allows the wagon to climb a 27 percent grade or pull stumps up to 18 inches in diameter, it means that the car runs abruptly out of revs at 15 mph in first gear, at 25 mph in second, 50 mph in third, and in fourth gear horsepower matches drag at a true 68 and an indicated 72 mph. It also means that it can and usually must be driven flat-out on the freeways.

Torsion bar suspension is used all round. Spring rates have been softened from the rock-hard setting used on earlier VW wagons. The dreaded

rear swing axle is a thing of the past, having been superseded by double-jointed halfshafts located by trailing arms and diagonal links. A front stabilizer bar is standard equipment.

One of the major 1971 changes, and a most welcome one, is the switch to power-assisted front disc brakes, augmented by a 20% increase in rear lining thickness and by a brake-force regulator in the rear brake circuit which functions as an anti-skid device by helping to prevent premature rear wheel lock. Brake cooling is aided by the use of perforated wheels, and handling has also been improved by increasing the wheel width half an inch to 5½ inches.

When comparisons are made between station wagons, though, it's what's inside that counts. And what's inside the VW Type II is room—lots of it. We regard the interior room and accomodation as its most outstanding feature. The model we used for our test was the three-door, seven-seat version with a pair of bucket seats in

front, a rear bench seat which accommodates three and a bench seat for two between them. Even with this much seating there's enough room left over to virtually walk around. Other interior options include a nine-seat wagon (the "bus" of VW advertising) and a camper arrangement. The seats can be removed by loosening a few wing nuts to make a rapid conversion to a delivery van configuration. When this is done there is a total of 176 cubic feet to fill with furniture, gardening tools, camping gear or baseball teams. If the assigned task includes transporting totem poles or grandfather clocks, an optional sliding sun roof is available.

In addition to this space, there is also a 35 cubic foot luggage compartment reached through an upward swinging rear door. This space can hold a substantial number of suitcases (provided that some provision is made to restrain them from flying forward in the event of a sudden stop) at the price of completely blocking the view through the rear window.

such that the driver is unable to see the horizon behind him, and in fact a car immediately following is cut off at about the belt line. No amount of squirming or adjustment could correct this situation, which could be potentially dangerous. It does appear that the inside mirror could be mounted lower; this, coupled with a change to a larger mirror should solve the problem.

The driver is provided with the traditional VW instrumentation and control package, consisting of speedometer with fuel gauge and warning light cluster and an array of push pull switches for headlights, wipers, inside light and electric rear window defroster. The Type II shares with the balance of the '71 VW line a "memory" switch which turns the headlights off while leaving the parking lights on when the ignition switch is turned off without turning off the headlights. After years of production, all operational problems have been solved save for the distance between the gear shift

New power front disc brakes pull the VW Station Wagon to swift, sure stop in only half the distance required to accelerate to 60 mph. The new brakes have special cooling scoops.

Double link rear suspension keeps both rear wheels on the road. The old swing axle caused the inside rear wheel to lift in situations like this one.

Unfortunately, access via the front doors to the commodious interior leaves something to be desired. The front seats, which are positioned directly over the front wheels, are 39 inches above the road, and the front floor is 22 inches above it. To climb into the front, it is necessary to step forward of the seat, not an easy task unless the door is at its maximum opening, bend the body into a question mark, grab something convenient like the steering wheel or top of the door and haul away until elevated sufficiently to assume a seated position. It's about as easy as it sounds. Dismounting is done in the reverse manner, though possibly a little more gracefully. Although this is a rather harsh condemnation, we can't honestly suggest how the situation could be improved; the seats are really in the right place.

Once seated, comfort is top level. With all the interior height available, the seating position is fully upright, and the front bucket seats are curved enough to provide a good degree of lateral support. The driver's seat is provided with a back-rake adjustment

in addition to the forward and back adjustment.

Access to the rear seats is a different story. The sliding side door exposes a 3½ by 4 foot opening through which either rear seat may be reached conveniently. Actually the front seats can be reached by this means also, since there is a foot-wide opening between them which also allows easy transfers within while on the road.

With the massive array of side windows and the large windshield located close to the driver, visibility is great in all directions save directly to the rear through the rear window. Here the placement of the inside mirror is

and transmission which introduces some uncertainty into the linkage.

There is a very effective ventilating and heating system. Fresh air is supplied through six outlets controllable from the dash with two supplying the windshield, two outlets in the dashboard, and two supplying the rear compartment through ducts located on the inside of the front doors where they also double as arm rests. Flow-through design allows exhaust and a comfortable air flow through the car while cruising without the need to lower any windows. Heat is supplied from an exhaust manifold heat exchanger in the traditional manner. There are five heated air outlets be-

30

It's a long way, and all of it usable space from front to rear. Luggage area behind rearmost seat holds 35 cubic feet if properly strapped down.

Two extremes of accessibility: Entrance to the front seats requires the skill of a contortionist, while the rear seats can be virtually entered in a wheelchair.

side the two defroster outlets at the windshield. Each heater outlet can be separately controlled.

Thanks to the revised spring settings the VW Station Wagon delivers an acceptably comfortable ride over any paved road surface that we could find, and holds its own on the dirt stretches we encountered. However, any attempt at brisk cornering will probably strike terror into the heart of a driver inexperienced in the operation of van type vehicles. A seating position above the front wheels and less than two feet behind the front bumper permits an unusual degree of awareness of what the front end of the vehicle is doing. Once armed with this realization, the VW wagon's cornering performance is revealed to be on a par with its class.

Straight line performance is either suitable or unsuitable, depending on driving habits. Sixty horsepower will only accelerate 3,000 pounds so fast. In this case we departed from our normal practice and took the acceleration times with four people on board. Thus, although they don't represent the car's absolute performance potential, they do give a very honest picture of what the average owner can expect to achieve when he has the whole family with him. Top speed, 72 mph indicated, is reached after a genteel wait, and getting up to this velocity in less than a minute is accom-

plished only by taking the engine to or past the maximum recommended speed in each gear. Freeway cruising at 65 mph or better requires nearly constant use of full throttle on anything but a dead level surface. Although the owner's manual assures you that the normal cruising speed is the same as top speed, we can't help but wonder what a steady diet of this would do to engine life. Incidentally, any acceleration through the gears is accompanied by noticeable drive train noise in the three lower gears.

The owner's manual suggests a limit of 1,00 pounds on the weight of any trailer, and we question the use of any trailer at all, although we've seen many of them over the years.

If the acceleration is not impressive, the braking performance certainly is. On both a qualitative and a quantitative basis the operation of the power

assisted disc brakes is nothing short of overwhelming. The favorable impression starts with the feel of a swift sure stop with no directional instability or lock-up as soon as the brakes are applied. It's almost as though the proverbial great hand is reaching out to take hold of the car. The numbers bear out the feeling, with the stopping distance of 167 feet from 60 mph being equivalent to a deceleration rate of about 23 ft./sec. or .72 g. While reducing our field test data to the proper format for the data sheet we became intrigued with comparative acceleration and deceleration rates, and came up with the interesting fact that the average deceleration rate from 60 mph to stop was exactly twice the average acceleration rate to 60 mph from a standing start. It is comforting to know that you can stop in

half the distance that it took you to reach a given speed.

After the fact that the engine is accessible from the rear rather than from the top has been accepted, one realizes that all components are indeed readily servicable, although its a longish reach into the battery which nestles just to the right of the engine. The service of this without spillage requires a special pitcher which normally is found only at a station specializing in Volkswagens.

Gas mileage claimed by VW is 23 mpg, this being achieved at 75% of maximum speed, or 53 mph. Since we can't imagine anyone driving on any state or interstate highway at less than 65 mph when weather and traffic conditions permit, we took our fuel economy data at that speed and recorded a figure of just under 19 mpg. This is very comparable to the city fuel economy which averaged out at

ters and camping families. Its principal drawbacks are power-to-weight ratio, front seat entry and exit, an unacceptable visibility through the rear window. These are countered with truly outstanding comfort for seven passengers complemented by a capability for movement inside the vehicle while on the road. (Don't knock this feature if you've never taken a long trip with small children) It has great visibility to all points of the compass except the rear, an effective ventilation and heating system which distributes heat to all parts of the interior, and a favorable purchase cost followed by reasonable operating costs and unusually low depreciation. And, of course, the styling is not likely to become obsolete in the foreseeable future. The VW Station Wagon is bound to continue in heavy demand. If you don't believe us, go to a dealer and see if you can buy one off the floor.

Ron Hickman

This is the reason that few VW Station Wagon pilots will ever find the limit of adhesion—the seat of your pants tells you when you're going fast enough.

60-horsepower engine buried at rear occupies absolute minimum of space, but is still conveniently accessible for maintenance. Oil bath air cleaner is used instead of paper cartridge found on other Volks.

just over 18 mpg, and the country mileage is only marginally better than the city mileage because it was nearly all recorded at full throttle.

On a price per pound or per foot of length, the VW wagon costs about the same as a domestic station wagon or van. This is to the great advantage of the VW which can be bought for under $3,000 if you supply your own music, or for $3,095 POE Los Angeles (plus the usual destination, dealer prep, tax and license) with the optional side vent windows and an AM radio as installed on our test car.

The VW Station Wagon will not appeal to boat owners, drag racers or arthritics. It can be an outstanding conveyance for commuters in large ride pools, den mothers, Scoutmas-

Volkswagen themselves call the Type II "a loaf of bread," but being functional, the bus is attractive. The best of the Beetle combined with family style room and long-legged performance.

1970 wagon may be identified by reflectors added to each corner. Except for minor carburetion modifications, the 1600-cc engine with 57 hp remains the same.

VW Type II Wagons, Campers and Trucks

Real ride improvement, beefed-up front structure and a longer gearshift handle are the important changes.

Volkswagen's Type II station wagons and trucks have been outfitted with a number of structural as well as convenience improvements which help make them both more rugged and more comfortable than in the past.

For example, the passenger compartment was made stronger by reinforcing the front-end frame and VW engineers also developed a new safety steering column which will tilt away from the driver in the event of a front-end collision.

In addition, the front axle assembly was improved to help dampen road shock and smooth out the ride. This was accomplished by modifying the front axle torsion bars and redesigning the shock absorbers.

The exterior styling introduced for all models in the line two years ago remains unchanged this year. However, four tell-tale additions on the outside of each 1970 vehicle set it apart — but only for the VW expert. These are rectangular side-marker reflectors mounted near the front and rear ends to provide better night-time visibility.

Visible improvements inside the vehicles include a new gear shift lever, its

1-3/4 inches of added length making it easier to change gears in the fully-synchronized transmission. Also new on the inside is nylon velour carpeting for the station wagon's 33-cubic-foot rear-end luggage compartment.

Other improvements added for 1970 include a day-night rear-view mirror and a buzzer which sounds a warning if the driver begins to leave his vehicle without removing the ignition key. This, coupled with the steering column lock which was introduced last year, gives the vehicles a high anti-theft factor.

Measuring only 174-inches overall, considerably less than most conventional sedans on the road today, both VW's station wagon models and panel truck pack 177 cubic feet of passenger and cargo space inside. Station wagons are available with sliding steel sunroofs.

Both the panel and single-cab pickup trucks are rated for 2,370-pound payloads while the double-cab pickup which carries six passengers is rated for a 2,259-pound load. Both pickup mod-

Factory-built camper with optional pop-up roof sleeps two adults and three children, will cruise at 65 mph. Another factory option is a free-standing tent.

els can be equipped with bows and tarpaulins to convert their open cargo beds with their three "tailgates" (one along each side as well as a conventional one at the rear) into a sort of modern-day covered wagon.

The carbureted 1600-cc engine, rated at 57 hp, remains the same except for minor emission-control modifications. Claimed cruising speed is 65 mph on regular gasoline for all types including the relatively heavy camper version. ●

For Sale:
Holiday Home.

One room. All steel exterior. Fibre glass roof.
2 louvred screened windows. Curtains all around. Wood panelled interior.
Sleeps 2 adults, 3 children. Clothes closet. Linen closet.
3-shelf storage cabinet. Pantry. Dinette. Icebox. Water supply.
2 utility tables and reading lamp. Pop-up top with luggage rack.
Folding tent optional.
Changes into a family bus for everyday use.
Open for inspection at our Volkswagen showrooms.
Let us show you through the Kampmobile.

VOLKSWAGEN KAMPMOBILE R2995
(suggested retail price)

VW bus range : Microbus, Microbus L, Microbus L with sunroof, Kombi and Kampmobile.

PNB369:

Put a Truck *IN* Your Bus

Notes and Photos by Bill McClure

leave-ho! Toss anything you like into the cargo box without fear of scratch or splatter.

Slightly separated here to illustrate details, the folded box can be stored in a space less than a foot wide.

Sides and tailgate are held in place by stakes attached to panels and slipped into sockets.

Tailgate is keyed into place as on a pickup truck and built lower than the sides to facilitate shoveling.

Do you itch to use all that cargo space in your VW bus for all the dirty hauling jobs that go with home ownership but hesitate to subject the interior of your wagon to such treatment?

Well, you can start shoveling. Sand, gravel, trash — even mud or ashes — can be heaved into her with never a qualm about scratches or smudges on her upholstery or dirt and mud on her floor.

How? Simply put a truck in your bus!

There's plenty of room for a lightweight, take-down cargo box that rivals a small pickup in capacity, and that barn-size sliding door on your bus is made-to-order for shoveling. Your truck-in-a-bus can be assembled in place in about five minutes after the center seat is removed and best of all, when you're through with the dirty work you can store the take-apart truck body along the wall of the garage by standing the floor, three side panels and tailgate in a space less than a foot wide.

You can build the whole thing with about $25 worth of plywood, light angle iron, some 1x4-inch and 1x2-inch strips and a little hardware. For another $10 you can line the truck floor with sheetmetal to make a smooth and long-lasting shoveling surface.

The base of the truck box is a piece of half-inch plywood for the floor elevated on 1x4-inch strips to clear the safety-belt lugs and to accommodate the stakes that slip into sockets to hold the side panels and tailgate in place. A 1x4-inch joist or two can be added to handle extra-heavy loads.

Side panels are of 3/8-inch plywood reinforced along the top with 1x2-inch strips and fitted with light angle irons at the corners to make a dribble-free box. And that's about all there is to it. Exact dimensions and design are up to you. A few hours' work with simple tools can put you in the dirty hauling business and also keep your bus passenger-clean.●

35

A MOVABLE FEAST

Vans. Suddenly everybody wants vans. Mini-vans. Normal-size vans. Super vans. Godzilla vans. Vans for hauling nine-kid families. Vans for hauling snowmobiles or ATV's. Vans for mobile TV shops or blood banks or dope dens or camping. Detroit wakes up in 1971 and discovers that, again, Volkswagenwerk was ahead of their time, selling vans — creating a whole cult — before Detroit even realized there was a Grand Canyon of a gap in their strategy.

But even though Volkswagen was first in the field, they still have one crack in their armor. For despite the addition of disc brakes and a miniscule power increase in the '71 Van, VW still persists with their tiny 96 cu. in. engine — less than one-third of the size

Vans are different from cars — something it takes a while to discover

of the engine available on any of the Detroit designed vans we drove. So, while the '71 VW mini bus radiates the glories of smaller-outside, nearly-as-big-inside accommodation, more maneuverability, better brakes, far superior control, no rattles, easier steering, greater gas mileage, lower upkeep, higher resale and rock-bottom investment — the thing still needs more performance.

The three big Detroit-made vans, the Chevy, the Ford and the Dodge, are so alike as to be practically indistinguishable except for the colors and the fact that the Chevy had a VW-style sliding side door. All three had adequate power — with the optional V8 they had stuffed under the shroud between the two front buckets — but a three seemed excessively large to each of the members on our staff.

The largeness of the Detroit vans, though, is partly the fault of the people who make up the van market. Detroit used to make small vans — Chevy had the Greenbrier, a Corvair based van; Ford had a cute little job that has been inflated into the house-sized beast we drove; and Dodge, the best of the American lot, the A100 Sportsman. The thing is that, each year, the people *out there* (speaking through the medium of the salesmen, we guess) demanded *more* on their vans. Power steering. Power brakes. Camping rigs. Extra seats. Air conditioning. Trailer towing packages. And on and on. The result was that Detroit overreacted and overbuilt what they thought people wanted and so now we're stuck with mini-Greyhounds if we want a native brand. If

steering wheels in most vans lie practically horizontal, in the manner of those found on large Greyhound scenicruiser buses. This means you sort of tug on the wheel to turn — a practice which takes getting used to. Our Ford van had jumbo wide-oval tires installed — partly for show and partly for a wider track. Yet it didn't have the needed power steering.

Another point — vans with stick shifts have the clutch pedals mounted in a manner which requires up and down movements of the clutch foot rather than in-and-out as in an ordinary car. This soon develops pains in muscles you didn't know you had. We think that when vans become more refined, the whole cockpit area will become like a car so van drivers won't be so "psyched out" by the awkward features of the controls.

manufacturers whose rigs we drove had renamed their vehicles to avoid the stigma of the word "van" or "bus." VW calls their micro-bus the "VW Station Wagon." Ford terms theirs a "Club Wagon" and Dodge's is a "Sportsman wagon." Only Chevy has the courage to call theirs a van but they couple it with the word "Sport" for Sportvan.

Rather than run a detailed test of these vans, we've presented the collective impressions of the entire staff of the four major brands. The performance of the Detroit vans was so repetitive — with all of them so closely matched — and the performance of the VW van so miserable, that we decided vans have to be approached from a different viewpoint than we're used to looking at cars from. In fact, vans require a whole new marketing strategy. Where

Volkswagen Station Wagon came out best in terms of size, finish, quality and ease of handling. But, for sheer load space, VW couldn't hope to match Ford, Dodge or Chevy vans. VW was also at a distinct power disadvantage, with an engine less than one-third the size of the optional V8s available in the Detroit-made vans. For everyday driving, though, staff still preferred VW van over rest of the group.

you want a smaller van, there is the VW — which seemed just the right size to the M/T staff and handled more like a car than any of the others for the very simple reason it is just 15 inches longer than a Beetle. But the VW van discovered hills — with a resultant slowing down — where the other vans didn't even notice. This is because its engine is just adequate to keep it up to freeway speed when empty, let alone loaded. And yet we see vacationers driving VW buses stocked to the gunnels and towing a boat besides!

Driving a van is not like driving a car. This may sound deceptively obvious but there should be a moment of thought required before the average car driver steps into a van for the first time. For one thing vans are long — most of them close to fifteen feet from bumper to bumper. For another, they're wide — almost too wide for the average parking space at the average shopping center and non-expressway traffic lanes.

Then, there are the controls. The

Another hang-up with vans is their height. We discovered this drawback rather abruptly when trying to pull into our office building's underground parking lot. The bus cleared the ceiling — but it didn't clear the sprinkling system. We also found our vans — even the VW — made us *persona non grata* at all the local car washes. Either the tracks were too wide to fit their rail or the buses stood so tall they would shear off their brushes.

After a while, van drivers develop a little-disguised disdain for ordinary cars. They began to wonder why they ever drove cars with five feet of hood and five feet of rear deck lid and so little usable room in between. Their van might be 15 feet long but they've fit 14-foot boards into it. Long-time van drivers have the air of long-distance tractor-trailer drivers who sneer at "civilians" in ¼-ton pickups. "If you ain't had a van, buddy, you don't know nothing about driving," is their attitude.

As if to disguise the commercial origins of vans, three of the four van

cars can still be sold by the addition of status-conscious badges (the crest on Monte Carlo, etc.), van buyers are utilitarian. They want to know how much of a load you can tote, how big an engine you can order and maybe how many beds or snowmobiles you can squeeze inside.

All the mystique that Detroit has built up for years about "formal rooflines" and "power dome hoods" and "die-cast precision-made grilles" falls upon deaf ears when it comes to the incredibly competitive van market. That's why the independents — like Travco in Michigan and Contempo and Red-E-Kamp in California — are making a mint in selling customized camper and cargo conversions to buyers who want *their* van set up *their* way. Occasionally the auto-makers will underwrite a particular conversion, like VW's Campmobile, but more often it's the individual dealer who buys the bare vans from the auto-maker and has them set up for the buyers in his area.

Continued on page 40

VW Station Wagon

Royal Sportsman B300

VW Station Wagon — Volkswagenwerk, Wolfsburg, West Germany

Powered by flat four, only 96 cu. in. in size. Oil cooler is stock. Weight is lightest of all vans tested. Size — in height and width — is also smallest. Boasts torsion bar front suspension, front discs, unitized body.

Wheelbase: 94.5 in.
Length: 14 ft. 6 in.
Width: 5 ft. 7 in.
Height: 6 ft. 3 in.
Fuel tank capacity: 16 gal.
Load capacity: 1,764 lbs.
Cubic feet of space: 176
Weight: 2, 888 lbs.
Suggested retail price: $3,164 — Including sunroof, radio.

Good Points
Good mileage for a van — over 17 mpg
Size seems just right for city travel
Good road feel and easy steering
Sliding door on side works perfectly, is solid
Finish on interior and exterior is best of lot
Sunroof availability adds sportiness to van concept and, more important, improves already excellent ventilation.
Disc brakes provide best stopping of all vans though more anti-dive is needed up front
Air-cooled engine doesn't overheat
Best visibility
Lowest initial investment
Highest resale value

Points That Need Improvement
Narrow track and narrow tires make van *seem* unstable, top-heavy, although it has adequate stability.
Engine in rear makes loading from rear impossible.
The 1.5-liter engine size is hopelessly inadequate. At least double that size is needed.
Driver/passenger seats have awkward positioning.

Royal Sportsman B300 — Dodge Division, Hamtramck, Mich. 318 cu. in. V8 available.

5-seat, 8-seat or 12-seat versions to choose from, automatic transmission available, 26-gal fuel tank. Concealed doorstep on side. Car-style instrument panel. Independent front coil suspension. Wide choice of colors. Choice of 109″ or 127″ wheelbase. West-Coast style outside mirrors and deluxe interior trim standard on Royal Sportsman.

Wheelbase: 109 in.
Length: 14 ft. 8 in.
Width: 6 ft. 7 in.
Height: 6 ft. 7 in.
Fuel tank capacity: 26 gal.
Load capacity: (V8) 2,445-3,245 lbs.
Cubic feet of space: 208.2
Weight: 3,455 lbs.

Suggested list price: $5,347 — Including V8, 4.10 axle, power brakes, automatic trans, tinted glass, air conditioning, 70 amp battery, 60 amp alternator, AM/FM radio, power steering, wide tread tires, special moldings, dual mirrors, and other options.

Good Points
Good power with optional 318
Fairly wide track
Easy power steering
Good visibility

Points That Need Improvement
Engine cover gets hot on long trips — better insulation or cooling needed.
Overall length and width seem too large for city driving and parking.
Not enough feel in power steering
Dismal gas mileage

Beauville Sportvan

Chateau Club Wagon

Beauville Sportvan — Chevrolet Division, Warren, Michigan.
Powered by standard (1 ton series) 250 hp 350 cu. in. V8.
Available with 3-speed automatic transmission. Sliding side
    door is standard. Coil springs up front. Heavy-duty rear
    shocks and springs available.
Wheelbase: 125 in.
Length: 16 ft. 9 in.
Width: 6 ft. 7 in.
Height: 6 ft. 8 in.
Fuel tank capacity: 24.5 gal.
Load capacity: 2,710 lbs.
Cubic feet of space: 286
Weight: 4,590 lbs.
Suggested list price: $4775.50 — Including tinted glass, H-D
    shocks, H-D rear springs, no-spin axle, 61-amp generator,
    TurboHydra-matic, H-D battery, push-button radio, instru-
    mentation, two-tone paint.

Good Points

Super response (for a van) with standard 350 V8
Best point is sliding cargo door, copied from VW, but copied
    without VW's quality rattle-free installation
Most dealers — over 7,000 Chevy dealers in U.S.
Comfortable seats

Points That Need Improvement

Again, the length and width overkill
Brakes require high pedal pressure and do not provide
    straight stops
Adequate-to-poor quality control
Poor ventilation and heating
Low gas mileage
Awkward step-up-into seats
General tin-can rattle
Echo chamber effect on anything but glass-smooth roads

Chateau Club Wagon — Ford Motor Co., Dearborn, Michigan
302 cu. in. V8 available.
Twin I-beam front suspension, wide track design, choice of
    body lengths, full carpeting.
Bias-belted fiberglass tires are standard, as is a 24 gallon
fuel tank. Engines include two sixes or a V8. Options range
from movable vent windows to tinted glass and air condi-
tioning. Three heavy-duty packages are available to raise
load capacity.
Wheelbase: 105.5 in.
Length: 14 ft. 1 in.
Width: 6 ft. 7 in.
Height: 6 ft. 5 in.
Fuel tank capacity: 24 gal.
Load capacity: 950-2,505 lbs.
Cubic feet of space: 220 (approx.)
Weight: 3,595-4,590 lbs. (depending on number of seats and
    options)
Suggested list price: $5,175 — Including special paint,
    302 V8, instruments, Cruise-o-matic, optional rear axle,
    heater, defroster, radio, tinted glass, rear door lock, wheel
    covers, H-D radiator, H-D shocks, power steering.

Good Points

Adequate power with optional V8
Wide track provides stability in crosswinds
Good visibility

Points That Need Improvement

Overall length and width seem excessive
Engine compartment cover gets excessively hot
Air conditioning dumps air only on driver
Not enough instrumentation
Rattles not controlled

VW's air-cooled flat 4 won't steam up as you take the mountain passes and serviceability is far and away the easiest of other vans.

Ford's 302 cu. in. V8 is a necessary option in our view. Standard axle ratio is 3.73 but you can order up to a 4.10 rear gear.

Dodge's 318 cu. in. optional V8 gives almost twice the horsepower of their standard six. A speed-set control is an available option.

Chevy's 250-hp 350 cu. in. optional V8 had plenty of power, even with optional Turbohydramatic. Tires were rugged 8-ply 16-inchers.

 1    2    3    4

1. VW Station Wagon interior was roomy for people but high-mounted rear engine prevented loading from rear. VW alone offers sunroof. 2. Dodge van was roomy, practically identical to Ford and Chevy vans. 3. Chevy van had handy sliding door, was wider between wheelwells than others, permitting two snowmobiles to ride side by side. 4. Ford van had AC but it seemed to dump all the air only on driver.

A MOVABLE FEAST

For specific reactions to the conveniences and inconveniences of these mass-produced "custom camper" set-ups, we advise you to read our companion publication, *Wheels Afield*, which regularly tests these super-vans. We used ours for hauling snowmobiles, toting our families and just plain commuting. Overall, we were disappointed to find vans, in spite of their popularity, still more *trucks* than cars, but that is to be expected when one looks at their mechanical origins and at the short lead time Detroit had in order to be able to come up with a product to blunt VW's long-established mini-bus Blitzkreig.

Vans are seldom bought because of the emotional charisma they churn up in the eye of their beholders under the bright lights of the car dealers. Most of them are ordered by customers who know just what they want. Accordingly, each of the major auto-makers offers different packages to suit the needs of the buyers. Ford, for instance, offers

three heavy-duty packages on their Club Wagons — each with progressively stiffer springs, stronger tires and heavier brakes. Their ultimate package — called simply "HD package C" — adds not only the H-D springs, tires and brakes but an extra cooling radiator, alternator, and special instrumentation. Dodge offers a trailer towing package, a school bus package or extra seats (for the longer wheelbase van) plus a list of options a yard long, including a 60-amp battery, power steering, heavy duty shocks, automatic speed control and the like. The important thing to remember when buying a van is that you've got to order *all* the parts you need to carry your projected weight load. Many states consider a van a truck and require the G.V.W. (Gross vehicle weight which includes the vehicle weight plus load) to be listed on the side. If they put you on the scales, and you're over your weight, you are fined. So if you plan to carry a big load, order the H-D springs and shocks. Because of the varying uses for vans — from camping to commuting — we can't recommend one basic package for everyone. A van is what you make of it (or order for it). A couple of general

rules are — don't settle for less than a V8 and power steering in an American-made van, or it'll be undriveable for anybody but a muscleman.

The future may see the incredibly competitive Japanese pop up with a van that'll knock VW right out of the ring by having an economical engine at least 3 liters in size — most likely a six powering an ultra-quality chassis that handles and stops. Until that happens, Detroit will be working at a feverish pitch to come up with more van models — super-super long vans, vans with TVs, vans with stereos, maybe even a big van with a mini-ATV-based van inside.

On balance, the VW van (bus) has a severe power shortage, and if you have two snowmobiles, it may not carry them but at nearly $2,000 less ($50 a month for 36 months) it has to be the best value, never mind the fact that on any snowy or ice-slick surface, the front-bias American vans will not move. VW sales success in 1970, over 65,000 units, was ahead of Dodge but behind Ford and Chevy. This shows the public prefers large size and power over all. Now if Detroit could only offer VW's quality at a competitive price . . .   /M

Volkswagen's Latest

For Light Duty Trucking, Volksvan's Still Tops — And Still Underpowered.

THE NEW VOLKSWAGEN TYPE II bus ("...it's a station wagon, more or less," says VW's recent ad campaign) is the fourth model in the "new look" series which first appeared in 1968. That debut came about just before domestic makers began moving into production with their "second generation" vans—models with front wheels forward of the driving position and wheelbases and overall lengths stretched well beyond what had been regarded as the limits for compact vans.

While domestic production concentrated on much heavier duty and higher gross vehicle weight class vans, Volkswagen kept its changes more modest. Company literature referred to them at "one-tonners," and post-'68 vans have had GVW ratings in excess of 4500 lb. The 1971 model, incorporating as it does its changes in the running gear, is rated at 73 lb. shy of 5000 lb. GVW. Though hardly a threat in the gross weight stakes, the VW van still provides all the useful capacity a Volksvanner could want.

The latest bus is the best model from this mold which the company has produced, too. That's an obvious thing to say, given Volkswagenwerk's rigorous policy of making gradual improvements rather than changes for the sake of change. The question is, how good is "best?"

For starters, there has been the increase in power. Not much, true, at only a modest 3-bhp boost, but every little bit helps. The 96.6-cu. in. flat-Four air-cooled engine tucked in the back locker turns up an even 60 bhp at 4400 rpm. Torque peak at 3000 rpm measures 81.7 lb.-ft. Increased power is responsible for a 3-mph increase in the official top speed which the company also lists as cruising speed) at 68 mph.

Along with Go, the Type II now has Stop: The best brakes that ever have been put on the vans, and they haven't been too bad in the recent past. For 1971, front disc brakes are combined with rear drums in a dual brake system which has an anti-lockup limiting valve in the hydraulic hosing. The brakes are power-assisted from an integral vacuum booster can, as standard equipment.

During trials of the new van, staff members actually got excited over the braking qualities. Pedal feel was sensitive and progressive, despite the power assist, so that there never was a question about what was going to happen with a given level of stomp. When incipient wheel-lock telegraphed itself (yes, it still could—and on one occasion did—happen), the slightest feathering of the brake pedal left it behind like an afterthought. Stopping distance was judged extremely good under the lightly-loaded test conditions, and testers could suggest no reason why it would not remain so throughout the weight range.

Additionally, there have been other running gear improvements. Sturdier constant-velocity universal joints now adorn the rear half-shafts, better able to withstand the guff of hard usage. And the typical Volksvan gets hard usage, indeed. To complement the brakes, 5.5x14 wheels, perforated around the outer edge of the centers for brake cooling, now carry the 7.00-14 tires, planting a full 5-in. wide tread patch on the pavement.

In combination with the new brakes (10.9-in. discs in front, 9.92 x 2.17-in. drums behind, and the necessary hub changes), the new running gear results in a slight change in van track. Front now is 54.6 in. and rear is 2-in. wider at 56.6 in. Aside from the perforated wheels, about the only exterior appearance clue to the model year identification is the flared lip of the rear fender, added to accommodate the wider track.

Wind wander has been brought under more effective control in the latest models, perhaps because the fully articulated rear axle is a more compliant means of keeping the wheels flat on the ground. Yet, in substantial wind conditions (30 kt. with gusts to 40) the bus is still a handful to handle. Constant and continual corrections are the only way to maintain lanes when tooling along in a stiff breeze.

van test

Wind effect—or more precisely, rolling resistance—also takes its toll in forward motion. Despite the gentle rounding of the edges of the front, the bow remains a great slab presented flat-side-first to the wind (the relative wind, created by forward motion). Although the van now is capable of building up a head of steam to charge down the freeway at an indicated 75 mph, achieving the final 5 or 10 mph is an exercise in brute force subduing a resisting medium. And a stiff gust straight on can slow the van perceptibly.

This lack of power is perhaps the most obvious drawback and the most frequent complaint from Volksvan owners. Even the slightest hills will slow the van's pace, and long grades can drag the vehicle down to the point where a downshift is demanded. On our test grade (5.5 per cent and exactly 1 mile in length), the van was slowed to 48 mph (actual) from a 55 mph entry speed. Though it maintained that speed, it was the only new van tested (aside from the Subaru, of course) that suffered from the grade.

Coming down the test grade, the VW—in neutral—coasted to 45 mph to stabilize (from the 55 mph entry speed), again showing the effect of its frontal area.

Sitting high, as one does, over the front wheels makes some rather odd feelings for the first-time vanmaster. There is the sense of insecurity present as the body leans, either in cornering or in wind effect. This is more apparent than real, however. Staffers pulled over 0.5g side loading around the 100-ft. radius turn circle with no problem—and felt comfortable enough to suggest that that figure could be substantially improved with a serious trial. That was indeed good enough to prove that the Volksvan was neither as top-heavy nor as tippy as it feels—and sometimes appears.

There is a choppiness in the ride, almost a loping sort of gait, that quickly is assimilated. And naturally, the driver in front of the wheels that do the steering must develop the habit of turning wide around corners and easing into parking slots lest something midway back scrapes. This too soon becomes an ingrained habit pattern. With surprisingly brief practice, one ceases to be so hesitant about pulling up against walls or stationary vehicles, knowing that the driver himself, in effect, is the extent of the overhang for this vehicle.

The VW has continued its consistent production of what essentially is a light-duty, highly maneuverable, and tautly smallish vehicle. The new vans still sit on the Beetle's 94.5-in. wheelbase and, though lengthened a few more inches four years ago, it still snakes through city traffic like a minicar. Besides that, it's a vehicle that permits (encourages, even) jumping into and jumping out of, making around-town shopping errands a joy to conduct. This aspect of it alone caused our test drivers to consider the Volksvan far superior to the domestic competitors where its primary use would be in the urban environment.

Internal capacity of the van body has been increased to 177 cu. ft., mostly achieved by reducing the engine compartment

NEAT AIR conditioner installation (above and right) is bett than all but Dodge among vans. Controls (reflected in mirrc are easily operated by touch from driver, and unit rapia cools 177 cu. ft. window wagon interior.

intrusion in the late models. The space is eminently usab despite that intrusion that prevents a flat load floor the f length of the inside. If the length of a stretched-out sleepi bag is the criterion, there is adequate level floor space. Whe special equipment and conveniences are to be built in (as ir camper conversion), the cargo box shape is merely somethi to be worked around—and often put to best advantage by t van modifier. And there are advantages to having a highe separate storage shelf in the rear. The rear engine compa ment, in fact, cannot be considered much of a penalty.

van test

The rear engine layout obviously continues its inherent superiority in two areas: Traction and braking. Where snow and ice are regularly encountered facts of life, VW vans prove their virtuosity over and over against just about anything else on wheels. In really treacherous types of non-tractive situations—deep sand, swampy bog land, etc.—the simple selection of proper tires is all with which the VW owner must contend. (It might be mentioned, in this regard, that Bruce Meyers developed most of his conceptual ideas for the dune buggy that started that whole movement from a clapped-out old van he was driving at the time.)

The van's brakes, as noted, are excellent. Its braking qualities, additionally, are improved and enhnced by the rearward weight bias of the design. This is because the brake forces tend to equalize on all four wheels as the rears unload during quick deceleration. But you still have the hinder binders contributing substantially to the work of stopping, a "have-your-cake-and-eat-it-too" situation.

Despite the appearance of the hog-nosed second generation domestic vans, Volkswagen's continual refinement to its basic van cannot be decried as a "lack of progress." It has, instead, proven itself to be a prudent, far-sighted determination to serve an existing and expanding market, rather than hop-scotching on to greater, grander, longer, wider, and heavier things. And the undeniable proof of that is the dealer's showroom: Volksvans have waiting lists that *start* at six months and stretch from there, and when they arrive they go out the door for full sticker price—despite the inane 25 per cent tariff penalty our illustrious Congress has slapped against the windowless ones. (At that, list still is below what Detroit offers for a fully equipped vehicle.)

For the simple fact is that if a buyer wants a small, simple, light weight, highly maneuverable, inexpensive, economical van for today's urban traffic ills, he has only one choice: Volkswagen. The simple fact is that American manufacturers have abandoned this market, as they did with the compact car market 10 years earlier. The simple fact is that no other European maker imports their vans in measureable quantities, and the Japanese makers, which may be expected to launch a drive for domination at any time, have yet to import competitive vans. The simple fact is that 66,188 Americans turned to Volkswagen in 1970 for the solution to their van and window wagon needs.

And the simple fact is that while the 1971 VW van is much different from the 1952 which first came into this country, in many major respects—on paper, if not in the feel of the steel or at the wheel—there remain great similarities and continuity.

The quality, the economy, the stamina are still there. And you can live with a little less power; it's better for the air we breathe that way. Domestic van addicts who snub or sneer at the Volksvan really are the ones who come off short. Volks bus drivers made the smarter choice.

SPECIFICATIONS

..ice, as tested	$3,460
..rb weight, lb.	2888
..st weight, lb.	3155
..distribution, percent, f/r	46.9/53.1
..ted GVW	4982
..e size	7.00—14
..rolling diameter, in.	25.5
..tread width, in.	5.0
..gine type	ohv, HO-4
..splacement, cu. in.	96.66
..e & Stroke, in.	3.36 x 2.72
..mpression ratio	7.5:1
..p @ rpm	60 @ 4400
..que, lb-ft @ rpm	81.7 @

Transmission type	4-sp. man.
ratios, 4th	0.82
3rd	1.26
2nd	2.06
1st	3.80
Final drive	5.375:1

DIMENSIONS

Wheelbase, in.	94.5
Tread f/r	54.6/56.6
Overall length, in.	174.0
width	69.5
height	77.0
equivalent vol., cu. ft.	539
Frontal area, sq. ft.	29.7
Ground clearance, in.	7.3
Steering ratio, o/a	14.7:1
turning circle, ft.	40.3

CALCULATED DATA

Lb/bhp, test wt.	52.5
@ GVW	83.0
Fuel consumption, test mpg	15-19
range, mi.	240-300

PERFORMANCE

Acceleration, 0-60, sec.	38.4
passing, 40-60, sec.	23.7
Braking, 60-0, ft.	215

O'KANE & THE

BY DICK O'KANE

I SHOULD BE uplifted by the scene today—made whole in the soul while my mind reclines on soft thoughts and nibbles at the little peeled grapes of delight that surround me. For the vista at this moment on this day is one many men dream of as they sit starched and confined on a cold winter Monday.

The scene is typical enough—for here. The cafe features the Mandatory Picture of the king, Optional Suggested Picture of the king's father, a sooty Moroccan flag, a roaring, hissing coffee machine with attendant harrassed attendant, and a flood of blazing, gold-white sunshine—hot and fine and welcome enough to bleach out almost any care. I say *almost* any care, for I'm beset by a malady, a longing, a certain madness that comes in recurring attacks, and needs only a reminder to trip off an episode. Like right now; I should be transported by the veiled ladies in white, and by the roaring towers of white spray where the sunlit surf crashes over the ruins of the ancient castle, but it's lost on me. Because *they* are there at the curb. Six . . . seven . . . ten of them. Ten Volkswagen vans. To me at this moment in history their presence, their being, the whirring, clittering bumble of their hopeless little engines is an affront, a cruelty, a taunt beyond endurance, because dammit, *I want one!* Gone is the low, snarling red fantasy, vanished in a cloud of rubber smoke and expensive fumes, to be replaced by dreams of . . . but you'd laugh.

Christ, it's like being infatuated with a fat, ugly woman.

And as with both women and cars, when you want one most, none are available.

I suppose I got into this Volksie van thing about the same way everybody does. At one point a while back I found myself with more than an E-Type could accommodate, i.e., a fallen-down farm and a woman possessed of all the best and worst qualities of mistress and magpie. See, Jeffi's a compulsive trash-picker, and many's the time I've answered the phone to an excited description of the perfectly good and excessively groovy 7-foot walnut and velvet couch simply sitting there on the sidewalk waiting for the trash man, and could I please get out the Jaguar and come help pack it on home. . .

Now, an E Jaguar has many remarkable abilities, but drayage is not one of them. So, typically, when a friend's clapped-out, clattering Volksie van came up for sale, we bought it, typically, for $400. It was one of the window vans with seats, about a '64, and we figured it would be nice to have around—you know, something to rumble down to the dump with every few days . . . or maybe to drive to town once a week to transport a few little sticks of furniture. . .

Anyway, that was the plan, and it soon got out of hand in predictable fashion—Jeffi and I squabbled daily over the thing while the E rusted silently in the barn. And by the end of the summer we were so captivated by that improbable conveyance that we were practically living in it. It may surprise you, but a Volksie van is one of the most delightful vehicles on the road—or off. And it is first, last and always eminently useful and sensible—a cheap, practical trundle-all for the Average Man—a veritable People's Truck, in fact, designed with the same quaint attention to Common Sense that guided the development of the People's Car.

Research the matter a little and you'll find that there are four kinds of Volksie vans—hundred-dollar ones, four-hundred-dollar ones, eight-hundred-dollar ones and new ones. A four-hundred-dollar one is actually a hundred-dollar one for which someone managed to get four hundred dollars, and an eight-hundred-dollar one is a four-hundred-dollar one with paint. A new one is any one with a one-piece windshield. And whether you get it new or used, you can take your choice or your chance and get it with or without windows, with or without seats, beds, a kitchen, whatever—there is a People's Truck and stuff to go in it for everyone. (Another fact of economics—when you have a Volksie van, everybody wants to buy it, except when you want to sell it; then you can't give it away.)

No matter what kind of body/interior it has, you can call it a bus, a truck or a van and no one will care, not even the parts man. Our first one had windows and we called it The Truck, while our second had none and we called it The Bus. See, it all depends on whether you come to regard yourself as the driver of a truck or a bus. The vehicle itself will force you into one of these roles because you sit *way* up high over all the other traffic, and the way your hands fall on the big horizontal wheel is . . . well, you just get into being a bus/truck driver, that's all.

Whether you're bussing or trucking, you can carry a prodigious load of goods and/or people; in fact, the thing has a bigger capacity than the average owner will ever use. With seats, it's cozy with nine, or you can take out the seats in about 2½ minutes and pack in an entire sub-culture. Other things you can put in a Volksie bus and take places include 12 to 18 great big dogs, sound equipment for a rock group, nine weeks' garbage or four weeks' trash, a winter's worth of firewood, two cows, most of your friends, a young elephant, 16 Arab ladies, or a big, hairy motorcycle. Though not all at once. And when you're through, you can simply hose the whole thing out.

Best of all, though, you can throw everyone and everything out and move into your truck to live. That's actually my rationale for wanting one here on the west coast of Africa. It'll accommodate a double bed, your camping stuff and all the crap you acquire in New Hope, Coney Island or Marrakech. And when you're through acquiring, you don't have to pay New Hope or Coney Island or Marrakech prices for a room—just drive until you find a place with a free view. And if the roadside doesn't suit you, leave it—the People's Truck stands tall and proud on its skinny tires, most of its vitals are tucked up out of reach of those big pointy rocks, and it can take you pretty far afield without damage or embarrassment to itself or its load.

And, mind you, it does all this on dainty sips of the gas-station man's most humble potion, with an engine that seems to require nothing more than privacy.

This is not to say that People's Trucking is *all* roses and light, though. For all this common sense, economy and space, one pays one's dues. For instance, consider the shape and size of the thing. It has all the aerodynamic purity of a sheet-iron cow shed, and if you like the sedan in a cross-wind, you'll just *love* the truck! It doesn't just meander around the road in the wind, either. It blows helplessly

PEOPLE'S TRUCK

around like a big empty box, it can meander clear *off* the road in a trice, and sudden bullish charges into the other lane are commonplace—but here, at last, after all these years, *you* get a chance to frighten all the oncoming traffic.

There are other wind hazards. For instance, there's headwind, which can turn a 2-hour trip into a 4-hour one, and there's tailwind, which can get you arrested for speeding, as it's the only way you can ever hope to exceed a turnpike speed limit. Then there's truck wind, which happens every time a truck passes you, which is quite often. This requires a high degree of hard left rudder, as the bow wave of a big truck can blow you right off into the ditch.

Without wind, the performance of the People's Truck will probably please Mom more than Dad. The handbook says the one-, four- and eight-hundred-dollar series will make a breathless 65, and it will—on the flat with no wind and after about fifteen minutes of gritting your teeth in sympathetic effort (sometimes it helps to lean forward in the seat and bounce gently up and down, too). Once underway, you drive flat out, and you soon learn to conserve headway like diamonds. You find yourself taking all kinds of wild chances, nipping through narrow openings, passing when you shouldn't, *anything* to save lifting your foot.

If you do any driving through hilly terrain, you'll learn something very valuable—how to enjoy scenery. This is something you'll *have* to learn to save your sanity, because there is precious little else to do—though on a *really* hilly road, you can always read.

Noise is something else you learn to take in stride, but not with all models. Some of them are all fancy and padded inside and are therefore pretty silent, but not all of them. See, the average garden-variety Volksie van is tastefully trimmed in booming, clanging sheet metal, and fast passage over a bumpy road is like rolling down a cobblestone hill in a galvanized garbage can.

There are a couple of remedies for this, though. One is to glue old carpeting, jute bags and foam rubber all over the interior, which will quiet things down some, and another is to overwhelm the clatter with a ruckus of one's own—like a good, big stereo tape system. In fact, one of the most impressive sound systems I've ever heard lived in a Volksie truck, along with an oriental carpet, an overstuffed armchair, a gigantic brass hookah and a Tiffany lamp. The truck was loud, but the tapes were louder, and a twist of the knob would drown out everything—the indigenous clatter, the leaky muffler, the hard metallic vibration and all that traffic blowing to pass. That's the thing—you don't dare get too quiet. I knew another guy who had a panel with a window in it right behind the front seats, and it made the cab so quiet that one day he got out on the turnpike, couldn't hear the engine screaming that it was still in third gear, and didn't even hear it when it finally blew up. He thought he was out of gas, and it wasn't until he tried the starter with the door open that he heard all the broken pieces churning around.

Yet another hassle you learn to live with is cops. You'd think that a vehicle capable of nothing more dangerous than a brisk trundle would be left alone by the fuzz, but it is not so. Because of its nature—cheap practicality with a highly mobile view—the Volksie van is rapidly becoming the Official Vehicle of the International Counter-Culture, which means young people with hair, bright clothing, rather loose

schedules and other such threats to God and Country. To the average cop, then, that big tin box full of hair gasping up the hill is nothing less than the Main Stash—a thousand-kilo brick of Panama Red disguised as a Volksie van, with windows and doors and freaks painted on it and *wow*, we're all gonna make sergeant! It isn't "Where's the fire?" anymore, it's "Where's the grass?" and unless you look like Mr. Clean going somewhere to scrub a floor, you can plan to spend some time by the side of the road explaining your identity, destination, political views and whatever's in your pockets with The Man.

A friend of mine gets his lumps in by always offering the cop the T-key to the engine compartment, the cop always goes to look, and he always gets all smarmy and greasy in the process, but beyond that there's nothing you can do . . . except vote for me and Stan Mott in '72. If elected, we will have all the drivers of port-hole Buicks stopped and hassled about income tax evasion.

But these are mere annoyances. The real danger—the Ultimate Hazard of People's Trucking is the Sorcerer's Apprentice Syndrome. Reduced to simplicity, this is where you say to your woman, "Behold, for I have brought thee a truck—go ye therefore and collect groovy things and bring them here to make our house fulsome and glad."

And she does.

Giving a truck to a compulsive trash-picker is like giving automatic weapons to Attila the Hun. Even with an empty 10-bedroom farmhouse we were soon overwhelmed with Stuff. After we'd owned the truck a month, for instance, George gave us a painting for the house—a small 2-ft-by-2-ft painting, already, and we couldn't find a place for it! And then there was all that stuff in the barn when we left . . . Lord! Your only consolation when this sort of thing starts is that you have a truck with which to cart it all away again —on days when your wife lets you use it.

Then there's the heater, and the matter of cold weather . . . but enough. You should have the picture by now. Still, you can't know the true, deep-down nature of the beast until you've lived with one for awhile—and then you begin to see that besides all its Teutonic sensibility and practicality and usefulness, there's just something about the People's Truck that's . . . well . . . *silly.* And fun. It's like owning a pack elephant that says and does droll things—a cartoon hippopotamus that brings you the paper and reads over your shoulder and agrees with you about important things, like where to go today, and where to spend the night and when to leave. I think Lewis Carroll would have owned one. Dammit, they *captivate,* that's all, and people respond by painting them colors and naming them things, like Fantasia and Moby Truck and Brunhilde. In fact, last night while dreaming over the fire I decided I'd get one without windows next, and paint it candy-apple red with a gigantic black Maltese Cross on the side, and put a big helmet spike on top of the cab and call it the Iron Chancellor. . .

High on a ridge about two miles up the beach, I can see a silver thread of road glistening with last night's rain, and on the thread like colorful beads are four . . . six . . . seven little dots. More Volkswagen vans. One of those dudes has just *got* to be for sale, I betcha.

Does anybody feel like taking a walk up the beach after breakfast?

VOLKSWAGEN 1700 Microbus 'L'

TEST HIGHLIGHTS

- Much-improved power and performance
- Discs and radials give fine braking
- Governed engine an irritation
- Verdict: the best Kombi ever . . .

BIG things have been happening to Volkswagen's well-loved ten-seater since we last tested it in June, 1968 (the Clipper 1600 L).

A considerable number of changes were made in the intervening three model years — including a small increase in power for the 1600 engine, and the introduction of disc front brakes and radial-ply tyres as options.

Now we have the 1972 model — designated the Microbus L — which has the discs and radials as standard equipment, plus the option of a slightly detuned version of the 1700 engine used in the VW 411 models.

There has been some play on names with this family-wagon vehicle through the years: Clipper, 10-Seater, and now Microbus. But it will always be known, universally, as the Kombi — though strictly speaking, this name is now reserved for the basic (and austere) 1600 model.

BIGGER ENGINE

Test vehicle was the Microbus L, with 1700 engine and all the trimmings, except for the sunshine roof. This is the Type 4 engine, but with compression dropped from 7,8 down to 7,3 to 1 to take regular-grade fuel.

In this form, it develops 55 kW, which is 74 bhp: 23 per cent more power than the uprated 1600 engine. It transforms the vehicle's performance, giving it real punch through the gears, a quite respectable top speed, and sound cruising ability.

VW has introduced governing on these engines, described as a "speed limiter".

It was stated that this would be on the 1600 motor only, but we found that the 1700 motor "dies" at 5 400 rpm in performance tests: very clear evidence that its limits are governed, as well.

Until the driver becomes accustomed to this, and restricts range to about 5 200 through the gears, this is irritating — and could be tricky in such situations as an overtaking operation. The Microbus 1700 picks up speed in lively fashion in 3rd, for instance, until it reaches about 95 km/h, when power is cut without warning. Very embarrassing — if it happens while overtaking on a short straight!

APPEARANCE CHANGES

There are some minor coachwork changes on the 1972 models: the engine air intake scoops at upper rear have been enlarged and squared to improve engine cooling; a bigger engine compartment lid is fitted, with improved locking mechanism; the tail lamp clusters are revised; and the front wheel arches have been flared to match those at rear.

It is a chunky, good-looking vehicle, with one aesthetic flaw: the front wheel arches are higher than those at rear, which emphasises the vehicle's tendency to stand nose-high when light.

The interior ventilation/heating system is improved by the fitting of louvred air outlets in the front doors, to extract air from the passenger compartment via slots in the leading edges of the doors.

SPACIOUS INTERIOR

The whole idea of a Kombi, of course, is space. The twin seats at front have a walkway between them leading to the rear, where there are two bench seats each capable of

KEY FIGURES	
Accel. 0–100 km/h .	24,3 seconds
Maximum speed . .	122,3 km/h
Optimum cruising speed	102 km/h
Cruising fuel range . .	450 km
Engine revs per km . .	2 448
National list price . . .	R3 298

IMPERIAL DATA

Major performance features of this Road Test are summarised below in Imperial measures, for comparative purposes:

ACCELERATION FROM REST
	(seconds):
0-60	23,4
¼ Mile	21,4

MAXIMUM SPEED (mph):
True speed	76,0

FUEL ECONOMY (mpg):
60 mph	22,7
75 mph	15,1

...aking three in comfort, or four at a squeeze. Access to the rear row is from the sliding side door, with the backrest of the left seat in the middle row tipped forward.

Right at the back, inside the tailgate and above the engine compartment, is a raised and (on the "L") carpeted luggage space bigger than the luggage trunk of most cars.

This vast interior, measuring about [?] cubic metres in total, is the basis of the load space on the commercial van model, and the caravan/sleeper conversion of the Kampmobile model. On the "L" Microbus, a step emerges when the side door is opened, to make access easier.

Front access is awkward, particularly as the seats are high above the ground and there are no grabhandles above the doors to help with the step-up.

STEERING AND BRAKES

Going to radials on wide-rim wheels for this vehicle was a courageous move by Volkswagen, and one which contributes materially to safety. Tubes are fitted in the 185 tyres: we would prefer tubeless, but presumably this is a concession to load capacity.

The steering wheel is very big — the biggest we have encountered on anything but a heavy commercial vehicle. This is obviously to provide lighter steering control, particularly with radials.

The boosted disc front brakes are a first-class feature, and in combina-

The twin-carburettor 1700 engine has a bigger engine compartment lid to improve access.

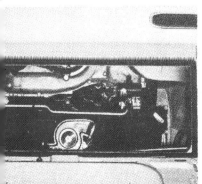

tion with the sure grip of the radials, enables the Kombi to stop almost as quickly as a light car, without wheel-locking or dramatics.

PERFORMANCE

VW has put all the increased power of the new Kombi 1700 into improving lugging power. Overall gearing remains the same as for the earlier 1600 models at 24,4 km/h per 1 000 rpm (roughly 15,2 mph/ 1 000). This is on the low side, and limits range in the gears during acceleration, quite severely.

It jumps away from rest with a bit of wheelspin, and upshifts are made at 30, 55 and 90 km/h.

This big-bodied vehicle is streets ahead of the earlier 1500/1600 models in performance. To give some idea, a brief comparison with the 1968 test (in Imperial measures):

			1600	1700
0–60	..	..	—	**23,4**
¼ Mile	..	..	25,5	**21,4**
Speed	..	..	61,8	**76,0**

In addition, gradient ability is substantially improved: the new model will take a 1 in 16 gradient in top, compared to the old model's best of 1 in 22.

FUEL ECONOMY

Surprisingly, with the twin-carburettor 1700 engine there is also a notable improvement in economy (figures in mpg):

		1600	1700
45 mph	..	25,6	**30,7**
60 mph	..	17,3	**22,7**

Taken to full-throttle cruising at the general speed limit of 120 km/h, the new model will drop right down to 15 mpg — one of the reasons why we suggest keeping to the optimum cruising speed of 4 200 rpm: which, on this vehicle, is a shade over 100 km/h.

STOPPING ABILITY

The Microbus has muscular stopping ability with its front discs and radials, marred only by the vehicle's marked tendency to pitch heavily under full braking: it feels almost as though it is trying to stand on its nose!

But it stops consistently well, with mild fade showing up in repeated stops and increased pedal pressure needed to counter this. The mass of engine at rear keeps the rear wheels on the road, so there is no rear-wheel locking to contend with. Directional stability, consequently, is first-rate, and the driver retains sensitive control. Congratulations to VW: those

NOISE LEVELS:	
Mechanical	Poor
Idling	Poor
Transmission	Good
Wind	Fair
Road	Poor
Coachwork	Good
Average	Poor
ENGINE:	
Starting	Very Good
Response	Good
Smoothness	Good
Accessibility	Fair
STEERING:	
Accuracy	Very Good
Stability at speed	Good
Stability in wind	Fair
Steering effort	Fair
Roughness	Very Good
Road feel	Good
Centring action	Very Good
Turning circle	Poor
BRAKING:	
Pedal pressure	Fair
Response	Very Good
Fade resistance	Good
Directional stability	Very Good
Handbrake position	Fair
Handbrake action	Good
TRANSMISSION:	
Clutch action	Very Good
Pedal pressure	Very Good
Gearbox ratios	Good
Final drive ratio	Good
Gearshift position	Good
Gearshift action	Fair
Synchromesh	Very Good
SUSPENSION:	
Firmness rating	Very Good
Progressive action	Very Good
Roadholding	Good
Roll control	Good
Tracking control	Very Good
Pitching control	Fair
Mass distribution	Fair
Load ability	Very Good
DRIVER CONTROL:	
Hand control location	Very Good
Pedal location	Very Good
Wiper action	Very Good
Washer action	Good
Instrumentation	Good
Rear-view mirrors	Good
Hooter	Poor
INTERIOR COMFORT:	
Seat design	Good
Headroom front	Excellent
Legroom front	Very Good
Headroom rear	Excellent
Legroom rear	Very Good
Lighting	Good
Accessories fitted	Fair
Accessories potential	Good
SEAT BELT EQUIPMENT:	
Type of belt	Fair
Belt mounting location	Good
Belt storage	Fair
ROAD LIGHTS:	
Headlamp penetration	Very Good
Headlamp spread	Good
Dipping control	Very Good
Reversing lamps	Nil
DRIVING COMFORT:	
Steering wheel position	Very Good
Steering wheel reach	Good
Visibility	Very Good
Directional feel	Poor
Ventilation	Good
Heating	Good
COACHWORK:	
Appearance	Very Good
Finish	Good
Space utilization	Very Good
Door access	Good
Load capacity	Excellent
Load access	Good

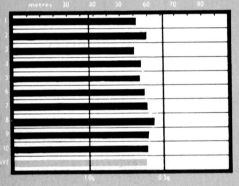

(The graph at top-left shows acceleration curve with 1st, 2nd, 3rd, Top gears, 400m marker, axes "km/h" vs "Time in seconds")

MAXIMUM SPEED 122,3

BRAKING DISTANCES

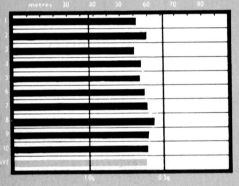

metres 30 40 50 60 70 80

(10 stops from 100 km/h)

1.0g   0.5g

ENGINE SPEED

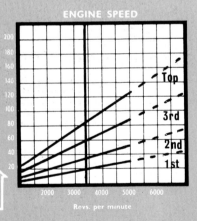

Top / 3rd / 2nd / 1st

km/h — Revs. per minute — 2000 3000 4000 5000 6000

GRADIENT ABILITY

MAX. TORQUE 3,400 RPM

1st / 2nd / 3rd / Top

(Degrees inclination)

PERFORMANCE

MAKE AND MODEL:

Make . . . . Volkswagen
Model . . . . . Microbus "L", 1700

INTERIOR NOISE LEVELS:

	Mech.	Wind	Road
Idling	57,5	—	—
60 km/h	73,5	—	—
80 km/h	78,0	—	—
100 km/h	82,0	—	—
120 km/h	86,5	88,5	89,5
Full throttle			See graph
Average dBA at 120			88,2

(Measured in decibels, "A" weighting, averaging runs both ways on a level road; "Mechanical" with car closed; "Wind" with one window fully open; "Road" on a coarse road surface.)

ACCELERATION FROM REST:

0–60	. . . . . .	7,6
0–80	. . . . . .	13,2
0–100	. . . . . .	24,3
0–120	. . . . . .	65,1
400 m sprint	. . .	21,4

OVERTAKING ACCELERATION:

	3rd	Top
40–60	4,6	10,5
60–80	5,7	11,5
80–100	—	14,0
100–120	—	40,7

(Measured in seconds, to true speeds, averaging runs both ways on a level road, car carrying test crew of two and standard test equipment.)

MAXIMUM SPEED:

True speed 122,3
Speedo reading 130
Calibration:

Indicated	60	80	100	120
True speed	56	76	95	113

FUEL ECONOMY (km/l):

60	. . . . . .	12,1
85	. . . . . .	10,1
100	. . . . . .	7,6
120	. . . . . .	5,5
Full throttle	. .	See graph

(Measured in kilometres per litre, averaging runs both ways on a level road.)

FUEL CONSUMPTION (litres/100 km):

60	. . . . . .	8,3
80	. . . . . .	9,9
100	. . . . . .	13,2
120	. . . . . .	18,2

(Stated in litres per 100 kilometres, based on fuel economy figures recorded at true speeds.)

BRAKING TEST:

From 100 km/h:

First stop	. . . . .	3,7
Tenth stop	. . . . .	4,0
Average	. . . . .	3,93

(Measured in sec. with stops from true speeds at 60 sec. intervals on a good bitumenised surface.)

GRADIENTS IN GEARS:

Low gear	. . . . .	1 in 3,3
2nd gear	. . . . .	1 in 4,7
3rd gear	. . . . .	1 in 8,0
Top gear	. . . . .	1 in 16,4

(Tabulated from Tapley (x gravity) readings, car carrying test crew of two and standard test equipment.)

GEARED SPEEDS (km/h):

Low gear	. . . . .	29,0
2nd gear	. . . . .	53,4
3rd gear	. . . . .	87,3
Top gear	. . . . .	121,9

(Calculated at engine peak rpm — 5 000.)

MECHANICAL NOISE

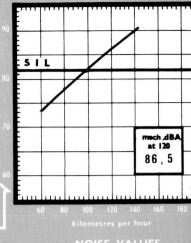

SIL

mech. dBA at 120 — 86,5

dBA — kilometres per hour — 60 80 100 120 140 160 180

NOISE VALUES

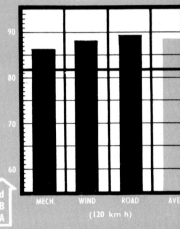

dBA — MECH. WIND ROAD AVE.

(120 km/h)

FUEL ECONOMY

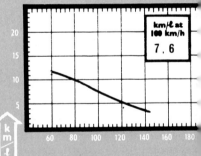

km/l at 100 km/h — 7,6

km/l — 60 80 100 120 140 160 180

FUEL CONSUMPTION

(litres/100 km)

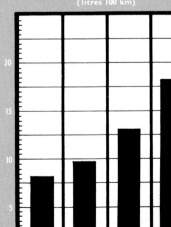

litres per 100 km — kilometres per hour — 60 80 100 120

NE:

nders	4 opposed, rear-mounted
burettors . .	Twin Solex single-choke
e	90,0 mm
oke	66,0 mm
ic capacity . . .	1 679 cm³
npression ratio . . .	7,3 to 1
ve gear . . .	Ohv, pushrods
n bearings . . .	Four
cleaners	Oil bath
l requirement .	91-octane Coast, 87-octane Reef
ling	Air, blower-driven
ctrics	12-volt DC

NE OUTPUT:

. power SAE (kW) .	55,1 (74,0 bhp)
. power net (kW) . .	46,9
k rpm	5 000
. torque (N.m) at rpm .	113,4 at 3 400

NSMISSION:

vard speeds . . .	Four
chromesh . . .	All
rshift	Floor
gear	3,80 to 1
gear	2,06 to 1
gear	1,26 to 1
gear	0,89 to 1
erse gear . . .	3,62 to 1
l drive . . .	5 375 to 1
e wheels	Rear

LS AND TYRES:

d wheels .	14 in. pressed steel discs
width	5½J
e of tyre .	Radial-ply, with tubes
size . . .	185 x 14
e pressures (front) .	2,0 to 2,2 bars (28 to 32 lb.)
pressures (rear) .	2,1 to 2,7 bars (30 to 38 lb.)

ES:

t	Discs
. . . . .	Drums
sure regulation . . .	Nil
ting	Vacuum servo
lbrake position	Centre dash, pull-out

RING:

.	Ross worm and roller, damped
to lock	2,8 turns
ing circle . .	12,0 metres

UREMENTS:

th overall . . .	4,45 m
h overall . . .	1,815 m
nt overall . . .	1,94 m
elbase . . .	2,40 m
track . . .	1,385 m
track . . .	1,426 m
nd clearance . . .	0,185 m
sing mass . . .	1 263 kg

ENSION:

. . . . .	Independent
. .	Torsion bar and stabiliser
. . . . .	Independent
. .	Torsion bar, dual-jointed half-axles

CITIES:

ng	8/10
tank	60 litres
age space . . .	1,0 m³ gross
y space . . .	5,0 m³ gross

ANTY:

ths or 10 000 km.	

CAR FROM:

outh Africa, Uitenhage, in conjunc-
with Motors Western Province Ser-
es, Paarden Eiland, Cape.

CRUISING AT 120

Mech. noise level . .	86,5 dBA
0–120 through gears .	65,1 seconds
km/litre at 120 . . .	5,5
litres/100 km . . .	18,2
Braking from 120 .	4,8 seconds
Maximum gradient (top) .	1 in 111,0
Speedometer error . .	6% over
Speedo at true 120 . .	127 km/h
Engine rmp (top) . .	4 830

discs and wide-boot radials pay off in safety!

VENTILATION AND NOISE

The ventilation and heating system on the Microbus is satisfactory, if not exciting. A weakness is that there are not enough fully-opening windows: only the two front door windows open wide: at rear, passengers have to depend on three hinged quarter-lights, which is not much. The new through-flow system does not have a noticeable effect.

Noise levels all round are fairly high, though the new sound-deadening has reduced mechanical noise levels slightly. Road noise is surprisingly high, considering that the wheels are radial-shod: it must be that the box-like body structure contains panels which pick up road noise.

HANDLING AND RIDE

Once one is accustomed to the very high driving position and big steering wheel, the Microbus is easy to drive. The floor gearshift on the test vehicle — a rather new one — was a bit stiff and vague: not nearly up to the usual smooth VW standard.

Ride is good, though subject to a fair amount of pitching action and while handling is fairly neutral with the dual-jointed rear-axle layout and radials, cornering ability is limited by the amount of high-up body mass and body roll: we took the test corner at a mild 50 km/h, and regard that as pretty well the limit for a tight turn in the Microbus.

Directional stability is good, though this big-sided vehicle is prone to wind-buffeting.

SUMMARY

This is easily the best Kombi ever: it sets new standards in performance and safety, and is a most endearing big-family vehicle. A family of six can get lost inside its big interior, yet its overall dimensions are those of a medium car.

Every inch of overall length and width is used to provide travelling and living space — which makes good sense for families who like to get around in comfort. ∎

PERFORMANCE FACTORS:

Power/mass (kg/kW net) . . .	40,8
Frontal area (m²)	3,52
km/h/1 000 rpm (top) . . .	24,4

(Calculated on licensing mass, gross frontal area, gearing and net power output.)

IGNITION SETTINGS:

Firing order	1–4–3–2
Ignition timing (coast) .	5° ATDC at 850 rpm
Spark plug gap	0,5–0,7 mm
Contact breaker gap . . .	0,4 mm

SERVICE REQUIREMENTS:

Sump capacity	3,0 litres
Change interval . . .	5 000 km
Oil filter capacity . . .	0,5 litres
Change interval . . .	10 000 km
Gearbox/diff capacity . .	3,5 litres
Change interval	Nil
Air filter service	5 000 km
Greasing points	Nil

(These basic service recommendations are given for guidance only, and may vary according to operating conditions. Inquiries should be addressed to authorised dealerships.)

STANDARD EQUIPMENT:

Electric clock, heater, exterior rear-view mirrors, twin dome lights, variable instrument lighting, boosted disc front brakes, radial-ply tyres on wide rims, rubber-faced bumpers, dash grabhandle, semi-reclining front seats, headlamp flasher, hazard warning switch, test wiring circuit.

TEST CONDITIONS:

Altitude	At sea level
Weather	Fine and hot
Fuel used	93-octane
Test car's odometer . . .	2 000 km

Cornered at 50 km/h, the Microbus leans a fair amount, but all four wheels stay put.

The forward-control driving position seen through the front seat walk-through. Steering wheel is very big.

VW CAMPMOBILE

THE POP TOP'S OPTIONAL BUT IT PROVIDES A BIG FIVE-FOOT-LONG UPPER BERTH FOR A 3RD CHILD.

■Volkswagen's Campmobile goes the vacation hideaway "three better." It not only provides living and sleeping space for a family of four or five, but does it wherever and whenever the owner wants and then promptly switches back to work-a-day use with the turn of its key.

One of the most versatile vehicles on the road, the VW Campmobile's 7.3-inch road clearance and rear-wheel traction enable it to reach spots far off the beaten track—and deliver a sedan-like ride in the bargain with its independent torsion bar suspension. That means that it can turn almost any spot into a secluded hideaway.

Heart of the Campmobile is VW's new 1700-cc twin-carburetor rear engine which delivers nearly 25 percent more power than last year's model.

That means faster get-up-and-go under all driving conditions, including improved hill-climbing performance.

Only about 15 inches longer than the familiar VW Beetle, the 1972 Campmobile—built on the same chassis as VW's bus-like Station Wagon—serves variously as living room, dinette, kitchen and bedroom while on vacation and during week-end get-aways.

The rest of the time it serves as a family auto—for shopping, driving to the commuter train station and other routine duties.

Convenience-designed "built-ins" include a clothes closet with inside-the-door mirror, a linen closet, two-shelf food locker, three additional storage cabinets and a hinge-mounted dinette table (Continued on page 71)

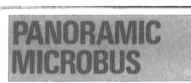

IMPRESSIONS

PANORAMIC MICROBUS

AN INTERESTING trend in South African motoring has been the swing towards de luxe family buses which have many advantages for weekends and holidays — and when mothers operate a car club to transport the kids to and from school.

Leading contender in the market, without a doubt, has been Volkswagen whose Combi and Microbus models — substantially similar but with differences in trim and equipment — have virtually coined the names for this class of vehicle in recent years.

When they brought out the Clipper model, with panoramic windscreen and far lighter, brighter styling, they built a new image for this type of vehicle and they are now reaping the reward with the 1972 Microbus L which for the first time is available with the 1700 cm³ motor to give it extra pep.

As I found when I drove one for a week in all sorts of going, it's a handsome, taut vehicle which has benefited greatly from its revamped suspension using double-joint rear axles and torsion bars all round. It handles with precision, and can be swung through the corners with confidence once you have got used to the high and forward driving position.

Women drivers have no trouble, for the steering is light and the clutch and brakes require no heavy pressures for smart operation.

Finish is superb — easily the best in this class of vehicle and everything about the Microbus seems made to last a long time.

A welcome surprise was the lively performance which comes from the 1 679 cm³ four-cylinder air-cooled engine, detuned from the car version to give 47 kW (net) (64 bhp) and able to run happily on the cheaper grade of petrol because of its 7,3 to 1 compression ratio. It gives the Microbus surging acceleration, so that it takes only 24 seconds to reach 100 km/h, and enables it to cruise at around its maximum speed of 122 km/h (76 mph) indefinitely when road gradients and traffic conditions allow.

The long-lever gearchange, placed left of the driver's seat within easy reach, is pleasant to use and the view from the Microbus in scenic surroundings, something to value.

Braking performance has gained considerably from the installation of boosted disc brakes on the front wheels in 1972 models and the switch to radials has aided the Microbus' ability to stop almost as quickly as a family sedan, without any danger of locked wheels.

At weekends, one can pack in four children, a dog and all the paraphernalia of fishing and playing gear and still have room for your friends and their brood, which allows the women to swop recipes or gossip en route to the beach.

Personally, I do not favour the fitting of the "speed limiter" now used on these engines, presumably to prevent damage from over-revving, and I find it irritating that the motor suddenly loses all urge at 5 400 r.p.m. If power were *sustained* under these conditions, at least you would be able to retire from an overtaking bid in good order. But I found on one occasion early on that the fall-off in "drive" was downright embarrassing. In future I restrained my enthusiasm to 5 200 rpm and resisted the temptation to hang on to third gear towards the 100 km/h mark.

Ventilation and heating are first class in the Microbus 'L', with a wide range of directional and temperature control and adequate power even for this cavernous interior. It was a good deal quieter than I expected, too, and the seats, better than those used in the Combi, earned high marks for comfort, with one exception — that the "front" passengers felt their seat too upright, even with full squab rake applied.

In a quick stop, they tended to slide forward too readily, calling for braking with the feet and arms to maintain position.

Access is remarkably efficient, with wide doors on both sides of the front driver and passenger seats and a double-width sliding door on the left hand side. On the Microbus, this door pulls a rubber-topped step into position as it opens and tucks it away again when it closes. There is a generous rear luggage compartment and this too has its own door.

They say the Microbus is selling mainly to upper income bracket buyers who normally use it as a second car and for open air weekends. So it's even become a status symbol!

Someday I might even buy this vehicle. And when I order, I'll stipulate the sunshine roof and a primrose-cream colour. At R2 998, the Microbus is a lot of car for the money. ●

Panoramic travelling for 10 people: the Microbus.

A rear door gives access to the luggage compartment.

A SUBTLE BULLET

IVERSON'S VAN

BY JOHN R. BOND, JR.

YOU MIGHT ASK what kind of Volkswagen van you can buy for $6000. If your taste in vans is for clean lines and excellent workmanship Chick Iverson, Inc., Newport Beach, Calif., would be happy to tell you. As a result of the favorable reaction to a personal van built for Chick's son, Chick IV, a limited number of similar examples have been built by this VW-Porsche-Audi dealer on special order.

"Bullet," as its owner calls it, took about five months to make its metamorphosis from stock into quality custom reflecting a great deal of good taste. The concept of its creators was to make subtle, tasteful changes rather than the other end of the spectrum.

The paint is actually four different shades ranging from gray to black and these were chosen not only to suit the owner's taste but to give the van something other than a "box-the-bug-came-in" look. The top is a 1958 Edsel silver, the upper side panels ebony, the bottom side panel Cadillac gray-silver and Porsche silver was chosen for the narrow ridge running around the sides between

he black and the gray.

The smooth steel flaring of the wheel-wells along with the redesigned bumpers were touches by Nell Emory, a well known craftsman who has been involved with custom work for many years. He and his son, Don, who sprayed the paint, both work for Iverson, Inc. The flawless acrylic truly enhances the van's otherwise functional styling.

The interior is in contrast to the often overdone, overcrowded insides of many custom vans. The rear area, including the ceiling, is covered with shag carpeting in blue tones and was kept very simple.

The LearJet AM-FM-Tape system is hidden in the rear behind the passenger seat although in reach of the driver. Two speaker boxes each containing two 6-in. J.B. Lansing speakers are mounted firmly in the rear corners. The rear window curtain is black velvet while the front and rear compartments are separated by hand sewn and fitted French calf hide. The floor of the front compartment is done in black cut pile carpeting. The seats are permanently

mounted fiberglass Solar units covered with black Naugahyde. Door panels are also of black Naugahyde. These are diamond pleated but without the heavy appearance which is common to this type of interior.

The mechanical disposition of the Bullet is surprising for a basically stock VW van. Whether streaking at near 100 mph or following buggies in the sand, Bullet's owner has had no back talk. The performance achieved at both extremes is due to only minor changes in its stock mechanics. The stock VW engine is an early '71 without the governor used on later models. The distributor is a Bosch mechanical-advance Porsche type rather than the stock vacuum-advance of the Volkswagen. A bigger main jet in the carb and colder plugs are the only other engine changes.

The suspension accounts for much of the van's improved handling. Gabriel Hi-Jacker air adjustable shocks are used all around, as are wide rims and tires. The wheels are Ansen, while the tires are Inglewood Pos-A-Tractions, E70-14s

on the front with L70-15s on the rear. With the wide tires, the steering effort has increased a bit but the driver has not found this bothersome.

These simple changes can make a great deal of difference in the handling characteristics of the Volks van. A major complaint of Volkswagen handling has always been the van's impromptu lane changing and other maneuvers in windy conditions. The harder shocks and the added rubber put the driver back in command when cornering or when cruising at highway speed. They also do wonders for the behavior when it heads through the brush. The Bullet has been there more than once and its owner has no trouble keeping up with friends in regular buggies.

For the future, Bullet's owner has plans for an electric sunroof and a few other niceties, but one thing he has no plans for is selling it. Those who like what they see can get a duplicate for around $6000. Iverson figures Bullet has cost him $5300, but not everyone has all the necessary talent in one shop—or gets wholesale prices.

VOLKSWAGEN VAN

WHEN HE DRIVES away in a 1972 model, anyone who is familiar with earlier model VW buses will realize that something pretty interesting has happened to the German bug box. It looks very much the same, to be sure, but on applying pressure to the accelerator pedal there is an unmistakable difference—something happens!

It has taken a long time. Back in 1952 when the first VW bus arrived in this country it was equipped with the crudest sort of crash-box transmission, no brakes to speak of, swing-axle rear suspension, lever shocks, skinny tires on 3½-inch rims, a magnificent total of 30 horse-power from an 1100-cc engine and a speedom-eter whose biggest number was 60 mph—and was dreaming even at that.

Only 10 of those 1952 buses were registered in the U.S. but they were the harbingers of much bigger things to come. By '55 there were 2000 VW buses and vans sold in the U.S. and the American manufacturers were beginning to

pay attention, realizing that there might be something them in this idea as well as for the German firm. Oh su American companies had been building delivery vans for ye but until Volkswagen came along none of th had realized that there was a worthwh market among private individuals for whom practicality of a small bus or van was immer ly appealing.

About the only thing that hasn't changed the Volksvan between '52 and '72 is its size shape. The reason for this is obvious; for purpose it is just about as close as you can to being perfect. The air-cooled, flat-4 eng goes into an unobtrusive compartment at rear, the wheels are located close to the corr of the box, everything is rectangular, the scarcely a cubic inch of wasted space anywh and it's as utilitarian as a box on wheels. Which is exactly w it is.

There have been modest increases in performance

The Volkswagen bus was given a thorough workout at Saddleback Park to test its hillclimbing ability. Although not built for going up grades like a 4wd vehicle, the VW bus we tested gave a good account of itself on the way up, but not down.

ontinuing improvements in handling over the years until the 972 model is far and away the best Volksbus yet. The old wing axles are gone, replaced by semi-trailing arms and ointed rear axles. The feeble brakes are no longer with us, ront disc brakes now doing the job. The gearbox is fully ynchronized. The skinny tires have been discarded in favor of air-size radials. The engine now has a rousing 74 horsepower. And the speedometer not only reads to 90 mph, it might even ome pretty close to that speed under favorable conditions.

The engine in the current model is the 1700-cc Type 411 ngine but the bus engine uses a pair of carburetors rather than he more sophisticated fuel injection of the 411 sedan. It got his new engine this year, replacing the dual-port 1600-cc, 0-horsepower engine of last year, and this 25-percent increase n horsepower makes the big difference.

ESTS & IMPRESSIONS

On climbing into the driver's seat, there are a couple things orth commenting about. You notice immediately that the eering wheel is very large and sits very flat in true bus-driver ttitude. You also become aware that the seating position is igh and commanding, the view of the road is very good and ie window glass of the bus affords excellent all-around vision.

The engine displays a host of examples of the effect that ie 1972 emission control regulations has on small engines. It ins poorly when cold, there are flat spots in the acceleration, has "lean surge" when running at part throttle and when ou release the accelerator pedal the engine continues to race r a second or two before dropping back. The 411 engine sed in the sedan is far better in these respects, the black-box el injection doing a better job of meeting the smog quirements with less loss of drivability. The bus engine seems work best when it is driven hard, the throttle kept pressed ell down. Then the additional power of the new engine is ost noticeable—and most appreciated.

Because this engine revs so freely, there's an engine-speed niting device built into the distributor to preclude over-

revving. This tells you exactly when to shift gears as the limiter makes its presence felt at 22 in first gear, 37 in second and 60 in third. These are good, practical speeds for a VW bus or van and a great improvement over the gentle waddle of earlier models when, at 45 mph, you had to shift into fourth gear and wait patiently for the speedometer needle to crawl across the dial.

Our resident van expert was greatly impressed with the performance of the '72 model. What didn't impress him was the softer front suspension. On applying the brakes, even for a relatively gentle stop, there is a lot of front end dive, and over humps and dips the front seat occupants get an unsettling amount of up-and-down action.

Our resident expert was also quick to volunteer that while the van's handling is markedly improved as a result of the new front and rear suspension, plus the larger tires, he would still classify it as "spooky." This is most apparent in straight-line highway motoring where the flat sides offer a tempting target for crosswinds or for the bow-wave blast of air from a big truck coming the other way on a 2-lane road. Admittedly the current model is far better than previous VW beetle boxes in this respect but the tendency is still unmistakably present.

The brakes, a combination of discs at the front and drums at the rear, are very good. Our test driver confessed to some trepidation as he prepared for the 60-mph panic stop but was pleasantly surprised that it responded with perfect control and reassuring surefootedness. It stopped in a respectable 158 ft during the panic stop and then, during our 6-stop-from-60 brake-fade test, displayed only a minimal quantity of fade.

One of the common complaints from drivers who have not gotten to know and love the VW bus is that in cornering it feels like it's about to fall over on its side. It isn't that bad, as our skid pad test demonstrated since it lapped the 200-ft circle at 14.5 seconds for a lateral acceleration reading of 0.58g, which is respectable. During this test there was a lot of body lean, as you would expect, but the tires would slide very nicely in a controllable breakaway rather than let the vehicle go

VOLKSWAGEN VAN

PRICES

Basic list, West Coast POE:
Station Wagon (7 seats)	$3299
Same but w/9 seats	$3329
Kombi	$3059
Campmobile (basic)	$2960

ENGINES

Standard	air-cooled flat 4
Bore x stroke, in.	3.54×2.59
Displacement, cu in.	102.5
Compression ratio	7.3:1
Horsepower @ rpm	74 @ 5400
Torque @ rpm, lb-ft	90.4 @ 3300
Type fuel required	regular

DRIVE TRAIN

Standard transmission	4-spd manual
Transmission ratios: 4th	0.82:1
3rd	1.26:1
2nd	2.06:1
1st	3.80:1

Optional transmission	none

Rear axle type	spiral bevel
Final drive ratio	5.375:1
Optional final drive ratios	none
Limited slip differential	none

CHASSIS & BODY

Body/frame: steel body with stamped/ unitized floor pan

Brakes: discs front; drums rear
Power brakes	std

Steering ratio	14.7:1
Turns, lock to lock	2.8
Power steering	none
Turning circle, ft	40.4

Wheel size, std	5½ x 14
Tire size, std	185SR14

SUSPENSION

Front suspension: trailing arms, torsion bars, stabilizer bar, tube shocks
Front axle capacity, lb	2227

Rear suspension: semi-trailing arms, torsion bars, tube shocks
Rear axle capacity, lb	2800
Additional suspension options:	none

ACCOMMODATION

Standard seats front buckets, 2 rear benches. Optional: 9-passenger seating
Headroom, in	38.0
Pedal to seatback, max	38.0
Steering wheel to seatback, max	15.5
Seat to ground	40.0
Floor to ground	21.0
Heater & defroster	std
Tinted glass	none

Unobstructed load space (length x width x height), in	60x41x48

INSTRUMENTATION

Instruments: 90-mph speedo, 99,999.9 odo, fuel level

Warning lights: oil pressure, alternator, directionals, high beam, parking, hazard, brakes

MAINTENANCE

Service intervals, normal use, miles:
Oil change	6000
Filter change	6000
Chassis lube	18,000
Tuneup	12,000
Warranty, months/miles	24/24,000

GENERAL

Curb weight, lb (test model)	2990

Weight distribution, percent, front/rear: 42/58
GVW (max. laden weight), lb.	4960
Optional GVW(s)	none
Wheelbase, in	94.5
Track, front/rear	54.6/56.4
Overall length	174.0
Height	76.4
Width	69.5
Overhang, front/rear	35/38

Ground clearances:
Front axle, in	10.0
Differential	10.0
Oil pan	10.0
Fuel tank	24.0

Fuel tank capacity, U.S. gal	16
Auxiliary tank(s)	none

OTHER OPTIONS

Campmobile equipment	$888
same plus pop top, roof rack tent	$1421

PERFORMANCE DATA

"Station Wagon" model with standard 7-passenger seating, AM radio. West Coast list price, $3375.

DRY PAVEMENT

Acceleration, time to speed, sec:
0-30 mph	5.7
0-40 mph	9.1
0-50 mph	14.0
0-60 mph	22.3
Standing start 1/4-mile, sec	23.1
Speed at end	60

Maximum speed in gears:
High gear	74
3rd	59
2nd	38
1st	20

BRAKE TESTS

Pedal pressure required for 1/2-g deceleration rate from 60 mph, lb	30
Stopping distance from 60 mph, ft	158
Fade: Percentage increase in pedal pressure for 6 stops from 60 mph	38
Overall brake rating	very good

CORNERING

Speed on 100-ft radius, mph	30.0
Lateral acceleration, g	0.58

INTERIOR NOISE

Idle in neutral, dBA	54
Maximum during acceleration	76
At steady 70-mph cruising speed	82

OFF PAVEMENT

Hillclimbing ability:
Climb test hill no. 1 (47% grade)	yes
Climb test hill no. 2 (56% grade)	no
Climb test hill no. 3 (63% grade)	no
Climb test hill no. 4 (69% grade)	no

Maneuverability	good
Turnaround capability	good

GENERAL

Heater rating	good
Defroster effectiveness	good
Wiper coverage	good

FUEL CONSUMPTION

Normal driving, mpg	18.3
Range, normal driving, mi	290-320

The interior of the Volkswagen Van is nicely done in simple good taste. The instruments are easily visible to the driver and the dashboard has an uncluttered appearance. The hand brake lever has been moved up under the dashboard.

alling over or doing anything strange to embarrass the driver.

The skid pad test brought out another characteristic and hat was for the driver to slide off the seat in hard cornering. 'he cross-over lap and shoulder belt has a lot to recommend it 1 a frontal crash but it doesn't do much about keeping you in osition in hard cornering.

There is conclusive statistical evidence that vans get into a igher percentage of accidents than conventional vehicles. 'hese statistics also reveal that the vast majority of these ccidents are the driver's fault. In hard cornering or in an mergency maneuver too many drivers have a tendency to let ff the gas or even hit the brakes if the tires start to slide. This, f course, is the worst thing to do at that point. What the river should do is keep the power on, letting it slide if it ants to, then get into a straight line again before decelerating r braking. In this respect, the Volksvan has a lot of "early arning" built into it; it will tell the driver long before he is ast the point of no return and the experienced VW bus or van river prefers this kind of handling to the numb understeer haracteristic of vehicles with a pronounced front-end weight ias.

We also took the bus to our usual off-pavement test area in addleback Park. There we found the ride and rough-road andling to be very good indeed. The generous suspension avel does a lot to soak up the road's irregularities and to give a reassuring sure-footed stance. The traction, because of the gine's weight at the rear, was also superior to any 2-wheel- ive vehicle we've ever had at Saddleback (excluding dune iggies, of course). Our only complaint resulted from the soft ont suspension that kept the driver bobbing up and down id we're sure that a good day's off-pavement motoring would nd a driver who would welcome a nice steady rock to sit on.

In trying the bus on our calibrated test hills, we made it up o. 1 with no trouble and got to within about 30 ft of the top No. 2. We were pleased at this, having expected it to make no more than about halfway. The cause for not making it to

the top was engine payout; it simply didn't have the beans to continue all the way up the 56-percent grade. For perspective, it should be mentioned that the mini-pickups we tested in the last issue would not climb our hill No. 1.

A lesson was learned when, after the bus was stopped on the slope, the driver put it into reverse to back down the hill. This, of course, is the proper procedure at such a point but he quickly discovered that reverse gear was too fast for safety and he estimated that he would arrive at the bottom of the hill going something like 60 mph, obviously a poor idea. So he applied the brakes and the front end, being very light at this attitude on the steep incline, locked the brakes so the tires had no grip and steering effectiveness was lost. This resulted in the front end starting to slide to the side. This could have been serious since the angle of the hill was such that the vehicle would roll over if it got sideways. Luckily, we had a Jeep CJ5 with a winch standing by and after the bus slid to a stop at about a 45-degree angle, we were able to hook the winch onto the front end of the bus and keep it straight for the balance of the let-down.

The lesson was clear. On short hills or in marginal traction, the rearward weight bias is a boon. But trying to back downhill with a light front end is likely to lead to serious difficulties.

On the highway or in the give-and-take of urban traffic, the '72 bus is not the perambulating chicane it once was. You can cruise with the fastest highway traffic, come a lot closer to maintaining headway on hills than you used to and you have the advantage of superior vision, good low-speed handling and good brakes.

All things considered, the '72 VW bus is still one of the very best buys in its class. It has the additional benefit of being fun to drive and eminently practical for almost any task to which it is assigned. With the increase in power, plus the established Volkswagen virtues of mechanical reliability and dependable service, you can't really go wrong. ●

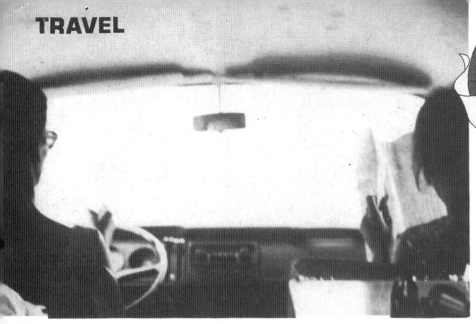

A World's Record In A

TOP LEFT: Carroll's wife and his daughter try to get back on course while heading for the pyramids. LEFT CENTER: The dirt road leading to the pyramid. LEFT: The brother and sister team who sold hand-woven hats and shell necklaces, typical of the area and worn by the Mexicans themselves. ABOVE: The pyramid and the VW camper meet! Actually the story is of what happens when you offer someone a lift in Mexico, especially if your Spanish is limited. The Carroll family is still arguing about how many people really got into the VW.

1970 VW CAMPER

BY RICHARD CARROLL

IT JUST HAS TO BE A RECORD IF YOU INCLUDE HIS FAMILY.

■ For weeks now, I along with my wife and two teenage children had been exploring the lush, tropical East coast of Mexico, living off the land, trying to converse with the elegant Indians who long ago convinced us that they are the true bohemians of the world because they work with the earth, speak their own language, eat what they raise and are almost untouched by the commercial world.

Often we would see them walking along the edge of the highway always in their bright white fabrics, rope sandals, and usually a large machete casually dangling at their side. We offered them rides but they always refused. The tremendous tropical heat didn't seem to bother them or else they didn't wish to bother with us. We felt rejected especially when we knew that they had a long distance to travel.

Our 1970 Volkswagen camper was taking the place of home and was our security blanket on wheels. She had already endured the terrific lashings of hurricane Cecilia and had been traveling the burro trails, fording small rivers and moving about in areas that were not even listed on our maps. The day before we had left Tihuatlan and driven eight miles up a dangerous washed out gravel road to the Pyramid of Castillo De Teayo. We noticed the Indian children peer-

1970 VW CAMPER

An Indian family (whose ancestors built the pyramid) disappearing into the jungle.

That evening we camped right on the Gulf at Tecolutica. A hot wind was blowing in off the water so we spent the night swimming and fighting off the pesky land crabs that covered the beach. Tomorrow would be the big day, a trip to the El Tajin archaeological zone. We had been looking forward to this for years, and we never realized that we also had the possibilities of breaking a world record.

The sky was filled with drifting, billowy clouds but the sun was penetrating and the heat and humidity were fierce. Excitedly we approached El Tajin moving onto the last one mile of road which was rough and unpaved. We had the side door open as we crept along the rocky trail. This is against the rules but we needed the breeze and the view was spectacular. We passed a family of Indians that looked more Oriental than Indian and then suddenly we saw the most beautiful ruins that we had ever seen in Mexico. It was deadly quiet and it seemed as if we were in another world, another time.

The Pyramid of the Nices has 365 niches, symbols of the days of the year and each of the four sides of the pyramid represents a season of the year. There is no question that the pyramid once was a part of a large center for there are foundations of dozens of structures in the immediate vicinity. The pyramid is today the best preserved building but there's also a ball court ninety meters long, surrounded by altars to the Totonac

ing out at us through the tall, dense growth. We would see an eye or a flash of black hair and then they would suddenly disappear, just fade away; it was uncomfortable.

Traveling on this road we had crossed over logs, moved around large boulders and at times we were not sure whether we were on a trail or just bulldozing through the jungle. Finally we came upon a huge pond that blocked the trail. Carson jumped out of the camper, shouting, "It's okay,

you can make it!", as he sank to his knees in water and mud. Somehow we always did make it, but a short time later our camper cast off all four hub caps as if to tell us that we were being unreasonable. But if she only knew what was in store for her.

The pyramid was beautifully preserved and stood squarely in the village plaza surrounded by ancient carved figures. It is located in the Totonac-Huastecan zone but Toltec and Mayan influences can be seen.

It was Indians like these that the Carrolls crammed into the VW and drove to town.

This view is from on top of one pyramid

The VW bus is dwarfed by the pyramids. Note the figure in the left foreground.

Gods. It's known that the Totonacs made their home in this region, but the Olmecs, about the year 600 A.D. were responsible for the construction of the Tajin and there is also a Toltec influence in construction.

Standing on top of the pyramid we noticed twenty or more large mounds that were covered with jungle growth which the archaeologists haven't had time to uncover or explore.

We had noticed the Indian family plus other Indians scattered about the area observing the buidings or just sitting staring out at the countryside. It was the core of the afternoon and the temperature was above 100 degrees. We climbed into the camper, sipped some water and headed slowly down the trail with the side door still open. We came upon the Indian family that we had seen earlier in the day. They were moving slowly and helping along an elderly grandmother or great grandmother who was perspiring profusely. She was not complaining but one could see that she was in pain.

In my very poor Spanish I asked them if they would like a ride. We had a complex now and my voice was shaky. They stopped and looked at us. One of the younger men spoke Spanish and smiled at me. They stood and spoke Indian among themselves looking in at the camper and

then at the old woman. We could see by the look in her eyes that the Grandmother wished to ride. We motioned to them and to our amazement, they climbed in. First the babies, then the children, followed by the women and finally the men. There were six of them. We started slowly down the trail when we came upon another couple. Our passengers yelled at them so I stopped and the couple climbed into the camper. We now had twelve people inside the Volkswagen. Further down the road we came upon another elderly couple, an uncle and an aunt. She was carrying a small child who was asleep and drooling. We all shifted and made room for them. We were wall to wall Indians plus four Americans. I suddenly discovered that it was a huge family that was spending the day at El Tajin, and that they were going to stick together. If one of them was going to ride then they all were.

I found out from one of them that they were going to Poza Rica which is 11½ miles from El Tajin. I could tell that the VW was upset with the extra 1000 or so pounds that I had put on her. As we drove to Poza Rica the Indians were very quiet. They didn't speak, not with us nor with one another and only smiled when I looked at them.

We pulled into Poza Rica and

stopped at the corner of their choice. The people in the city were amazed. We caused a horrendous traffic jam as the shocked people stopped to watch the eleven Indians unload from the VW. The family stood on the sidewalk and waved goodby to us. The man that spoke Spanish looked at our license plate and yelled "Viva California, Viva California!" They didn't move from the corner until we were out of sight.

We were on the road to Vera Cruz and everything felt good.

"I guess the Indians liked us after all, huh, Dad?" Stacy said. "There were eighteen of us in the car."

"No, I think there were only fifteen."

"Counting us?"

"Yes."

"Did you count the two babies behind the spare tire and the one fastened on the back of the lady with the long black hair that reached to her waist? There were eighteen of us, Dad, and it *has* to be a world record, at least for 11½ miles along a Mexican road in a 1970 VW camper."

We are still arguing about the count. But I know that it was more than fourteen and less than twenty. Either way it probably is a world's record for 11½ miles along a Mexican road in a 1970 VW camper. ●

THE VOLKSWAGEN van was the first to really get the van movement off the ground in this country. It was introduced in the U.S. in 1952 (10 were sold that year), it has continued to be a leader in sales through the years and there are now well over half a million plying the highways of America.

The Volksvan is one of the best vans available, offering many design features not found in other vans. The air-cooled engine placed over the driving wheels in the back offers outstanding traction both on and off the road. The 1968 and later model Volkswagen vans also feature fully-articulated independent rear suspension with universal joints at each end of the half shafts, instead of swing axles. This, coupled with independent front suspension, make the ride and traction characteristics of the later Volksvans superior to the traditional live-rear-axle design common to U.S.-built vans.

But from the introduction of the VW van to the U.S., owners have had one common complaint: lack of power. The special requirements of highway cruising in this country have always tested the Volksvan to its limit, not to mention getting onto freeways safely and over anything larger than a 5-percent grade. Some of the more talented and industrious owners began making various engine conversions but these were generally of the "backyard special" variety because there was nothing else available.

There are now, however, a number of companies which offer kits that enable Volksvan owners to replace the power plant of their box with something more potent. These range from the more common Corvair engine conversion right up to V-8s which can make the VW van a real barnstormer. Even the latest Volksvans can benefit from the increased torque and horsepower, especially if trailer towing is to be considered.

CORVAIRS

The most common and perhaps the easiest conversion is to put a Chevrolet Corvair engine into your van. The 6-cylinder Corvair engine is the only American-built air-cooled engine which was produced in significant numbers. Thanks to Ralph Nader, Corvairs are pretty cheap autos to buy nowadays. There are two basic ways to convert to Corvair power in your bus: one is to retain the VW transaxle, the other is to substitute that of the Corvair.

The conversion kit made by Paul Hadley of Hadley Chassis Engineering in Costa Mesa, Calif. uses the Corvair transaxle as well. Hadley's Transvair kit is for '68 and later buses since the earlier Volksvans call for a variety of mechanical changes which Paul believes are not worth the trouble. The basic reason for utilizing the Corvair transaxle, according to Hadley, is that the Chevy engine turns in the opposite direction of the VW engine. Therefore you have to either reverse the camshaft in the engine, which means a complete tear-down, or you must flop the ring gear in the VW transaxle, which cannot be done in the '68 and later models. Also, the greater power of the Corvair engine puts additional stress on the VW transaxle which can lead to mechanical problems and the lower gear ratios

VW VAN ENGINE CONVERSIONS

MAKING THE BUGBOX A GOOD PERFORMER

BY THOS. L. BRYANT

While the bumper sticker of Hadley Chassis Engineering is for fun, it also holds a lot ‹ truth. The Hadley VolksVan with Corvair conversion was peppier and more responsiv‹

sult in lower cruising speeds.

Hadley puts out a fact sheet for ɔspective converters who are not sure the best way to proceed in locating ajor components for the swap. He els the best thing to do is check the ant ads of your newspaper and drive ɔrvairs that are still running. Checking ɪt an engine and transaxle in a wreck-ɡ yard is best left to the true auto-otive expert. An engine that is still in vehicle and running will tell you more.

The '65 or newer engines are the best ɪd should be used along with the later ansaxle, although the '61 to '63 trans-ɪles offer lower first and second gear tios. Another added feature of the Transvair kit is that you can easily make your Volksvan automatic by using the Corvair Power Glide transmission and shift cables. This is a real boon to PV4'ers who spend a lot of time driving in the city.

Hadley Chassis Engineering made two of its Transvair-equipped vans available to PV4 for testing on the highway and at the Orange County International Raceway. The performance was exciting to those of us who have served time in stock VW vans, especially the older ones, laboring over hills in company with the big semi rigs and getting stuck behind Sunday drivers on 2-lane roads.

The first test vehicle was equipped with the 110-bhp engine and an automatic transmission. On a 400-mile weekend roundtrip the performance was pleasantly surprising. Cruising the freeways at 70 mph at half throttle and going up and over grades without appreciable slowing was fun, almost as much fun as seeing the expressions on the faces of other Volksvan drivers struggling along at much higher rpm and lesser speeds. The entire PV4 staff thoroughly enjoyed driving the automatic and felt that its performance was all it should be. On the highway the fuel consumption ran 18 mpg which compares favorably with the 18.3 mpg we got in the 1972 VW stock van reported in the last issue of PV4.

The other Transvair van was equipped with the 140-bhp engine and a 4-speed manual shift. It wasn't as quick off the line due to the higher 1st-gear ratio but once you get going it has surprising power. We took both of these Corvair-powered vehicles to the test track and ran acceleration tests. The 4-speed's acceleration was somewhat disappointing as it had 215-14 tires on the rear instead of the stock 185 size and these bogged the van down off the line. As a result, the acceleration was not as impressive as one would imagine. Another factor was that the second set of carburetors on the big engine was not kicking in properly at full throttle. The stock VW van we tested earlier ran the quarter mile in 23.1 seconds with a speed of 60 mph. The Transvair 4-speed did 70 mph with an elapsed time of just under 20 seconds. The automatic turned in a time of 21 seconds at 64 mph. The time-to-speed runs also showed increased performance for the Corvair powered vehicles as they generally took some 30 percent off the times of the stock VW to 50 and 60 mph. However, the stump pulling low gears of the stock van kept it competitive in the 0-30 tests.

As far as maximum speeds are concerned, the Transvair vans were not completely measurable due to the shortness of the track. The best we got out of the stock Volksvan was 74 mph wound out, while the Transvair automatic did 80 mph fairly comfortably and the 140 Transvair ran off the speedometer (which goes to 90) and kept right on going! We had calibrated the speedometers earlier so that the indicated speed was very close to actual.

The Transvair vans have another important feature, low end torque. The stock VW van in either the standard model or the Westphalia camper would make an ideal recreational vehicle if it had the power to pull a trailer. It does, of course, have as low a gear ratio in first as anything around, but after that you run out of power pretty quickly. With an engine conversion this is not the case.

thout the bumper sticker on the back no one would suspect that this VW van is any-ng but stock. However it has a Corvair engine and an automatic transmission.

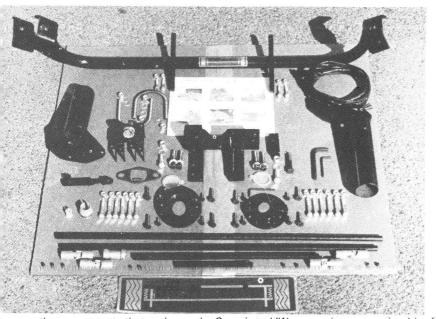

ɛse are the components that make up the Corvair to VW van engine conversion kit of ːdley Chassis Engineering. This kit is complete and will make for easy engine switch.

We also visited Crown Manufacturing Company in Newport Beach, Calif. another company making Corvair-to-VW adaptor kits. Crown offers three different kits. One is for those who want to retain the VW transaxle (pre-1968) and can take the trouble to disassemble it and reverse the ring gear; the second also retains the VW transaxle and is for those who are planning to tear down their Corvair engine completely to put in a backwards-running camshaft; and the third is for mating the Corvair transaxle and engine to the VW. Although we did not drive a van conversion done by Crown, we assume the performance will be similar to that of the Hadley vans, with the exception of those which retain the VW transaxle. In those the top speed will not be as high as the gearing will be lower.

V-6 AND V-8

For those who want optimum performance, Kennedy Engineered Products in Pacoima, Calif. offers conversion kits for stuffing a V-6 or a V-8 into the VW van. Obviously the project is going to be more complicated and time-consuming due to the need for a radiator. Hobert Kennedy can also provide the kit and instructions for placing a Saab V-4, Dodge Colt inline 4, '72 Ford Pinto OHC 4, Chevy Vega, Capri V-6 or Mazda Rotary engine in your bus. However, the most common conversions have been to the Buick V-6 or the aluminum V-8.

Kennedy suggests that the cast iron V-6 from the 1964-67 Buick Specials and the 1965-70 Jeeps (same engine) are readily available and make an easier conversion due to their smaller size. The drawback is that they are harder on the VW transmission than the V-8 because of the larger displacement per cylinder and the non-rhythmic firing order. The V-6 should give better gas mileage than the V-8, but strangely enough it doesn't.

The aluminum V-8 has some drawbacks too. It is not as plentiful, there is a tendency for the heads and block to be warped if the engine has been seriously overheated, and there may be corrosion caused by not maintaining anti-freeze in the cooling system. However, the aluminum V-8 will give more power and will be considerably quieter.

Kennedy points out, as did Paul Hadley, that the resale of VW engines is generally quite good and that you may offset much of the cost of your conversion by selling off the VW engine. The cost of the V-6 and the V-8s is generally quite moderate, probably ranging from a high of $325 to a bargain of $65 or so. The price of the kits from KEP is $190 complete or $155 for the aluminum V-8 kit less clutch and $150 for the V-6 kit without the clutch.

Three satisfied KEP customers brought their vans by for pictures and evaluation. Leon Leonardo of Burbank, Calif. has a '58 VW pickup on which he has mounted his own camper and has a Buick V-6 hidden in the rear. Previously Leon had the engine in a VW sedan, but after two years in the army in Germany driving VW vans, he found he liked them and decided to switch his V-6 into the larger vehicle. When PV4 talked with Leon, he had just returned from an 11,000-mile journey around the U.S. and Canada and reported no troubles with his conversion. He averaged close to 18 mpg throughout the trip, Leon said, and had no problems on the mountain roads, even crossing the Continental Divide. Unfortunately we were not able to get his van or the other KEP equipped ones to the test track but driving impressions showed that the V-6 and the V-8 conversions gave you more than enough power and acceleration.

The second KEP van was a '69 with a Buick aluminum V-8 belonging to Wolfgang Van Der Grinten who tows a trailer with boat weighing about 2000 lbs. Wolfgang says he gets about 17 mpg and can go over most grades at close to 80 mph with the trailer hooked up. He has put over 10,000 miles on his conversion since he did it. It has a VW sedan transaxle instead of the regular

The Corvair engine being set into the Volkswagen engine box. It is a close fit but can be made without too much alteration. The increased performance will be pleasing.

This is the Volkswagen pickup of Leon Leonardo of Burbank, Calif who has put a V-6 into it. The camper was built by Leon himself. The performance is fantastic!

...us unit and this provides somewhat ...gher gearing and closer ratios.

Harold Shands, the owner of the ...ird KEP van we inspected, has a '61 ...W with a Buick V-6 225-cu-in. engine ... which he has traveled some 60,000 ...iles. Harold states that most of his ...riving has been with a 2-car trailer ...tched to the back and he gets about ...2 mpg that way.

All three of these van owners agreed ...at the work was well worth it and that ...esides improved acceleration they ...lieved the increased weight of the ...gger engines provided better handling ...aracteristics.

The biggest problem in the V-6 or 8

conversion, as we mentioned, is the radiator. Wolfgang has his mounted on the front while Leon and Harold have mounted theirs on the rear. The radiator can be from any vehicle as long as it has sufficient cooling capacity. It may need some modification of the outlets so that the hoses go in the right places and you may have to do some work with angle irons to mount it.

PORSCHE SWAP

Another type of van conversion for VWs is the swap involving a Porsche engine. This is certainly one of the most common and the easiest conversions to

make in your VW van as the Porsche engine will generally slip right in without much work. The choice of Porsche engines ranges from a good sturdy industrial engine to the later high performance powerplants that will develop all the horsepower and torque you can use.

Kennedy Engineered Products makes available a kit for converting the Porsche 914 engine to the VolksVan for $90 including clutch. Most people who go the Porsche route, however, do so without the benefit of any type of kit as the engine will generally match up with the VW transaxle. The mounting of the engine usually requires some spot welding when installing the Porsche, but the conversion is still a simple one compared with the others. The biggest problems occur when putting in the 6-cylinder Porsche engine as it requires a bit more space than the 4-cylinder models.

CONCLUSION

As you can see there are a number of alternatives open to VW van owners who want the extra power. The Corvair conversion has long been popular and will continue to be. The V-6 and 8 conversions are the ultimate for hauling power and acceleration, although we have some reservations about durability since the greatly increased torque and horsepower put a lot of stress on the VW transaxle.

The VW van engine swap seems to us to be a good idea for a number of obvious reasons. You should also be aware that conversions may also change the handling characteristics of the vehicle to some degree, especially if an appreciably heavier engine is used to replace the original. Of the owners we have talked to concerning this, however, none have been disappointed in the end result and all describe an engine conversion as being the only way to go to make the bugbox into a good performer. ●

...is is the Volkswagen van of Hobert Kennedy of Kennedy Engineered Products in ...coima, Calif. It has a V-6 engine that is tight fit but only small rise for carb.

...olfgang Van Der Grinten and "friend" find it a pleasure to motor along in V-8 ...uipped VW van, even pulling 2000-lbs of boat and trailer. Can cruise at 80 easily.

Corvair Conversions

Hadley Chassis Engineering
1778 Monrovia
Costa Mesa, Calif 92627
$119.50 Complete

Crown Mfg. Co. Inc.
858 Production Place
Newport Beach, Calif 92660
$119.50 up

V-8 & V-6 Conversions

Kennedy Engineered Products
10202 Glenoaks Blvd.,
Pacoima, Calif 91331
Various prices depending
on engine. Request price
list.

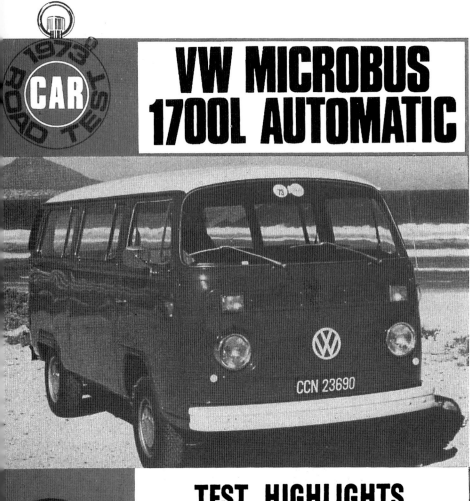

VW MICROBUS 1700L AUTOMATIC

CCN 23690

TEST HIGHLIGHTS

- Responsive in traffic, cruises well
- Smooth and easy-driving, good economy
- Lighter steering benefits handling
- Kick-down awkward, climbing is slower
- Verdict: Capable, and delightful to drive . . .

The Volkswagen Microbus, or Kombi, is a load vehicle, a light bus, a family holiday car. You don't put automatic transmission in that kind of vehicle — or so most people would have thought.

Well, Volkswagen has done it, and the result is truly amazing! Right at the start, we can report that the Microbus Automatic is a resounding success: responsive, smooth and infinitely drive-able.

KEY FIGURES

Accel. 0—100 km/h . 34,9 seconds
Maximum speed . . . 115,5 km/h
Optimum cruising speed 111 km/h
Cruising fuel range . . . 325 km
Engine revs per km . . . 2 255
National list price . . . R3 187

It can keep up with city traffic — and even set the pace — and it retains both sound cruising ability and fuel economy to match that of the manual-transmission model. In addition, it suddenly becomes easy-driving and relaxed-feeling on the road, thanks to both the accurate automatic transmission and the improved, lighter steering.

There is one penalty to pay: it becomes inferior to the manual transmission model in upper-speed and general gradient ability.

PIONEERING FEATURE

Since Volkswagenwerke began the modernisation and improvement of its Type 2 models — with the abolition of the wicked crank-axle rear suspen-sion layout seven or eight years ago — the Kombi range has made steady advances. Changing to the modern, dual-jointed half-axles at the rear lowered the rear roll centre consider-ably, and made the Kombi models much more stable and safe.

On the 10-seaters we have seen such pioneering features in their class as the introduction of disc front brakes with vacuum-servo boosting, wide-rim wheels with radial-ply tyres — and now, full automatic transmission. This last, we may add, is one of the biggest surprises to come from any manufac-turer in the first half of 1973 — a half-year packed with announcements of new and improved models.

NEW FEATURES

The 1973 models — including the Type 2 commercial models — incor-porate substantial styling, detail and mechanical improvements. To start with, the amber front indicator lights are bigger and are mounted higher (on either side of the air intake grille) to give clear signals.

The bumpers, front and rear, are deeper and heavier this year, to match standard car-bumper heights and give increased protection. They include an impact-absorbing element for safety.

The interior heating system has been improved by introducing outlets at the centre bench seat, and it works well — though the warm air from the engine-cooling system had a musty smell on a new vehicle.

The 1700 engine has been made standard right through the Microbus range.

LIGHTER STEERING

The steering wheel remains very large — the only truck-like feature in the controls of the Microbus — but steering itself has been made 20 per cent lighter by increasing the ratio of the worm-and-roller system. It now requires 3 turns from lock to lock in place of the earlier 2,8 turns, and

IMPERIAL DATA

Major performance features of this Road Test are summarised below in Imperial measures, for comparative purposes:

ACCELERATION FROM REST:
	(seconds)
0—60	31,2
¼ mile	23,1

MAXIMUM SPEED (mph):
True speed	71,8

FUEL ECONOMY (mpg):
60 mph	21,4
Full throttle	15,3

this benefits about-town handling considerably.

Engine access is improved on the 10-seaters by the introduction of a hatch under the load-space carpet, so that the engine can now be reached from above as well as through the rear engine-cover lid.

As on other disc-braked VW models, disc pad thickness has been increased from 10 to 14 mm, to give improved pad life.

DRY AIR-CLEANER

Another historic change is the introduction of a dry-element aircleaner in place of the traditional VW oil-bath cleaner, which will make for greater engine cleanliness and easier servicing.

The styling changes have made the new model 60 mm longer than before, though it is still only 39 cm longer than the Beetle. Inside this modest length is seating for 8—10 people, with a walk-through between the front seats, and a 990 dm³ load space at rear

The long T-handle selector replaces the gearlever, and is easy to operate. Steering has improved gearing, and is lighter.

Engine access is improved by the interior hatch, under the load space carpet.

above the engine. Rear access is by a sliding side door and counterbalanced rear tailgate.

In the new model, tools and jack are mounted under the front passenger seat, and the windscreen wiper control is on the steering column for easier operation.

3-SPEED TRANSMISSION

The 3-speed automatic transmission is the VW unit as used on the Type 4 models, with the same indirect ratios and direct drive in top, and mated with a well-balanced 4,45 to 1 final drive ratio.

Selection is made via a full-length T-handle control, which replaces the floor-mounted gearlever of the manual-shift model, with an indicator panel at the floor. Accelerator and brake pedal are close-mounted.

The A/T is very easy to use and effective: we found no stalling problem at all — thanks to the efficient automatic choke — and the creep action is very mild.

The single awkward feature is that second-stage pedal pressure is required for automatic kick-down, and this means tramping the accelerator pedal virtually flat onto the floor — needing a fairly acrobatic ankle action, and considerable pressure. A woman would find this extremely difficult to manage.

PERFORMANCE

As on the manual-shift models, the engine is governed to a limit of about 5 400 rpm, and we found that there was absolutely nothing to be gained by using manual override control in performance tests. In fact, the best figures were achieved by simply flooring the pedal and letting the gearbox computer do the work.

Natural full-throttle upchanges were at 50 and 80 km/h, and apart from a very gentle start from rest, the Microbus proved startlingly responsive in the up-to-80 range. Once top gear takes over at that point the acceleration eases off, as a comparison with the manual-shift model (CAR, June 1972) shows:

	MANUAL	AUTO
0—80	13,2	16,7
0—100	24,3	34,9
400 m	21,4	23,1
Speed	122,3	115,5

Because of its swift and accurate upshifts and easy use of full power, the Microbus Automatic proved surprisingly nippy in starts from robots and up to normal expressway speeds. It never held the traffic up, and could eat up expressways with the best of them.

TEST REPORT

NOISE LEVELS:	
Mechanical	poor
Idling	poor
Transmission	very good
Wind	fair
Road	fair
Coachwork	good
Average	poor
ENGINE:	
Starting	good
Response	good
Smoothness	good
Accessibility	fair
STEERING:	
Accuracy	very good
Stability at speed	good
Stability in wind	fair
Steering effort	good
Roughness	very good
Road feel	good
Centring action	very good
Turning circle	good
BRAKING:	
Pedal pressure	good
Response	very good
Fade resistance	good
Directional stability	very good
Handbrake position	fair
Handbrake action	good
TRANSMISSION:	
A/T action	very good
Gearbox ratios	good
Final drive ratio	good
Selector position	very good
Selector action	very good
SUSPENSION:	
Firmness rating	very good
Progressive action	very good
Roadholding	good
Roll control	good
Tracking control	very good
Pitching control	fair
Mass distribution	fair
Load ability	very good
DRIVER CONTROLS:	
Hand control location	very good
Pedal location	good
Wiper action	very good
Washer action	good
Instrumentation	good
Rear-view mirror	good
Hooters	poor
INTERIOR COMFORT:	
Seat design	good
Headroom front	excellent
Legroom front	very good
Headroom rear	excellent
Legroom rear	very good
Lighting	good
Accessories	fair
ROAD LIGHTS:	
Headlamp penetration	very good
Headlamp spread	good
Dipping control	very good
Reversing lamps	nil
DRIVING COMFORT:	
Steering wheel position	very good
Steering wheel reach	good
Visibility	very good
Directional feel	poor
Ventilation	good
Heating	good
COACHWORK:	
Appearance	very good
Finish	very good
Space utilization	very good
Door access	good
Load capacity	excellent
Load access	good

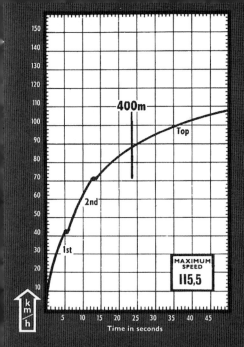

Time in seconds

MAXIMUM SPEED
115,5

BRAKING DISTANCES

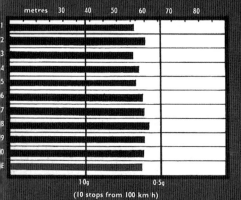

(10 stops from 100 km/h)

ENGINE SPEED

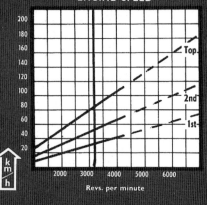

Revs. per minute

GRADIENT ABILITY

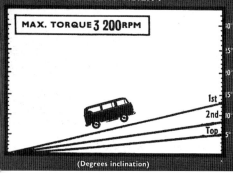

MAX. TORQUE 3 200 RPM

(Degrees inclination)

MAKE AND MODEL:
Make   Volkswagen
Model   1700 Microbus L Automatic

INTERIOR NOISE LEVELS:

	Mech.	Wind	Road
Idling	57,5	—	—
60	73,5	—	—
80	78,5	—	—
100	83,0	86,0	87,0
Full throttle	See graph		
Average dBA at 100	85,3		

(Measured in decibels, "A" weighting, averaging runs both ways on a level road; "Mechanical" with car closed; "Wind" with one window fully open; "Road" on a coarse road surface.)

ACCELERATION FROM REST:
0–60	9,3
0–80	16,7
0–100.	34,9
0–120.	—
400 m sprint	23,1

OVERTAKING ACCELERATION:
                             (A/T)
40–60.	4,5
60–80.	7,4
80–100	18,5
100–120	—

(Measured in seconds, to true speeds, averaging runs both ways on a level road, car carrying test crew of two and standard test equipment.)

MAXIMUM SPEED:
True speed	115,5
Speedo reading	124

Calibration:

Indicated:	60	80	100	120
True speed:	56	75	94	112

FUEL ECONOMY (km/l):
60	11,4
85	9,0
100	7,2
Full throttle	5,4

(Measured in kilometres per litre, averaging runs both ways on a level road.)

FUEL CONSUMPTION (litres/100 km):
60	8,8
80	11,1
100	13,9
Full throttle	16,6

(Stated in litres per 100 kilometres, based on fuel economy figures recorded at true speeds.)

BRAKING TEST (From 100 km/h):
First stop	3,7
Tenth stop	4,0
Average	3,93

(Measured in sec. with stops from true speeds at 30-second intervals on a good bitumenised surface.)

GRADIENTS IN GEARS:
Low gear	1 in 4,3
2nd gear	1 in 6,7
Top gear	1 in 10,2

(Tabulated from Tapley (x gravity) readings, car carrying test crew of two and standard test equipment.)

GEARED SPEEDS (km/h):
Low gear	42,1
2nd gear	70,2
Top gear	111,3

(Calculated at engine peak rpm — 4 200.)

MECHANICAL NOISE

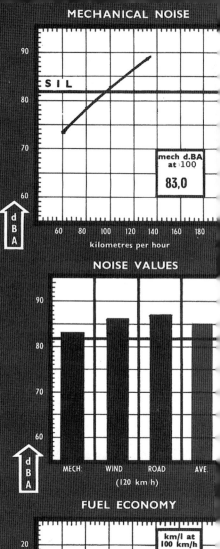

SIL

mech d.BA at 100
83,0

kilometres per hour

NOISE VALUES

(120 km/h)

FUEL ECONOMY

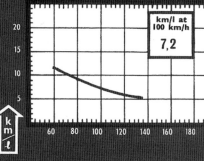

km/l at 100 km/h
7,2

FUEL CONSUMPTION
(litres 100 km)

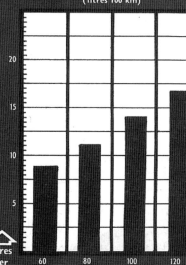

kilometres per hour

ENGINE:

Cylinders	4 opposed, rear-mounted
Carburettors	Twin Solex 32/34—PDSIT—2/3
Bore	90,0 mm
Stroke	66,0 mm
Cubic capacity	1 697 cm3
Compression ratio	7,3 to 1
Valve gear	ohv, pushrods
Main bearings	four
Aircleaner	paper element
Fuel requirement	91-octane Coast, 87-octane Reef
Cooling	air, blower-driven
Electrics	12-volt DC

ENGINE OUTPUT:

Max. power SAE (kW)	52 kW (70 bhp)
Max. power net (kW)	44,2
Peak rpm	4 200
Max torque (N.m.) at rpm	118 at 3 200

TRANSMISSION:

Forward speeds	three, VW Automatic
Selector	floor T-handle
Low gear	2,65 to 1
2nd gear	1,59 to 1
Top gear	Direct
Reverse gear	1,80 to 1
Final drive	4,45 to 1
Drive wheels	rear

WHEELS AND TYRES:

Road wheels	14-inch pressed steel discs
Rim width	5½ inch
Tyres	185 SR 14 radials
Tyre pressures (front)	200 to 220 kPa (29 to 32 lb.)
Tyre pressures (rear)	220 to 250 kPa (32 to 36 lb.)

BRAKES:

Front	discs
Rear	drums
Pressure regulation	dual circuit
Boosting	vacuum servo
Handbrake position	centre dash — pull-out

STEERING:

Type	worm and roller, damped
Lock to lock	3,0 turns
Turning circle	10,5 metres approx

MEASUREMENTS:

Length overall	4,505 m
Width overall	1,720 m
Height overall	1,955 m
Wheelbase	2,400 m
Front track	1,395 m
Rear track	1,455 m
Ground clearance	0,185 m
Licensing mass	1 280 kg

SUSPENSION:

Front	independent
Type	torque tube and stabiliser
Rear	independent
Type	torque tube and dual-jointed half-axles

CAPACITIES:

Seating	8—10
Fuel tank	60,0 litres
Luggage space	991 dm3
Utility space	up to 5 000 dm3 gross

WARANTY:

Six months or 10 000 km.

TEST CAR FROM:

VW South Africa, Uitenhage, in association with Motors Western Province Services, Paarden Eiland, Cape.

Its weakness is in hill-climbing: here, it falls down quite badly at higher speeds (90-plus) with little or no top-gear reserve, and having to drop back to the 80-km/h intermediate gear for extra torque. On a level road, it will cruise very happily at 100—110 km/h, which is as fast as most people would want to travel with a big-bodied family bus.

ECONOMY AND NOISE

The 1700 engine of the Microbus Automatic is a slightly down-rated version in terms of power, but strong on torque (this change is achieved, we are told, by amended camshaft profiles and flat piston crowns with recessed combustion chambers).

It proved very good on economy, as well, returning almost exactly the same figures as the manual-shift model at steady speeds — though owners would have to guard against the tendency to use the throttle extravagantly with the Automatic in acceleration.

Noise levels are much the same as those of the manual-shift model, with a slight increase in mechanical noise. The transmission — thanks to being set right at the back — is notably quiet.

BRAKING AND HANDLING

The combination of wide-boot radials, boosted discs at front, and engine mass at rear, contribute to first-class braking ability with the Microbus. It stops almost as well as a sedan, with no wheel locking or loss of directional stability, and fade is slight in repeated stops.

Ride is very sound: the torque-tube suspension front and rear has fine progression and load-ability, and the big radials hold the road well. A high-roofed vehicle like this one cannot be thrown about like a car, and is necessarily somewhat prone to buffeting by side-winds. But generally speaking, the Kombi is no problem on the road, and its only minor vice is a tendency to pitch end-to-end under acceleration and deceleration.

SUMMARY

The Microbus Automatic is a vehicle which, if anything, is ahead of its time. Motorists may find it difficult to accept, because it breaks so radically from traditions.

They can take our word for it that this is a most serviceable and pleasant-driving vehicle, much easier to use about-town than the manual-shift model, and quite eager enough for that once-a-year long holiday trip. Anyone who is prepared to pay the very nominal extra cost of the automatic transmission, is sure to be delighted with it in service. ∎

PERFORMANCE FACTORS:

Power/mass (W/kg) net	34,5
Frontal area (m2)	3,52
km/h/1 000 rpm (top)	26,5

(Calculated on licensing mass, gross frontal area, gearing and net power output.)

SERVICE REQUIREMENTS:

Sump capacity	3,0 litres
Change interval	5 000 km
Oil filter capacity	0,5 litres
Change interval	10 000 km
Gearbox/diff capacity	3,5 litres
Change interval	nil km
Air filter change	Up to 10 000 km
Greasing points	nil

(These basic service recommendations are given for guidance only, and may vary according to operating conditions. Inquiries should be addressed to authorised dealerships.)

STANDARD EQUIPMENT:

Electric clock, heater, exterior rear-view mirrors, twin dome lights, variable instrument lighting, boosted disc front brakes, radial-ply tyres on wide rims, dash grabhandles, semi-reclining front seats, headlamp flasher, hazard warning switch, test wiring circuit.

TEST CONDITIONS:

Altitude	At sea level
Weather	cool, overcast, windy
Fuel used	93-octane
Test car's odometer	4 100 km

The spacious interior seen from the tailgate, with seating for 8—10 people and 990 dm3 of load space.

Kombi handling and stability is good on wide radials, with dual-jointed rear half-axles. (Picture from 1972 Test.)

THREE SHOEBOXES IN SEARCH OF A SHELF

The Volkswagen van, above, was built by some rather shrewd marketing people in Germany. The Dodge, at left, has the market cornered in driver-design. But we don't suggest tossing the keys to the Ford to your wife and having her run down to the corner for a six-pack—it's that big. The password here is function. Just like the title says, they're three shoeboxes in search of a shelf.

The highly competitive van marketplace is filled with well-designed packages. Each of our three test vehicles did very well in all categories and each deserves a niche./by Kyle Given.

Supposing we take a very un-car book-like look at vans. Suppose we cut all the talk of wheelbases, rear axle ratios, lateral G forces, side loadings, and braking distances. Suppose we don't mention cubic feet of interior space—a dimension which is absolutely incomprehensible to me, anyway. Suppose we simply get three different vans from three separate manufacturers, in three sizes. Finally, suppose we look at them from the standpoint of the average consumer—as contrasted with special interest groupies who buy, drive and redesign vans to complement their life-styles. That means we get vans with windows—we want to see out, and we don't particularly care if anybody can see in or not.

Beginning at the small end of the si[ze] scale, *MT* ordered up a new Volkswag[en] van from VW Pacific. They call it a stati[on] wagon, of course, because it has w[in]dows. The one we ordered seats seve[n], has the 1700-cc engine, a four-spe[ed] (although an automatic trans was r[e]cently made available) and an AM/F[M] radio.

In the middle of the size range and f[or] no particular purpose, we got a half-t[on] package van from Dodge. It came w[ith] the options piled higher than Iowa cor[n] —including a 318 cu. in. V-8, automa[tic] trans, power steering, air condition[ing] radio, deluxe trim and sturdy vinyl uph[ol]stery. The Dodge seats nine people.

More bus than personal car, our Cl[ub]

Ford-Chateau E-300 derivitive van at the big end of the scale was also heavily laden with options—including a 302 cu. in. V-8, automatic trans, power steering, brakes, air conditioner, AM/FM radio, deluxe trim and combination vinyl and material upholstery. It seats 12.

Here's the way we saw them after trips of only a few miles (roughly five to 25, from where they were picked up, back to the Peterson parking areac):

1.) Volkswagen. Designed by some very shrewd marketing people a number of years ago, the VW van hasn't changed much in the last decade. It is still marketed for a buyer VW must think of as being a "concerned, sensible" *consumer*. It gets good gas mileage, it's easy to park, it's a handy size and it does not intimidate the new-to-vans driver.

2.) Dodge. From the guys who were first among domestic manufacturers to note an upswing of interest in vans by the general public, the Dodge van seems engineered for the *driver*. It is easy to drive and goes where it's pointed—both facts made obvious by a well-designed driver's seating position and steering wheel rake. For a van, the Dodge has impeccable road manners.

3.) Ford. Benefitting from one of the more successful truck and utility vehicle marketing and engineering groups, the Ford van seems designed for the *user*. It scares hell out of you the first time you drive it and, in fact, took *MT* staffers longer to get accustomed to than either the VW or Dodge. Once you're no longer leery of the thing, however, it really comes into its own. One driving peculiarity on the open road was the feeling the Ford gave of being more comfortable at cruising speeds of 70 to 80 mph than it was at 50 to 60 mph. Even in cross winds.

Immediately noticeable en route back to the office from the points of delivery was the fact that you can make good highway time in both the Dodge and the Ford. The VW seems more at ease in the suburbs and on moderately-trafficked city streets.

As vans are felt to be multi-usable vehicles we conceived of a three-part test that included trips to the supermarket, highway cruising—including mountains and desert—and some off road sorties designed to test the cars' abilities to get to those out of the way camping sites. Average mileage traveled was 750 miles. Here's the way that worked out:

Daily use: The Ford was simply too big. Its very bulk precludes the notion of toss-

ing the keys to your old lady and saying, "How about running down to the store for a six-pack?" The VW probably gets the edge in the daily-use category, although the Dodge is also easy to drive. Assume you're an average suburbanite and you want an automatic transmission and air conditioning and the nod goes to the Dodge. The VW's smaller engine would simply bog down (by comparison) under the horsepower robbing load of those options. Otherwise, VW.

Highway use: The Ford gets it. Easily. That big bus gobbled up highway miles in some of the worst weather ever encountered in the stretch between Las Vegas and Los Angeles. Rain, 45-mph winds, snow flurries and long, steep grades didn't make a dent in the Ford's unflustered stability. Conversely, the Dodge rated a close second in those tests and came out ahead in a portion of the run that encountered twisty mountain roads. The VW huffed, chaffed, sputtered, wheezed and averaged some 15 mph slower over the same stretch. *Ah-hah*, however, it got much better gas mileage. (About gas mileage: The VW averaged 18 mpg over the entire test, the Dodge got 10 and the Ford 9.) The VW ran well on low lead. The Dodge and Ford did not.)

Off-road use. (Divided into two parts—how well the vehicle drove through ruts, washes, desert sand and then wove through sparse timber country; and, phase two, how usable the vehicle was as a campsite center.)

Surprisingly, the VW seemed most at ease in the outback—in terms of getting through the rough stuff. The four speed gave precise gearing and was instantly selectable. Feathering the clutch (not conducive to long life) enabled the perfect blend of traction to be applied to any sort of terrain. Also, the VW's shorter wheelbase and tighter turning radius made for more maneuverability.

Still it was very, very close. Any of the three vehicles can go off road, albeit very carefully and very slowly. The Ford was clearly the most usable car once it was parked and turned into a camp site. You can sleep in any of the Ford's bench-type seats. You can't (because of seat width, length, seat bottom rake and upholstery material) in the VW or Dodge. It's that simple. All three vans are equal, if you take the seats out—with the exception that, of course, the Ford had more room.

How do we rate 'em all around? Well, it's a highly personal preference, but here goes: 1.) Ford, 2.) Dodge, 3.) VW. How do you rate 'em? We'd like to know. ∎

Winner in the size department seemed to be the massive Club Ford-Chateau E-300. It seats 12 and has an air-conditioning system that could cool Wrigley Field in August. While the Ford was not the ideal neighborhood car because of its size, it performed best on the highway and open road.

Continued from Page 50

which swings up from the left side of the center "cabin" to seat four people.

The vehicle's compact "kitchen" area is equipped with a 1.6-cubic-foot insulated ice-box, 7-1/2-gallon water tank, pump-equipped stainless steel sink which is recessed into the top of the ice-box cabinet and a collapsible utility table. Hingemounted to the wall of the ice-box cabinet, the table covers a two-shelf "pantry," swinging up into position to hold a camp stove.

—OUTSIDE POWER CONNECTION—

Power for interior lights is drawn from the vehicle's 12-volt battery while power for 110-volt electrical appliances is supplied from the outside through a socket installed in the outer wall of the vehicle itself.

At night the vehicle turns into sleeping quarters for four with a full-width 76-inch long double bed for two adults and smaller berths for two children. An optional "pop-top" which literally raises the Campmobile's roof provides a five-foot-long "upper" for a third child.

The "pop-top" itself is equipped with screening material to shut out insects while a snap-on collapsible screen also is provided for the vehicle's four-foot-wide rear door. All windows are curtain-equipped for inside privacy, the louver-type center windows on each side also equipped with screens.

—ADDED SPACE—

Optional in addition to the "pop-top" roof is a free-standing tent which can be left behind at a camping site whenever the vehicle is driven off on a short trip. In use, the tent provides a screened-in "living room" or extra bedroom measuring 9'8" by 6'6".

Easy-to-clean polyvinyl flooring is used wall-to-wall inside the Campmobile while both interior wall and ceiling paneling is backed by fiber-glass insulating material.

Braking power was increased for 1972 through the addition of larger rear-wheel brake cylinders. Already equipped with a power-assisted braking system for quick, easy stops, the 1972 Campmobile features radial ply tires as standard equippment.

As with all new Volkswagens, the Campmobile is backed by a 24 month or 24,000-mile—whichever comes first—warranty and is delivered with coupons good for free VW diagnosis at 6,000-mile intervals during their first 24,000 miles of operation.

VOLKSWAGEN AUTOMATIC VAN

THE VAN THAT STARTED IT ALL NOW HAS AN AUTOMATIC TRANSMISSION

THE THOUGHT OF a VW bus with an automatic transmission doesn't do too much for the imagination. In fact, about the only image it conjures up is a snail with wheels. Volkswagen was never in the horsepower race even before the government pressured car factories to quit racing.

The last VW bus tested by PV4 (December 1972) was a '72 model with a 4-speed manual transmission. The '73 Type 2 station wagon is little changed over the '72 but an automatic transmission has been made optional. This is truly an automatic transmission, not like the automatic/stick in the Beetle series. It's a good one, borrowed from the 411 Series; the same source in 1972 of the 1679-cc engine currently in the Type 2.

Last year's test report was favorable with the 4-speed manual transmission and power was considered adequate. What happens, then, when an automatic is mated to a powerplant that is already just adequate? Well, usually the

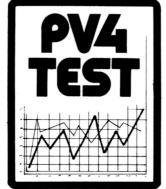

vehicle will turn out to be a stone. But in this particula[r] case—not so! The performance figures of the automatic va[n] rival those of the stick shift bus.

Just what black magic did VW perform [to] accomplish this neat trick? First off, as me[n]tioned earlier, it's a good transmission. The[re] seems to be little power loss through the bo[x.] The shift is positive and snappy. The 2.65 rat[io] of first gear is low enough to move the V[W] away from stoplights at a brisk pace. Couple[d] with the automatic is a rear axle ratio chan[ge] from the 5.37 with the 4-speed to a 4.45 f[or] the automatic. At first glance this wou[ld] indicate a lower cruising rpm for the automati[c,] probably resulting in the engine lugging a[t] highway speed. However at 70 miles per ho[ur] both vehicles are turning about the same rp[m.] This is because the top gear in the automatic is 1.00 to 1 [or] straight through whereas top gear in the 4-speed is actually a[n] overdrive ratio of 0.82 to 1. Using simple arithmetic we fi[nd]

The engine compartment is accessible from the rear and also from the parcel compartment inside the VW bus.

The interior is spacious and typical Volkswagen—quality materials and attention to detail and workmanship.

82 times 5.37 equals 4.40, almost identical to the 4.45 ratio used with the automatic.

The engine in the Type 2 has a rating of 63 horsepower at 4300 rpm for the 4-speed and 59 at 4200 for the automatic. Although the automatic loses four horsepower over the manual, the torque of the automatic is greater at 3200 rpm—83 as against 81.

Something we noticed that was surprising was the external dimensions of the bus have changed slightly. The wheelbase was the same but the overall length was changed from 174 to 177.4 inches. This can be attributed to the crash-type bumpers (5 mph front/2.5 rear) but the overall width of the vehicle has changed as well. Overall body width has decreased from 69.5 to 67.7. The slight decrease in body width should improve the handling somewhat.

The VW bus comes in several configurations, such as our test vehicle which is the station wagon, the Kombi, the campmobile and delivery van. The station wagon lies in between the sparsely outfitted delivery van and the plush campmobile which is a home on wheels complete with an icebox, sink, beds, closets, paneling, pop-up top, etc. The station wagon is available in either the 7- or 9-passenger version. A sunroof is optional with the 7-passenger.

Fittings for headrests have been built into all seatbacks, so owners who want restraints can install them. VW voluntarily provided the head-restraint fittings and energy absorbing bumpers although not required to do so under Federal regulations.

Fresh air and heater outlets have been relocated and enlarged. The wiper/washer switch mounted on the right side of the steering column has a position for intermittant wiping. The engine compartment lid remains on the outside rear of the vehicle, however, a second opening—over the engine in the luggage compartment—offers greater accessibility and ease of service.

TEST AND IMPRESSIONS

We were pleasantly surprised to find the automatic version of the timeless VW bus to be just about as quick as its stickshift brother. It doesn't have throw-you-in-the-backseat acceleration, but it moves out smartly and would have to be rated acceptable in this category. The shift lever must be three feet long and grows out of the floor in the same location as the 4-speed. Some automatics tend to shift themselves too quickly, however, the reverse is true of the VW. It hangs in the gears to a high rpm to take advantage of the engine's torque

The instrument panel is simple but has a certain beauty. The steering wheel is almost flat and is close to driver.

curve. Hand shifting the box made little if any difference; it goes ahead and shifts when it wants to.

The smog equipment has made the engine rather erratic. The idle is totally unpredictable. One time it's right on the money and another time it wants to buzz about 2000 rpm. Cold or hot makes no difference. Slight changes in speed around 45 mph cause funny things too. Letting off the accelerator slightly results in the vehicle speeding up a tad, whereas depressing the pedal will cause the vehicle to slow. All this is very minute, mind you, but a little unnerving until you get used to it.

The day at the raceway produced some figures to back up our earlier impressions that this vehicle was nearly as quick as the 4-speed. The quarter mile standing start took 23.6 seconds for the automatic as against the '72 stick shift time of 23.1. The difference is so slight as to be hardly noticeable during normal driving.

The braking test popped a few eyeballs; four to be exact. The two belonging to the driver and those baby blues belonging to our number one instrument watcher. The panic stop from 60 mph used up just 123.5 feet! The bus came to a nose-diving halt in a straight line without screeching a tire. Due to the rather soft suspension on the VW, we had thought some tailwagging might occur in the panic stop causing a few nervous moments. But it never happened. Just to see if it was a one-time thing, we ran the VW back down the strip and tried it again. This time with our foot through the floor. The g-meter indicator dropped clear out of sight and we came to another

Off road is where the VW bus really shines. The fully independent suspension soaks up the bumps very well.

The handling in the dirt is very good and predictable, even better than driving on the pavement.

stop in about the same distance with just a little tire screeching and slight side skid at the end. Fantastic! Brake fade tests during 6 stops from 60 produced no recordable difference with the pressure required for a ½-g stop staying about 45 pounds.

When driving this vehicle at speed it gives the impression of being somewhat unstable, but it really isn't. Rounding curves at speed results in some oversteer but it's predictable. Side winds and big trucks do have a noticeable effect on handling, however. This can be traced to the rather soft suspension. Straight-line driving is smooth and effortless and 70 mph is an easy speed to maintain.

The flow-through ventilation is very good although somewhat noisy. During cold weather the rear window defogger should be a great help in keeping visibility to a maximum. And the visibility from the driver's seat in all directions is very good. The almost horizontal steering wheel is big and right where it should be for comfortable driving.

The interior trim is typical Volkswagen—second to none. Their attention to detail is to be commended. The instrument panel is simple but has a certain beauty to it and all the controls are within easy reach and legible.

The trip to Hillclimb Valley at Saddleback Park was not made without some apprehension. The '72 4-speed VW bus had to be winched down Test Hill No. 2 (63%) because the front end began weaving back and forth when backing down. The lack of weight on the front axle and not enough engine compression braking in reverse made for some anxious moments.

We really didn't believe the automatic would make it up Test Hill No. 1 (36%) so we weren't overly concerned about backing down No. 2. But lo and behold, the bus motored up No. 1 like it was a Sunday drive. The tires never slipped nor did the engine sputter as it crested the top. No. 2 was next and even though the first hill was topped rather easily, no one thought the automatic stood a chance of getting halfway up No. 2. Well, were we wrong. It not only made it halfway, we came within an eyelash of going over the top. For a minute there it looked as if we would make it but a little wheelspin caused a loss of momentum and the engine simply ran out of horses. So there we were at the crest of No. 2 and thoughts of backing down flashed into our mind. The erratic idle precluded any thoughts of putting the automatic into reverse. That would have been worse than using neutral. Easing slightly off the brake while still in low forward produced as leisurely a backwards ride downhill as you would want. Just to double check our suspicion on going down in reverse we tried it. Never again! Almost instantly the vehicle got squirrelly and out of shape.

We haven't had but one 2-wheel-drive vehicle make it over No. 2 (the VW Thing), which makes the automatic bus pretty impressive even though it didn't make it either. It must be remembered that we don't make banzai runs at the test hills. The vehicle is stopped close to the base of the hill and driven from there.

The handling of the bus off road is where it really shines. None of the bone-jarring jolts are present even on the roughest of roads. We flogged the VW around the outbacks of Saddleback Park with the greatest of ease. Of course this box on wheels won't climb over huge rocks or out of holes but there's a great many areas of off-roading that the VW is suited for.

Volkswagens have always been noted for fairly good economy but the '73 automatic falls a little short in this area. Our test vehicle averaged just 16.1 mpg during normal driving. This is a couple of miles per gallon less than the 4-speed delivered. However if you compare this figure to a domestic van the mileage isn't all that bad. It's just that you expect VW to do better than this.

Everything considered the VW bus is a good vehicle. It's well built, handles beautifully off road, gets reasonable economy, acceptable on the highway and has enough power for most people. The price has crept up in the last few years but at a basic list of $3799, it's still competitive.

VOLKSWAGEN AUTOMATIC VAN

PRICES
Basic list, West Coast POE
  Type 2 with 7-passenger seating . .$3799

Standard equipment: 102.5-cu.-in. 4-cyl engine, 4-spd manual transmission, adjustable driver's seat and backrest, 2-spd windshield wipers/washers, electric rear window defogger, outside rearview mirrors, heater/defroster, 185R x 14 tires, power brakes

ENGINES
Standard: 102.5-cu.-in. horizontally opposed 4-cyl
Bore x stroke, in. . . . . .3.54 x 2.59
Compression ratio 7.3:1
Net horsepower @ rpm 63 @ 4800 (4-spd)
                     59 @ 4200 (auto trans)
Net torque @ rpm, lb-ft 81 @ 3200 (4-spd)
                        83 @ 3200 (auto trans)
Type fuel required . . . . regular

Optional engines . . . . .none

DRIVE TRAIN
Standard transmission . . . . 4-spd manual
Clutch dia., in 8.0
Transmission ratios: 4th 0.82:1
  3rd 1.26:1
  2nd 2.06:1
  1st 3.80:1
Synchromesh . . . . .all forward gears

Optional 3-spd automatic $235
Transmission ratios: 3rd 1.00:1
  2nd 1.59:1
  1st 2.65:1

Rear axle type: spiral bevel gears and two double-jointed rear axles
Final drive ratios 5.37:1 (4-spd)
                              4.45:1 (automatic)
Overdrive .none
Limited slip differential . . . . .none

CHASSIS & BODY
Body/frame: unitized body frame plates reinforced with side and cross members

Brakes
Brakes (std): 11.2 x 2.9-in. front disc, 10.1 x 1.6-in. rear drums
Brake swept area, sq in 252
  Swept area/ton (max load) 101
Power brakes . . . . std

Steering type (std) . . . . . .worm & roller
Steering ratio 14.7:1
Turns, lock to lock 2.8
Power steering . . . . .none
Turning circle, ft 40

Wheel size (std) . . . . 14 x 5½J
Optional wheel sizes . . . . .none
Tire size (std) . . . . 185R x 14
Optional tire sizes . . . . .none

SUSPENSION
Front suspension: independent with trailing arms, transverse torsion bars, stabilizer bar & tube shocks
Front axle capacity, lb 2227

Rear suspension: independent with trailing arms, diagonal links, transverse torsion bars & tube shocks
Rear axle capacity, lb 2800

Additional suspension options . . . . .none

ACCOMMODATION
Standard seats: front buckets, 2-passenger center seat, 3-passenger rear seat
Optional seats . . . . 9-passenger seating

Headroom, in 36.5
Pedal to seatback, max 39.3
Steering wheel to seatback, max 15.0
Seat to ground 39.0
Floor to ground 22.5

Heater & defroster . . . . std
Tinted glass . . . . .none
Air conditioning $510

Unobstructed load space (length x width x height) in . . . . .36 x 41 x 48
Rear folded or removed . . .60 x 41 x 48

INSTRUMENTATION
Instruments: 0-90 mph speedometer, 99,999.9-mi odometer, fuel gauge
Warning lights: oil pressure, alternator, brake warning, hazard warning, high beam
Optional . . . . .none

MAINTENANCE
Service intervals, normal use, miles:
  Oil change 3000
  Filter change 6000
  Chassis lube 18,000
Minor tuneup 6000
Major tuneup 12,000
Warranty, months/miles 24/24,000

GENERAL
Curb weight, lb (test model) 3045
GVW (max. laden weight) 4961
  Optional GVWs . . . . .none

Wheelbase, in 94.5
Track, front/rear 54.8/57.2
Overall length 177.4
Overall height 76.4
Overall width 67.7
Overhang, front/rear 43/41

Approach angle, degrees 23
Departure angle 17

Ground clearances (test model):
  Front axle 11.0
  Rear axle 10.3
  Oil pan 10.0
  Fuel tank 26.0
  Exhaust system (lowest point) 11.0

Fuel tank capacity (U.S. gal) 15.8
Auxiliary tank . . . . .none

OTHER OPTIONS
AM radio $72
Leatherette interior $50

PERFORMANCE DATA

TEST MODEL
Type 2 station wagon with 7-passenger seating, automatic transmission, AM radio, leatherette interior
West Coast list price $4156

ACCELERATION
Time to speed, sec:
  0-30 mph 6.6
  0-45 mph 13.3
  0-60 mph 26.8
  0-70 mph 46.5
Standing start, 1/4-mile, sec 23.6
  Speed at end, mph 58

SPEED IN GEARS
High 3rd (4000 rpm) 65
  2nd (4000 rpm) 42
  1st (4000 rpm) 25

BRAKE TESTS
Pedal pressure required for 1/2-g deceleration rate from 60 mph, lb 40
Stopping distance from 60 mph, ft . 123.5
Fade: Percent increase in pedal pressure for 6 stops from 60 mph . . . . .nil
Overall brake rating . . . . .excellent

INTERIOR NOISE
Idle in neutral, dBA 61
Maximum during acceleration 81
At steady 70-mph cruising speed 83

OFF PAVEMENT
Hillclimbing ability . . . . .good
Maneuverability . . . . .good
Turnaround capability . . . . .good
Handling .good
Ride . . . . .excellent

GENERAL
Heater rating . . . . .good
Defroster effectiveness . . . . .good
Wiper coverage . . . . .good

FUEL CONSUMPTION
Normal driving, mpg 16.1
Off pavement 13.7
Range, normal driving, miles 254
Range, off pavement 216

A Bus Lover Looks At The NEW...

VW STATION

The shift mechanism seems to take up **more** room in the middle of the floor than it did on previous models but that's progress!

Optional sunroof is worth the extra cost, this writer feels. Slide it back and you've got a true, breezy summertime car.

By NANCY COGGINS

EDITOR'S NOTE—You've probably seen the ad that triggered this story. A woman is kissing a Volkswagen station wagon just because it now sports an automatic transmission. There happens to be a female VW bus lover right in the editor's family so we turned a new one with the automatic over to her, stood aside and watched her reactions. This, we thought, might produce a unique "owner's evaluation" for these pages.

The first thing she said was, "Why, they've made the VW emblem in the front smaller!"

We made her jot down all her impressions, anyway and we have come to the conclusion that Volkswagen knew what would happen when they pitched their campaign for the automatic bus to the women among us. Here's what one thinks about the latest offering from Wolfsburg. . . . .

■ Well, Volkswagen has done it again—with an automatic bus this time! It was a joy to drive after shifting our bus for these past two years. I'd like to call it "the People's Lib Bus" for those men and women who prefer exercising only when they feel like it. I'm not like my husband who likes to "go through gears" as he calls it. He said he thought there was a little less acceleration with the automatic but it seemed to go right along for me, as fast as I wanted it to, anyhow.

You hear a lot of talk about things not being built as well as they used to build them, these days but, to me, the new bus is definitely a better vehicle. It took

Look, Ma. No Clutch! Step has also been reworked so that it doesn't protrude. (The Automatic bus is shown below.) Writer approves of the addition of automatic transmission to the bus.

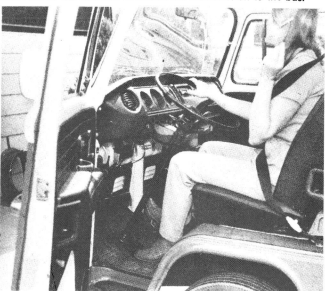

VAGON AUTOMATIC

eater tunnel pipes air along the door into the nether regions the VW bus. Heat control has been moved right onto door.

The old (on the left) and the new. Directional lights have been moved, wipers dechromed and bumpers have been stiffened.

a while for me to get used to the seats in my bus but the new ones are very firm and give good support where I need it most-in my aching back. The whole car feels as though it would give many rugged, serviceable miles. We've had no real problems with our old one and never had to take advantage of the 24 month/24 thousand mile warranty. Since this applies to the new automatic the VW people must be doing something right.

One of the first things I look for is adequate heating in a car. We've never frozen in our wagon, of course, but the changes in the new bus should make it a lot cosier. No one can convince me that it was a simple task to fix up a vehicle big enough to carry nine people so that they all got enough heat. This has always been a little more difficult in Volkswagens, I understand, yet they have accomplished it admirably.

The love of my life is the bus's sliding door. That it is wide enough to admit a small elephant continues to amaze me. I am always pleased with being able to park close to another car and open the door without knocking the paint off either vehicle. Our sliding door gets almost continual use because it is so easy for our little girl to get in and out of it. Her "Grandma" finds it a cinch, too and rides with us much more frequently than she did when we had our Beetle.

With or without an automatic the wagon is such a versatile vehicle. To me it is two rolling platforms. Sometimes I prefer the high one over the engine in the rear to the one you get to through the sliding door. I guess I instinctively gauge this on how much

weight has to be lifted and, of course, how bulky the object is. When we first got our bus we delved right in and removed the rear seat. Things that have seen the inside of that bus include a console television, shelving boards (astride the seat tops from front to back), a minibike and, at another time, of course, a load of partying children going for hamburgers!

The various control knobs are much handier in the new automatic. The high and low beams for the headlights are at one's fingertips on the

left side of the steering column. The wiper/washer is a corresponding right hand "wand." Even the ventilator knob can be reached easily by hand.

When we contemplated buying our bus we were told to wait a while because the new ones would have more horsepower. The new engine develops more horsepower than ours but some of it is lost because of the automatic. I saw a specification sheet that rated it at 59 hp at 4200 rpm. While driving it, however, it seemed to me that there was a definite increase in power all the way from a standing start right up to turnpike speeds. Gas mileage has gone down some, a fact that is very important to me, and most women, I guess. I make it a practice to keep my speed down to fifty miles an hour feeling that this way I make an already economical vehicle even more so.

The automatic bus is fitted with the diagnostic plug and even the dealers in our neighborhood have finally installed the computer. I insist on those periodic inspections and honestly believe it has saved us time and money. The diagnosis, incidentally, is faster and cheaper now that the computers are in.

We have learned since we moved out into the suburbs to take a little walk around the car before backing it out of the driveway. This prevents screams of anguish from the kids who may have left bicycles, scooters or other toys in the driveway. A walk around the new automatic reveals the new placement of the directional lights (up above the headlights on either side of the grille). The little front step is now completely invisible when the door is closed and although you can't tell too well just by looking, the bumpers have been strengthened—a reinforcing structure added.

One thing we did notice about the front is that the VW emblem is smaller and, somehow, I would have been happier if they had left it alone. Maybe it's not important, since my husband wants to put the spare tire up there some day on our bus. And a friend of ours hung a Christmas wreath over it during the holidays. Imagine her surprise when her husband wouldn't let her take it off because he could spot her on the road much quicker whenever he was driving in the other direction!

The automatic has a sunroof and it sure made things bright. It also made

the bus seem larger inside. They tell me the sunroof is an option but we certainly would order it.

Now if this all sounds too ultra positive I can mention somethings I consider drawbacks. The sliding door that I love so much is not only still hard to open but it's not easy to explain its operation to someone else. A chivalrous man has to be a VW bus owner or he begins to look puny when he tries to close it for you. Then there is still the wind to contend with. The

wagon, automatic or not, is literally a "box on wheels" when the wind comes up so I just slow down and take it easy for awhile. But then show me the sleeker, heavier car that offers the wagon's seating and enconomy.

The current seat belts are a pleasant change from those in our bus. The old ones had a squeeze mechanism which the littler kids just could not work. Now all they have to do is press a finger into an indented square on the buckle and out pops the end of the belt. I think this encourages them to use the belts.

I read somewhere that thirty-one people have been stuffed into and onto the VW bus. I just hope it was the automatic because I wouldn't want to shift anything in a situation like that. In any event, while I thoroughly enjoyed driving the new automatic We're not rushing out and buying one. Our present bus has plenty of years as well as miles in it. But if you need more space than you get in the Beetle go all the way with the automatic wagon. The visibility alone, will delight you and it's really no more difficult to park then the sedan, you know. The first time I ran the bus up beside the kitchen door and transferred the groceries without bending my back I knew I was hooked on the bus. It could happen to you!

VOLKSWAGEN PANEL VAN

IT'S BEEN AROUND A LONG TIME BUT MAY STILL BE THE BEST ON THE ROAD

WITH THE ENERGY crisis there has been a resurgence of interest in the Volkswagen van as a good alternative for getting the best possible fuel economy with the spaciousness of a van. Volkswagen was the first to get into the van movement in any numbers back in the days when American-built vans were still being used only by the plumber and the hardware store. After a few years of rising VW van sales, the U.S. manufacturers realized that they were missing a great potential sales area and began to construct more vans so that the public would have access to them for recreational purposes.

So, the VW van is the forerunner of the van boom which continues mostly unabated with the manufacturers building them as fast as they can and the dealers, by and large, selling them almost that quickly. In the street van world today, the VW van has taken pretty much a back seat to the domestics, as most customizers and converters have not shown much inclination

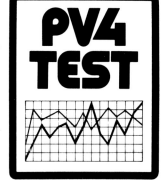

to make high-zoot custom vans out of VWs. Nevertheless, there is a sizeable group of people who think that VW vans are the best around and we have seen some exciting custom ones from time to time.

The latest model of the VW has a larger engine with an increased power output. The air-cooled horizontally opposed 4-cylinder unit now has a displacement of 109.5 cubic inches versus the 102.5 of the previous model. The net horsepower rating has increased from 63 to 65 in the manual transmission model, but it feels like more.

The standard transmission is the manual 4-speed with synchromesh in all forward gears. About a year ago, the VW people introduced the 3-speed automatic transmission into the van line and it is still available as an extra-cost option for $275.

The VW van comes more fully equipped at the base price than most U.S.-built vans and the list of standard features ➤

VW dashboard is simple and uncluttered. We would like more gauges rather than idiot lights.

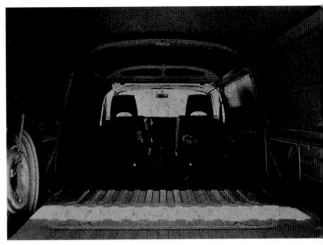

Interior has raised platform at rear to cover the engine. Air conditioner mounts above and behind front seat passengers.

The horizontally-opposed 4-cylinder engine in latest model VW van has slightly bigger displacement

includes two front bucket seats, electric rear window defogger, outside rearview mirrors and power brakes. Also, 185SR x 14 radial tires are standard equipment.

The Volkswagen uses a transaxle in the rear with spiral bevel gears. The rear end ratio for the 4-speed model is 4.86:1 while for the automatic transmission it's 4.45:1. The VW is the only van with fully independent suspension both front and rear which is reflected in its superior ride characteristics. The front has trailing arms, transverse torsion bars and tube shocks while the rear is pretty much the same with the addition of diagonal links. There are no heavy-duty suspension options available with the Volkswagen.

The brake system is composed of disc brakes at the front and 10.1 x 1.6-in. drums at the rear with power assist as standard equipment. The steering is by means of a worm and roller assembly and has a ratio of 14.7:1 with no power steering available nor necessary. The steering requires 2.8 turns, lock to lock, and the turning circle measures 41 feet.

Most VW vans are sold in the bus configuration, that is with seats and windows. In addition, the buyer can order the panel van with a bare-bones interior behind the two front bucket seats. However, due to some conflicts in trade between the U.S. and the European Common Market countries, the panel van has a rather stiff penalty in the price tag which makes its basic list price almost as much as the fancier bus models.

The Volkswagen is the smallest of the vans available in this country in wheelbase dimension. It sits on a 94.5-in. wheelbase and has an overall length of 179 inches. The short domestic vans have wheelbases of 105 to 110 inches but the overall length of the U.S. vans in the short versions is generally about the same as the VW or a bit smaller. As long as we are making comparisons, it seems appropriate to note that while the Volkswagen has a basic list price several hundred dollars higher than the domestics, it's pretty difficult to get out the door with all of the features found on the Volkswagen at the list price in a U.S.-built van.

TEST & IMPRESSIONS

Our test model this time was the panel van which had nothing aft of the front bucket seats. It came to us with all of the standard equipment including the 4-speed manual gear box and had only two accessories; air conditioning and an AM radio. The West Coast list price was $4925. We were a bit shocked at the final price tag, but then the currency manipulations around the world have taken their toll of imported vehicles in all shapes and sizes. The last VW van we tested was in our December '73 issue and it was a bus with the automatic transmission. We were curious to see what differences there might be.

Right away we noticed that the new VW van was considerably more spirited in performance. Much of the difference can be attributed to the 4-speed transmission and the lack of seats and windows which add weight, but the new engine with its larger displacement also helped. Even with the air conditioning in operation, we found the VW was sufficiently lively to get us onto the freeway without misgivings and we were easily able to keep up with the traffic in the fast lane.

The steering effort and the feel are superb. The controllability is better than the average American van. Also, the brakes work quite well and don't exhibit the fish-tailing effect at the rear wheels in the unloaded condition. At Orange County International Raceway during our brake tests, the Volkswagen came to a safe and sure stop in a mere 151 feet from 60 mph. Also, the brakes only faded 15 percent during the six consecutive stops from 60 mph test and we have to rate them as probably the best of any vehicle we have tested.

VOLKSWAGEN PANEL VAN

PRICES

Basic list, West Coast POE:

Panel Van	$4380
7-seat Station Wgn	$4350
9-seat Station Wgn	$4400

Standard equipment: 109.5-cu.in. 4-cyl engine, 4-spd manual transmission, adjustable driver's seat and backrest, 2-spd electric wiper/washers, electric rear window defogger, outside rearview mirrors, heater/defroster, 185SRx14 tires, power brakes

ENGINES

Standard ... horizontally opposed 4-cyl	
Bore x stroke, in	3.66 x 2.59
Compression ratio	7.3:1
Net horsepower @ rpm	65 @ 4200
Net torque @ rpm, lb-ft	91 @ 3000
Type fuel required	91 octane
Optional engines	none

DRIVE TRAIN

Standard transmission	4-spd manual
Clutch dia., in	8.0
Transmission ratios: 4th	0.89:1
3rd	1.26:1
2nd	2.06:1
1st	3.78:1
Synchromesh	all forward gears
Optional 3-spd automatic	$275
Transmission ratios: 3rd	1.00:1
2nd	1.59:1
1st	2.65:1

Rear axle type: spiral bevel gears and two double-jointed rear axles

Final drive ratios: 4.86:1 (4-spd), 4.45:1 (auto. trans)

Overdrive	none

CHASSIS & BODY

Body/frame: unitized body, frame plates reinforced with side and cross members

Brakes (std): front, 11.2-in. dia. disc; rear, 10.1 x 1.6-in. drums

Brake swept area, sq in	252
Swept area/ton (max load)	101
Power brakes	std
Steering type (std)	worm & roller
Steering ratio	14.7:1
Turns, lock to lock	2.8
Power steering	none
Turning circle, ft	41
Wheel size (std)	14 x 5.5J
Optional wheel sizes:	none
Tire size (std)	185SR x 14
Optional tire sizes:	none

SUSPENSION

Front suspension: independent with trailing arms, transverse torsion bars and tube shocks

Front axle capacity, lb	2227
Optional	none

Rear suspension: independent with trailing arms, diagonal links, transverse torsion bars and tube shocks

Rear axle capacity, lb	2867
Optional	none
Additional suspension options.	none

ACCOMMODATION

Standard seats	front bucket seats

Optional seats: 2-passenger center seat, 3-passenger rear seat

Headroom, in	37.5
Pedal to seatback, max	39.5
Steering wheel to seatback, max	15.2
Seat to ground	38.5
Floor to ground	21.9
Heater & defroster	std
Tinted glass	none
Air conditioning	$510

Unobstructed load space (length x width x height) in ... 72 x 59 x 56

Tailgate (width x height)	49 x 29

INSTRUMENTATION

Instruments: 10-90-mph speedometer, 99,999-mi. odometer, fuel gauge

Warning lights: oil pressure, alternator, hazard warning

Optional:	none

GENERAL

Curb weight, lb (test model)	2760
GVWR (test model)	5072
Optional GVWRs	none
Wheelbase, in	94.5
Track, front/rear	54.9/57.3
Overall length	179.0
Overall height	77.0
Overall width	69.3
Overhang, front/rear	44/35
Approach angle, degrees	22
Departure angle	23

Ground clearances (test model):

Front axle	10.8
Rear axle	9.8
Oil pan	10.5
Fuel tank	17
Exhaust system (lowest point)	10.8
Fuel tank capacity (U.S. gal)	15.8
Auxiliary tank	none

PERFORMANCE DATA

TEST MODEL

Panel Van, 4-spd manual transmission, air conditioning, AM radio

West Coast list price	$4925

ACCELERATION

Time to speed, sec:

0-30 mph	5.4
0-45 mph	11.2
0-60 mph	20.0
0-65 mph	25.8
Standing start, 1/4-mile, sec	21.7
Speed at end, mph	61.5

SPEED IN GEARS

High: 4th (4000 rpm)	67
3rd (4000 rpm)	53
2nd (4000 rpm)	32
1st (4000 rpm)	18

BRAKE TESTS

Pedal pressure required for 1/2-g deceleration rate from 60 mph, lb	36
Stopping distance from 60 mph, ft	151
Fade: Percent increase in pedal pressure for 6 stops from 60 mph	15
Overall brake rating	excellent

INTERIOR NOISE

Idle in neutral, dBA	62
Maximum during acceleration	82
At steady 60-mph cruising speed	81

OFF PAVEMENT

Hillclimbing ability	good
Maneuverability	very good
Turnaround capability	excellent
Handling	very good
Ride	excellent

GENERAL

Heater rating	very good
Defroster effectiveness	good
Wiper coverage	good

FUEL CONSUMPTION

Normal driving, mpg	20.9
Off pavement	15.6
Range, normal driving, miles	330
Range, off pavement	246

The Volkswagen is king of the vans in terms of off-pavement performance and ride. The placement of the engine over the driving wheels gives it superior traction and the independent suspension at all four corners makes the ride smooth.

Although a bit short on power by American standards, VW van will get you there and use less gas than U.S. vans.

The overall handling of the VW received very high marks from all the staff members who drove it, with the exception of the wind resistance. Because of the design, there is a lot of that and getting sandwiched between two large trucks on the freeway on a windy day can be a real treat. Without wind, the VW tracks arrow-straight down the road and gives an excellent ride. The off-road performance and handling are head and shoulders above all the domestic vans and the ride is better than just about any vehicle we have driven. The independent suspension at all four corners is responsible for this and allows the wheels to travel a good distance up and down to absorb the bumps and shocks rather than transmitting them directly to the occupants.

The accelerative ability is adequate and we timed it at 20.0 seconds for the zero to 60 mph run. In the quarter mile, the VW gave a reading of 21.7 seconds for covering the distance and went through the lights at 61.5 mph. While we felt that the engine was developing ample horsepower for all driving conditions, we did note that the emission control equipment on the 4-cylinder powerplant does exhibit some strange quirks. For example, the engine continues to rev when the clutch is depressed for gear changing and we are curious about the effect this will have on the clutch over extended periods of use. It seems to us that the clutch must be receiving a stiff jolt with every gear change since the engine does not rev down. At the same time, the engine always fired right up no matter how long the vehicle had been sitting.

The quality of the workmanship in the Volkswagen is nice to behold. Everything fits as it should and there are no rattles or squeaks. It is a bit on the noisy side with no insulation in the cargo area and with the air-cooled engine, but we suspect that most buyers would fill the back with carpeting or paneling and cut down the noise considerably.

All in all, we like the VW van and think that it is outstanding in many areas. However, there is one great qualification which must be made. For carrying a sizeable load of gear inside or pulling a trailer behind, the small engine has to struggle a lot. The reserve power is simply not there and this is the area where the U.S.-built vans get the nod.

In terms of fuel economy, the VW achieved 20.9 miles per gallon in our test which includes both highway cruising and short trips in city traffic. Off the pavement, the figure was 15.6 mpg. So, the VW has an effective range on the road of more than 300 miles between fill ups, making it the longest hauler with the stock fuel tank setup.

Our overall conclusion about the VW is that it has more outstanding features than it has drawbacks. The ride, handling, durability and quality far outweigh the relative lack of power. In addition, the fuel economy is hard to beat. It may still be the best van on the road. ●

VOLKSWAGEN 1800 KOMBI KAMPER

The Kamper is identical to the Microbus externally and mechanically, but has caravan conversion at rear.

The Volkswagen Kombi Kamper — a Microbus 1800 which doubles as a motorised caravan — has been introduced in the Republic by Volkswagen South Africa, priced at R4 490.

The Kamper conversion is carried out on the assembly line to produce a five/six-seat family holiday vehicle, with light woodgrain furnishings in the style of a caravan. There are storage lockers, a full-length wardrobe with mirror, a folding dining table, and Formica working surfaces, with storage drawers and soft lighting.

FOLDING DOUBLE BED

The rear seat folds and extends to form a double bed, and a child's hammock is provided. There are curtains in all the windows, and insulated woodgrain panelling all round.

In the daytime, the rear space can be used as a dinette, and it converts into a bedroom at night.

OPTIONS AVAILABLE

Several options are available:
● A battery and gas-operated refrigerator, R151,32. (Part No. 996069113).

● A 3,6 x 2,1 metre side tent, R180,56. (Part No. 996069732).
● A 2,7 x 4 metre side tent, R181,28. (Part No. 996069734).

The prices given are subject to change without notice.

Mechanically, the Kamper is the same as the Microbus 1800, with the 1 795 cm³ engine producing 50 kW DIN at 4 800 r/min. Overall dimensions are the same, and four-speed manual gearbox is standard. Tyres are 185 x 14 radials on 5½ J wide rims.

The Kombi Kamper is a South African-developed addition to the Microbus range.

●

Left: View of the dinette space through the side door. The Kamper has motorised caravan status for caravan park purposes.

Below: The double bed conversion seen through the tailgate. Optional side tents and stretchers or sleeping bags can be used to increase living and sleeping space.

ROTARY-POWERED VW VAN

KENNEDY ENGINEERED PRODUCTS is located in Pacoima, Calif. and is the shop of Hobart Kennedy, a man who specializes in making Volkswagen vans into better performing vehicles. Kennedy was good enough to give us some input for a feature in the February 1973 issue of PV4 about how to improve the horsepower in VW vans through engine swaps. At that time he mentioned that he had an RX-2 Mazda rotary engine which he was planning to slip into a VW van sometime in the future. Sure enough, he did it and gave us a call when the project was completed so we could come and look at it and drive it.

The rotary engine was put into the KEP delivery truck which Kennedy uses as a test vehicle for comparing engines. Because the vehicle has had a variety of powerplants in it, Kennedy is able to get a good evaluation of new engines because the variables are kept to a minimum. Thus far, Kennedy has put six

---

ONE MAN'S ANSWER TO SMOOTHER PERFORMANCE

BY THOS. L. BRYANT

---

different engines into the van and after having the RX-2 engine around for a year or so, he decided it was time to drop it in and see the results. He had a bias against the engine before installing it, feeling that the rotary design configuration is inherently inefficient.

The Mazda engine which Kennedy had was built from a variety of borrowed pieces which disturbed the original factory balance. Thus, there is a low frequency vibration at the bottom end

of the power curve but there is n vibration at the top end due to th design of the engine which has n connecting rods. Hobart says th smoothness of the engine is reminiscen of a V-8 motor in the Volksvan and no at all like the 4 and 6-cylinder engine he has also installed.

The exhaust system for the Mazd engine was made from standard exhaus tubing as it was only going to have t last for a month for test purpose Normally, Kennedy says, stainless ste should be used. Also, the thermal rea tor portion of the exhaust system wa not available so the bus was run withou it which gave it an extra 10 horsepowe

One of the other chores involved the conversion was the installation of radiator for the water-cooled RX-2 e gine. Kennedy picked out a '56 For core with special small header tanks allow it to fit beside the steering ge box under the front of the bus. He to us that if he were doing it again would mount the radiator upright in front of the nose of the bus on the outside. The installation under the bumper has not proven all that satisfactory but a scoop does pull air into it when driving and an electric fan is there to help during idle situations.

Following the hook up of all the parts, Kennedy discovered that the maximum torque curve was between 3500 and 5500 rpm, which nicely suited the VW bus shifting range. At 70 mph, the Volkswagen transaxle was allowing the engine to turn at 3500 rpm.

Acceleration tests at Irwindale Raceway produced a pleasant surprise as the VW with the Mazda engine was able to run through the quarter-mile at 74 mph with an elapsed time of 18.2 seconds. There was no opportunity to test the top speed of the Mazda bus but it is certain, according to Kennedy, that it will be well over 90 mph.

In summing it all up, Kennedy says that the only engine he has tested in a Volkswagen bus that compares with the Mazda for driveability is the aluminum V-8 which was used in GM cars from 1961 to 1963. While the V-8 gives better acceleration, is equally smooth and also gives better gas mileage, the

Mazda RX-2 rotary fits neatly into the engine bay of the VW van. Kennedy says that installation of the rotary is one of the simpler ones he's done.

Kennedy's try-out Volkswagon van. Since he has been developing engine kits for VW van, he has had six different engines in this one. Mazda Rotary offers considerably more power than stock VW engine and gets about 16 miles per gallon.

RX-2 engine gets the nod in ease of installation. Extensive modification is necessary to slip the V-8 into the VW but this is not the case with the Mazda powerplant. Also, the Mazda engine has the advantage of a slightly wider rpm range and should be easier on the parts

in the stock VW transaxle which can have difficulty accepting the torque of the V-8.

It's quite a conversion and the gas mileage, around town and highway cruising combined, is about 16 mpg. What you lose in economy, however, is

made up for in not having to inch up mountain passes and labor when towing a trailer behind. It's a pretty slick conversion. If you'd like more information, write to Kennedy Engineered Products, 10202 Glen Oaks Blvd., Pacoima, Calif. 91331. •

VW KOMBI 1800 KAMPER

The perennial Volkswagen Kombi, first of the family buses, never seems to run out of surprises. There is always something new coming up to maintain the popularity of this well-loved 10-seater.

It has been growing steadily in performance and all-round capability, always seeming to keep a clear jump ahead of the opposition.

Last year, the engine was increased in size from 1700 to 1800 cm^3, giving it more steam for general driving ability, without detracting from economy — in fact, this test showed better fuel economy

than did that of the 1700 model in June, 1972.

KAMPER VERSION

Also in 1974, VWSA introduced a locally-developed motorised caravan version, known as the Kombi Kamper, with 1800 engine and 4-speed manual transmission. Based on the 10-seater, it has caravan-style furnishing in the vast rear space, in place of the conventional two rows of rear seats.

This furnished area is primarily a dinette, with fold-down table and foam-rubber-cushioned seating on either side of it, opposite the sliding side door. Just inside the door — behind the front passenger seat — is a kitchen locker, and behind the side door is a full-depth wardrobe with mirror. There are storage shelves,

and luggage lockers in the seats, to provide standard holiday accommodation.

The dinette converts (in somewhat awkward fashion, by normal caravan standards) into a large double bed, and a wide hammock can be slung above the

KEY FIGURES

100 metres sprint	8,9 seconds
Terminal speed	63,5 km/h
1 km sprint	42,9 seconds
Terminal speed	114,0 km/h
Litres/100 km at 80	9,2
Fuel tank capacity	60 litres
Fuel range at 80	648 km
Engine revs per km	2 170
National list price	R4 670

The new Microbus 1800 is very much as the 1700 tested earlier, except for the increased engine capacity and improved gearing. The engine gains 100 cm³ by increasing the bore of the 1700 motor from 90 to 93 mm, to give a small increase in power output, and a sizeable (about 16%) jump in torque.

The improved pulling power is evident as soon as one drives the new model — the 1700 was pretty zestful by 10-seater standards, and the 1800 is even better, particularly up hills.

VW has taken advantage of this to improve gearing by changing from a 5,375 to 1 final drive to 4,86 to 1. With the indirect top gear (0,89 to 1) this gives overall gearing of 4,33 to 1 in top, making the new Kombi more long-legged — it now pulls 27,6 km/h in top at 1 000 r/min.

PERFORMANCE

In actual acceleration, the new Kombi is very much the same as the 1700 model. With more leisurely gearing, it is a bit slower away from rest, for instance. But it pulls a better gradient in top, and has a much-enhanced top speed potential, becoming the first Kombi to top a true 80 mph (130 km/h).

As with earlier Kombi models, the engine is governed mechanically to about 5 400 r/min, but we found that the 1800 would go to 100 km/h in 3rd — perhaps a trifle unwillingly. But it romps to 80 in 3rd, to have full climbing and overtaking ability.

The test car proved prone to engine-stalling, possibly because its idling speed was set low. It proved very steady at speed, except that a buffeting side wind on those high sides caused deflection — which is understandable on a vehicle of this type.

ECONOMY AND BRAKING

The 1800 showed surprisingly good economy at steady speeds well ahead of the figures achieved by the 1700 in 1972. In part it would be the improved gearing which is responsible, though there may well have been some economy tuning in production, too, since fuel consump-

tion became extra-important 18 months ago. Driving carefully, owners might get 10 litres/100 km on the open road at 80, to give a range of about 600 km on the 60-litre tank.

Brakes use discs at front, drums rear, boosted, and in good balance. The big-bodied vehicle stops cleanly and safely, though it pitches heavily and the steering tightens up in a hard stop.

WITH ROOF RACK

As a matter of interest, we did brief tests with the big roof rack in place, and found that it creates a substantial amount of drag — something like 8 per cent loss in performance resulted, with just the bare rack without luggage.

Even at middle speeds, the whistle set up by the unloaded rack was evidence that it caused turbulence above the roof — sufficient to reduce maximum speed from about 130 to less than 120 km/h, for instance.

So we have reservations about this roof rack, particularly as it would increase high-up mass and add to that mild out-of-balance feeling that characterises Kombi handling in tight situations.

LIVING COMFORT

The Kamper qualifies as a motorised caravan for admission to caravan parks, and provides comfortable living for a couple, or a family with one or two young children. The double bed and hammock are both spacious, and the daytime living space compares well with a conventional caravan, except for head-room.

There is abundant stowage space, and when staying on site for any length of time, the optional side tent would double the available living room.

On the road it is very much a car, except that the number of rear seats is reduced — making it a 6/7-seater — and that the window curtains reduce rearward vision slightly, even when open. The rear view mirror on these Kombi's, incidentally, is set too high and — even when riding light — only gives rear view up to about 80 metres behind. It would be a good idea if VWSA reverted to a pair of

front seats for a child (it would even take two very little ones).

OPTIONAL FEATURES

The Kamper can be extended from its standard 3/4-berth sleeper role to cater for bigger families, by using the optional frame side-tent (there is a choice of two in the VW accessory range). There is also a compact battery-and-gas-operated refrigerator offered as an extra, besides the normal range of VW Kombi and camping accessories.

The test car was equipped with tent and refrigerator, and a massive, full-length roof rack was also fitted. We removed all these extra items during performance tests, so as to make this test valid for the normal 1800 Microbus/Kombi, in terms of mass and frontal area.

The twin-carburettor 1800 engine, which is notably strong on torque.

ACCELERATION

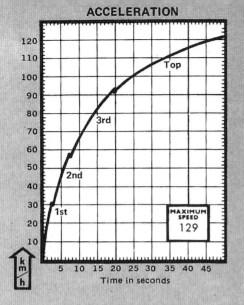

MAXIMUM SPEED
129

Time in seconds

BRAKING DISTANCES

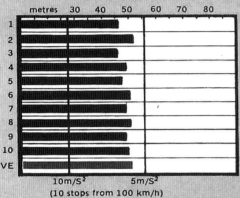

10m/S² 5m/S²
(10 stops from 100 km/h)

ENGINE SPEED

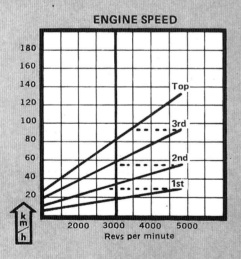

Revs per minute

GRADIENT ABILITY

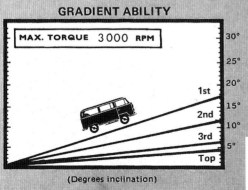

MAX. TORQUE 3000 RPM

(Degrees inclination)

PERFORMANCE

MAKE AND MODEL:
Make . . . . . . Volkswagen
Model . . . . . Kombi 1800

INTERIOR NOISE LEVELS:

	Mech.	Wind	Road
Idling . . .	55,5	—	—
60 . . .	73,0	—	—
80 . . .	78,0	—	—
100 . . .	82,5	85,0	86,0
Average dBA at 100 . . .			84,5

(Measured in decibels, "A" weighting,
averaging runs both ways on a level
road; "Mechanical" with car closed;
"Wind" with one window fully open;
"Road" on a coarse road surface.)

ACCELERATION FROM REST:
0-60 7,7
0-80 13,9
0-100 24,6
400 m sprint 8,9
1 km sprint 42,9

OVERTAKING ACCELERATION:

	3rd	Top
40-60 . . .	5,6	9,6
60-80 . . .	6,1	10,3
80-100 . .	13,5	18,3

(Measured in seconds, to true speeds,
averaging runs both ways on a level
road, car carrying test crew of two and
standard test equipment.)

IMPERIAL DATA

Major performance features of this
Road Test are summarised below in
Imperial measures, for comparative pur-
poses:

ACCELERATION FROM REST
(seconds):
0-50: 14,2
0-60: 22,7

MAXIMUM SPEED (mph):
True speed 80,4

FUEL ECONOMY (mpg):
30 mph 41,1
40 mph 35,5
50 mph 30,4
60 mph 26,8

MAXIMUM SPEED:
True speed 129,2
Speedo reading . . . 136

Calibration:

Indicated	40	60	80	100
True speed	35	56	76,5	97

FUEL CONSUMPTION
(litres/100 km):
40 6,4
60 7,7
80 9,2
100 10,8

(Stated in litres per 100 kilometres,
based on fuel economy figures recorded
at true speeds.)

BRAKING TEST:
From 100 km/h:
First stop 3,7
Tenth stop 4,0
Average 3,93

(Measured in seconds with stops from
true speeds at 30-second intervals on a
good bitumenised surface.)

GRADIENTS IN GEARS:
Low gear . . . . . 1 in 3,2
2nd gear . . . . . 1 in 4,8
3rd gear . . . . . 1 in 8,4
Top gear . . . . . 1 in 14,1

(Tabulated from Tapley (x gravity)
readings, car carrying test crew of two
and standard test equipment.)

GEARED SPEEDS: (km/h)
Low gear 31,2
2nd gear 57,2
3rd gear 93,6
Top gear 132,3

(Calculated at engine peak r/min —
4 800.)

NOISE VALUES

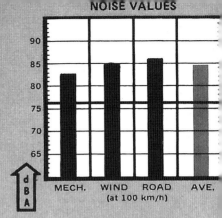

MECH. WIND ROAD AVE.
(at 100 km/h)

LUGGAGE CAPACITY
(dm³)

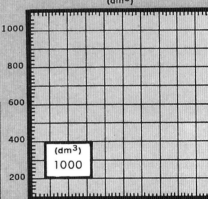

(dm³)
1000

FUEL RANGE
(km)

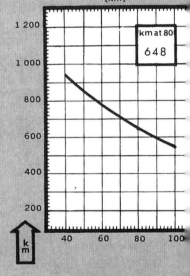

km at 80
648

FUEL CONSUMPTION
(litres/100 km)

litres
per
100 km

kilometres per hour

SPECIFICATIONS

ENGINE:
Cylinders . 4, horizontally opposed, rear mounted
Carburettors . twin Solex 32-34, PDSIT
Bore . . . . . 93,0 mm
Stroke . . . . . 66,0 mm
Cubic capacity . . . 1 795 cm³
Compression ratio . . 7,3 to 1
Valve gear . . . ohv, pushrods
Main bearings. . . . . four
Aircleaner. . . . paper element
Fuel requirement 93-octane Coast, 87-octane Reef
Cooling . . air, blower-driven
Electrics . . . . 12-volt AC

ENGINE OUTPUT:
Max power SAE (kW) . 56 (75 b.h.p.)
Max. power net (kW) .48 (50 D.I.N.)
Peak r/min 4 800
Max torque (N.m) at r/min . 132 at 3 000

TRANSMISSION:
Forward speeds . . . . four
Synchromesh . . . . . all
Gearshift . . . . . floor
Low gear . . . . .3,78 to 1
2nd gear . . . .2,06 to 1
3rd gear . . . .1,26 to 1
Top gear . . . .0,89 to 1
Reverse gear . . .3,78 to 1
Final drive . . . .4,86 to 1
Drive wheels . . . . rear

WHEELS AND TYRES:
Road wheels . 14 inch pressed steel discs
Rim width 5½J
Tyres . . . 185 SR 14 radials
Tyre pressures (front) . 200 to 220 kPa (28 to 32 lb)
Tyre pressures (rear) . 210 to 250 kPa (30 to 36 lb)

BRAKES:
Front . . . . . discs
Rear . . . . . drums
Pressure regulation . . . .nil
Boosting . . . vacuum servo
Handbrake position . fascia pull-handle

STEERING:
Type . . . Ross worm and roller, damped
Lock to lock . . . . 2,8 turns
Turning circle . 10 metres approx

MEASUREMENTS:
Length overall . . . 4,505 m
Width overall . . . 1,720 m
Height overall . . . 1,940 m
Wheelbase . . . . 2,400 m
Front track . . . 1,395 m
Rear track . . . 1,455 m
Ground clearance . . . 0,185 m
Licensing mass . . . 1 265 kg

SUSPENSION:
Front . . . . . independent
Type . torsion bar and stabiliser
Rear . . . . independent
Type . torsion.bar, dual-jointed half-axles

CAPACITIES:
Seating . . . 8/10 (Kamper 6/7)
Fuel tank . . . . . 60 litres
Luggage trunk . .1 000 dm³ gross
Utility space . .5 000 dm³ gross

WARRANTY:
Six months or 10 000 km.

TEST CAR FROM:
VW South Africa, Uitenhage, in conjunction with Motors W.P. Services, Paarden Eiland, Cape.

CRUISING AT 80

Mech. noise level . . .	78,0 dBA
0-80 through gears .	.13,9 seconds
km/litre at 80 . . .	. 10,8
litres/100 km . . .	. 9,2
Braking from 80 . . .	. 3,3 seconds
Maximum gradient (top)	. 1 in 17,0
Speedometer error . .	. 4% over
Speedo at true 80 . .	. 84 km/h
Engine r/min (top) . .	. 3 896

door mirrors instead of the single fitted in current production, to imporve rearward vision — particularly on the Kamper.

SUMMARY

This 1800 Kombi/Microbus/Kamper model shows a substantial measure of improvement over earlier models in performance and economy, making it even more driveable than before, and better value.

The Kamper is a clever car/caravan model at lower cost than the earlier Kampmobile. It is built in comparatively small volume to fill a special need for a double-purpose family car, less expensive than a full car/caravan combination.

VW has shown great enterprise in developing and improving the Kombi range in recent years, pioneering the establishment of a new and exciting category of family car.

TECHNICAL

PERFORMANCE FACTORS:
Power/mass (W/kg) net . . . 37,9
Frontal area (m²) 3,34
km/h per 1 000 r/min (top) . 27,6
(Calculated on licensing mass, gross frontal area, gearing and net power output.)

SERVICE REQUIREMENTS:
Sump capacity . . . . 3,5 litres
Change interval . . . .5 000 km
Oil filter capacity . . . 0,5 litres
Change interval . . . 10 000 km
Gearbox/diff. capacity . 3,5 litres
Change interval . . . . . .nil
Air filter change . Up to 20 000 km
Greasing points . . . . .nil
(These basic service recommendations are given for guidance only, and may vary according to operating conditions. Inquiries should be addressed to authorised dealerships.)

STANDARD EQUIPMENT:
Electric clock, heater/demister; driver door mirror; twin dome lights; disc front brakes; brake booster; radial-ply tyres on wide rims; rubber-faced bumpers; dash grabhandle; semi-reclining front seats; headlight flasher; hazard warning control; test wiring circuit.
Kamper: rear space furnished with dinette (convertible to double bed); wardrobe, cupboards, drawers and lockers; removable child's hammock; curtains in windows.
Extras provided on test car; full-length roof rack, frame side tent, gas/battery refrigerator.

TEST CONDITIONS:
Altitude . . . . . At sea level
Weather . . . . . fine and hot
Fuel used . . . . . 93 octane
Test car's odometer . .2 929 km

Without roof rack, the Kamper returned representative Kombi 1800 performance in this test. Curtains are a Kamper identifying feature.

Thrown into a tight turn at 50 km/h, the Kamper responded neatly enough — in spite of that big roofrack!

Controls are simple and easy to use, including the large, almost horizontal steering wheel.

VW KOMBI FLEETLINE 1600

E ven Volkswagen of South Africa has
been surprised at the demand for the
VW Fleetline Kombi.

This humble vehicle is hardly likely
to shape in any "Car of the Year" nomin-
ation — yet in many ways, it is one of the
most important of many new models
announced in South Africa this year.
If the yardstick were to be sheer value and
a counter to inflation — rather than
glamour and performance — the Fleetline
models from VW would be leading con-
tenders.

The Fleetline models — pick-up, van
and Kombi — are something quite exceptional in the South African motor indus-

try. They are plain, basic vehicles of
obsolete pattern, built to traditional VW
standards and fitted with modern engines.
The result is a range of vehicles which may
be quaint in some respects — but which are
thoroughly workable and thrifty to operate.

DERIVED FROM BRAZIL

In brief outline, the Fleetline models
are based on the commercial vehicle
models built by the largest VW manufacturing concern outside Wolfsburg —
VW do Brasil. Brazil, with a rigid local-
manufacture programme, adopted a policy
of freezing vehicle models at the beginning
of the last decade.

So the local VW plant has been building Beetle and Type 2 models since
about 1963 without any change in design.
In the case of the Kombi, in fact, a local
adaptation was the addition of extra

windows in the rear quarters, so th
this Rip-van-Winkel 10-seater has 15 wir
dows — including the split windscree

There are no frills to the car: th
windows slide or hinge open (includir

KEY FIGURES

100 metres sprint . .	9,2 seconds
Terminal speed . .	. 61,5 km/h
1 km sprint	43,8 seconds
Terminal speed . .	.109,0 km/h
Accel. 0-80 km/h .	15,3 seconds
Fuel tank capacity .	. .43 litres
litres/100 km at 80 .	. . . 9,4
Fuel range at 80 . .	. . 466 km
litres/100 km at 90 .	. . . 10,7
Fuel range at 90 . .	. . 400 km
Engine revs per km .	. . 1 805
National list price .	. . R3 095

have kept the cost of the Fleetline models down to a remarkable level.

MODERN FEATURES

But this is not just an obsolete car resuscitated in modern manufacture — it also has some very up-to-date features. VW South Africa wisely decided not to use the old, low-performance Brazillian engine, and instead, fits the modern 1600 unit from Germany, complete with oil cooler and electronic diagnosis plug-in point.

Then there is the transmission: traditional VW Porsche-type with standard Kombi ratios, but with a brilliant innovation: the Beetle's former 4,125 to 1 final drive ratio, instead of the 4,86 used in the Kombi 1800, for instance.

Over the years we have pleaded for higher gearing for 10-seaters, and the Fleetline is the first to go to a really effective overall ratio. With the 0,89 to 1 of the indirect top, its overall gearing works out to 3,67 to 1 — giving 33,2 km/h per 1 000 r/min, in top.

As a final touch, the Fleetline models are fitted with semi-widerim wheels which would take 175 radials.

PERFORMANCE

The Fleetline Kombi is lighter than its modern counterparts, and has some of the disabilities of the old Kombi models: severe wind-up of the rear crank axles at a sprint start (resulting in the tail jacking up as it jumps away from rest), plenty of engine noise because of minimal insulation, and engine governing at 4 000 r/min.

But it goes through the gears very quickly and has quite reasonable range — thanks to its good gearing — so that it reaches 80 km/h in 15,3 seconds: only 1,4 seconds behind the modern Kombi 1800 (CAR Road Test, April 1975), and 100 inside 30 seconds.

Maximum speed is a quite remarkable 117 km/h (the best we have recorded with a 1600 Kombi).

Gradient ability, understandably, is not exciting — but third gear is long-ranging enough to enable the Fleetline to climb strongly at 85 km/h.

FUEL ECONOMY

The Fleetline proved very much more economical than 1600 Kombi models tested earlier (CAR June 1968 and October 1969), returning 9,4 litres/100 km (about 30 mpg) at 80 km/h — though this drops fairly sharply to 11,8 litres/100 km (22,4 mpg) at 100 km/h. At 90, the big-bodied vehicle registered 10,7 litres/100 km (26,3 mpg).

With its 43 litre tank, we calculate that it should have an effective range of 400 km per tankful at cruising speeds, driving economically and without load. With this single-carburettor engine, the speed factor is important: full-throttle driving can drop the return to as little as 16,5 litres/100 km (17mpg).

NOISE AND BRAKING

Mainly because there is less body insulation in this low-cost model, noise levels tend to be higher all round — even road noise shows a rise, as the crossply tyres do not have the sound insulating properties of radials. This is far from a quiet car, exceeding speech interference levels all the time once 80 km/h is passed.

It stops reasonably enough under normal conditions, but the unboosted brakes need considerable pedal pressure for good results. The drum brakes are not nearly as effective as the disc/drum combination used on the modern German-sourced models, but they resisted fade quite well in spite of becoming smoking hot during our series of 10 crash stops.

Finish and equipment are basic, but include heater, exterior mirrors and other essentials.

ront quarterlights) and do not wind down; the windscreen wipers park high, and have old-fashioned mechanical washers, for instance.

OLD SUSPENSION

Brakes are drums all round, without boosting, and the wicked old crank-type swing axles are used at rear — so the Fleetline is not as stable and controllable as its modern, German-sourced counterpart, which has had a dual-jointed rear axle system since way back in 1968.

VW do Brasil was able to take over old body-pressing dies from VW Germany at minimal cost, and carry on stamping out body panels for more than a decade without change, so that amortisation costs are negligible. At the same time, the Brazilian Cruziero offers a more favourable rate of exchange with the Rand than does the Deutschmark, so these two factors

ACCELERATION

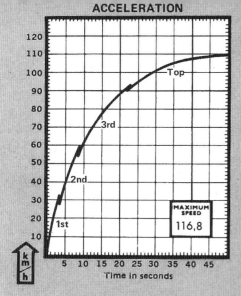

Time in seconds

MAXIMUM SPEED
116,8

PERFORMANCE

MAKE AND MODEL:
Make . . . . Volkswagen
Model . . Fleetline 1600 Kombi

INTERIOR NOISE LEVELS:

	Mech.	Wind	Road
Idling	58,5	—	—
60	75,5	—	—
80	81,5	—	—
100	86,5	87,0	89,0
Average dBA at 100			87,5

(Measured in decibels, "A" weighting, averaging runs both ways on a level road; "Mechanical" with car closed; "Wind" with one window fully open; "Road" on a coarse road surface.)

ACCELERATION FROM REST:
0-60 8,6
0-80 15,3
0-100 29,6
100 m sprint 9,2
1 km sprint 43,8

OVERTAKING ACCELERATION:

	3rd	Top
40-60	4,4	7,7
60-80	6,2	9,3
80-100	—	14,5

(Measured in seconds, to true speeds, averaging runs both ways on a level road, car carrying test crew of two and standard test equipment).

MAXIMUM SPEED:
True speed 116,8
Speedo reading 117
Calibration:
Indicated: . . 60 . 80 . 100
True speed: . . 59 . 78 . 97

NOISE VALUES

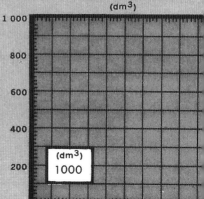

MECH.   WIND   ROAD   AVE
(at 100 km/h)

LUGGAGE CAPACITY
(dm³)

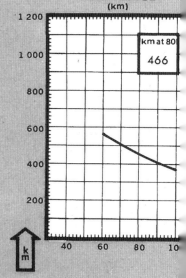

(dm³)
1000

BRAKING DISTANCES

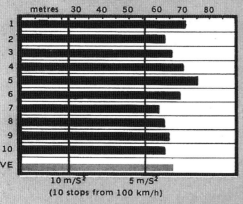

10 m/S²   5 m/S²
(10 stops from 100 km/h)

CRUISING AT 80

Mech. noise level . . . .81,5 dBA
0-80 through gears . .15,3 seconds
km/litre at 80 10,6
litres/100 km 9,4
Braking from 80 . . 4,1 seconds
Maximum gradient (top) . 1 in 19,2
Speedometer error . . 2,5% over
Speedo at true 80 . . 82 km/h
Engine rpm (top) 2 410

FUEL CONSUMPTION (litres/100 km):
60 7,6
80 9,4
100 11,8
(Stated in litres per 100 kilometres, based on fuel economy figures recorded at true speeds.)

BRAKING TEST:
From 100 km/h:
First stop 5,7
Tenth stop 5,0
Average 5,31
(Measured in sec. with stops from true speeds at 30-second intervals on a good bitumenised surface.)

GRADIENTS IN GEARS:
Low gear . . . . . . 1 in 3,6
2nd gear . . . . . . 1 in 5,1
3rd gear . . . . . . 1 in 7,4
Top gear . . . . . . 1 in 12,4
(Tabulated from Tapley (x gravity) readings, car carrying test crew of two and standard test equipment.)

GEARED SPEEDS: (km/h)
Low gear 31,2
2nd gear 57,4
3rd gear 90,5
Top gear 132,8
(Calculated at engine peak r/min — 4 000.)

FUEL RANGE
(km)

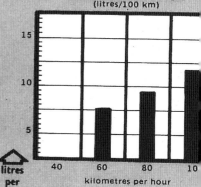

km at 80
466

ENGINE SPEED

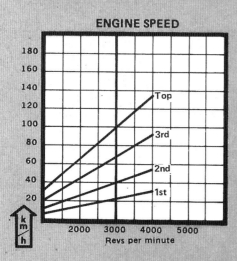

Revs per minute

GRADIENT ABILITY

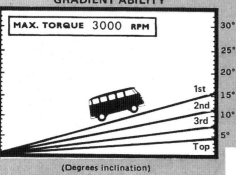

MAX. TORQUE 3000 RPM

(Degrees inclination)

FUEL CONSUMPTION
(litres/100 km)

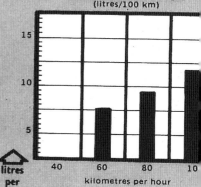

kilometres per hour

SPECIFICATIONS

ENGINE:

Cylinders . .	4 cylinders opposed, rear mounted
Carburettor . .	single choke Solex downdraught 34 PICT
Bore	. . 85,5 mm
Stroke	. . 69,0 mm
Cubic capacity . .	1 584 cm³
Compression ratio . .	7,5 to 1
Valve gear . .	ohv, pushrod
Main bearings . . .	4
Aircleaner	oil bath
Fuel requirement.	.93-octane Coast 88-octane Reef
Cooling . . .	air, blower-driven
Electrics	12-volt AC

ENGINE OUTPUT

Max. power SAE (kW)	. 43 (57 bhp)
Max. power net (kW)	. 37 (37 DIN)
Peak r/min	.4 000
Max. torque (N.m.) at r/min	. 111 at 3 000

TRANSMISSION:

Forward speeds . . .	. four
Synchromesh	.all
Gearshift	. floor
Low gear . . .	.3,80 to 1
2nd gear . . .	.2,06 to 1
3rd gear . . .	.1,32 to 1
Top gear . . .	.0,89 to 1
Reverse gear . . .	.3,88 to 1
Final drive. . . .	4,125 to 1
Drive wheels . . .	rear

WHEELS AND TYRES:

Road wheels .	14 inch pressed steel discs
Rim width	. 5 JK
Tyres . . .	775 X 14 crossply
Tyre pressures (front)	. 200 to 220 kPa (28 to 32 lb)
Tyre pressures (rear).	. 220 to 250 kPa (28 to 36 lb)

BRAKES:

Front	.drums
Rear	.drums
Pressure regulation . .	.nil
Boosting	.nil
Handbrake position . .	under dash

STEERING:

Type	worm and roller
Lock to lock . . .	. 2,8 turns
Turning circle. . .	11,4 metres

MEASUREMENTS:

Length overall . .	. 4,289 m
Width overall. . .	. 1,746 m
Height overall. . .	. 1,883 m
Wheelbase. . . .	. 2,400 m
Front track . . .	. 1,375 m
Rear track. . . .	. 1,360 m
Ground clearance. .	. 0,225 m
Licensing mass . .	. 1 065 kg

SUSPENSION:

Front	.independent
Type . .	link pins, torsion bars, stabiliser
Rear	independent
Type	.crank swing axles, torsion bars

CAPACITIES:

Seating	. .8–10
Fuel tank	. 43 litres
Luggage space .	.1 000 dm³ gross
Utility space . .	5 000 dm³ gross (seat removed)

WARRANTY:
12 months

TEST CAR FROM:
Volkswagen of South Africa, Uitenhage, C.P.

IMPERIAL DATA

Major performance features of this Road Test are summarised below in Imperial measures, for comparative purposes:

ACCELERATION FROM REST
(seconds):

0-50	. . 15,6
0-60	. . 26,6

MAXIMUM SPEED (mph):

True speed . . .	. . 72,6

FUEL ECONOMY (mpg):

40 mph	. . 35,7
50 mph	. . 29,8
60 mph	. . 23,8

SUMMARY

This economy Kombi has conventional arrangement of three rows of seats without the walk-through facility from the front found on later models, and with the spare wheel placed behind the front seats.

In deference to the simple swing-axle layout, it needs to be driven more sedately than the dual-joint axle models, and firm tyre pressures are needed to aid directional stability.

The fact that this is our third VW Kombi test this year is an indication of how the demand for this class of vehicle has grown. The Fleetline models were originally intended for the fleet owner as economy models, but the Kombi in particular, has been "adopted" as a good-value family car by hundreds of motorists.

Priced about R800 lower than any other 10-seater model, it is notable value — and may well point the way to other ventures in the "basic car" field. ∎

TECHNICAL

PERFORMANCE FACTORS:

Power/mass (W/kg) net . .	. 34,8
Frontal area (m²) . . .	. 3,30
km/h per 1 000 r/min (top).	. 33,2

(Calculated on licensing mass, gross frontal area, gearing and net power output).

SERVICE REQUIREMENTS:

Sump capacity . . .	. 2,5 litres
Change interval . .	.5 000 km
Gearbox/diff capacity .	. 2,5 litres
Change interval . . .	. .nil
Air filter service .	up to 10 000 km
Greasing points . . .	. 9
Greasing interval. .	10 000 km

(These basic service recommendations are given for guidance only, and may vary according to operating conditions. Inquiries should be addressed to authorised dealerships).

STANDARD EQUIPMENT:
Heater with forced draught; mechanical windscreen washers; bumper overriders; twin exterior rearview mirrors; headlight flashers.

TEST CONDITIONS:

Altitude	. At sea level
Weather . . .	fine and warm
Fuel used	.93-octane
Test car's odometer . .	.3 142 km

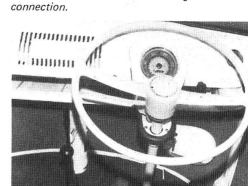

The rear swing axles are twitchy, and we cornered the Fleetline smoothly at 50 to avoid provoking them.

Engine is the modern 1600 from Germany, with oil cooler and electronic diagnostic connection.

Nothing luxurious about the Fleetline dashboard, but equipment is functional.

The car is a mass of windows, and has old-style Kombi tailgate access.

MICROBUS DRIVING IMPRESSIONS

We'd like to have one 'cause there may not be another

BY PAUL DEXLER

Years ago, we remember reading in The Flat Four, (the magazine of the Volkswagon Owner's Club) a fictional article about the VW of the future. Thoughts of it came back to us as we lived with the 1976 deluxe station wagen for two weeks.

"It will have automatic transmission, and air conditioning," said the story, " but the familiar tick-tick from the rear tells us that it still has the same old air cooled flat-4." So did our bus—almost. The super smooth 3-speed automatic transmission was there. The powerful air conditioner was there. And the flat-4 was there, but it wasn't quite the same flat-4 that was powering VW's in 1957 when the story was written.

People have always accused the VW bus of being underpowered. "It can't pull the skin off a rice pudding," they would say. Ah, yes, but now, it can. As with the Beetle, the final fading years of the rear engined VW bus have seen it reach a state of perfection. The flat-4 used in the '76 model bus was lifted directly from the late lamented Porsche 914. With two liters of displacement, even our automatic version could easily keep up with traffic, and even out-accelerate a car or two. We loved it. The feeling of driving a VW bus that was *fast* was marvelous.

Aside from the "big" engine, there

is little new in the latest version of the bus. The power front disc brakes from the 1971 model, and the automatic transmission from the '73, fit nicely into the basic box that first appeared in 1968. Yes, Virginia, we know that the first VW bus appeared on these shores back in the '50s, but the second generation version was introduced in '68. The last version of this design may well be the present one, because its successor is already running around in Europe, and it is only a matter of time before it comes here. So if you want the last of the classic VW busses, now's the time to buy.

The VW is also the last of the van-type vehicles that you can buy in this country in which the driver sits in front of the front wheels, as is done in large busses. This makes for a subtle difference in driving style from vehicles where the front wheels are well ahead of the driver. As for cornering, well, the bus will

go around a corner. Actually, if you can get past the strange swaying sensation caused by the high driving position and the high center of gravity, the bus can be cornered with considerable verve. Most people we know will tend to approach corners gently, however.

The big engine and automatic transmission didn't cut down the gas mileage too much. The engine has fuel injection, and the transmission is well mated to it, something that couldn't be said of earlier automatics. We got about 15 miles per gallon in traffic, and over 17 mpg on the highway. A 1966 model (1600cc engine and 4 speed transmission) that we owned when it was new, only got 19 mpg on the highway, so

it appears that the new engine is really efficient.

One of the nicest features of the bus is that its gas mileage doesn't change much with load. Driving solo or loaded with people and their things, we still got our 15 mpg in town and 17 mpg on the highway. The bus doesn't balk at carrying any load that you might want to put inside it. The wide sliding side door, and the fold-down rear seat backrest allow large loads to be carried or slide in without much strain. With a sunroof model, you could even haul a giraffe.

Our test model was equipped with the factory air, mounted in the roof just behind the driver's seat. A housing extended forward to distribute cool air into the driving compartment, reminding us in a way of the roof-mounted fresh air distribution system on our '66 model. The air unit only got in the way if someone was coming up the aisle from the rear compartment to the front, in which case they usually banged their head on it. The air unit made up for this deficincy by putting out a great volume of cold air, enough to keep the interior of the box comfortable even on a sunny, hot day.

Fresh air ventilation is not quite so effective with the front windows rolled up, but some air does move through the dash vents and the vents at the back of the front seats that are connected to them. Our unit had the optional opening vent panes in the middle side windows and in the left rear side window. They were great forgetting a little more air to the rear passengers.

Seven or nine passengers can be accommodated in the bus, depending on the seat style ordered. Ours was a 7-seat version, with individual front seats, a 2-passenger seat in the middle, and an aisle so that passengers can move around without opening the doors. The 9-seater has three abreast benches in all positions, giving seating capacity in return for restrictions.

The VW bus is still the best buy in a van type of vehicle for passenger use. Recent currency fluctuations have caused its price to rise a lot, but you can't get the same thing anywhere else for less, and you certainly can't run anything else for less. 🐛

1. *Addition of bigger engine for 1976 has increased the acceleration and speed capabilities of the bus without drastically increasing fuel consumption.*

2. *From the rear, the bus is still the same basic box as always. No external changes mark the new model.*

3. *The driving position is high and forward, with excellent visibility. Blank dial on dash can be used for an optional clock or tach.*

4. *The center of gravity is high, making brisk cornering seem scarier than it really is.*

5. *Much chrome trim has been removed from the exterior in recent years in order to hold costs down.*

6. *The VW bus is still the most maneuverable vehicle on the market for its capacity.*

7. *The 7-seater configuration provides an aisle between the two front seats for passengers to circulate.*

8. *Plenty of glass area keeps the interior bright. Seat belts are supplied for all passenger positions, with headrests optional.*

9. *The two liter engine is a carry-over from the Porsche 914. It is the best improvement the bus could have had.*

6

7

8

9

VW MICROBUS 2000

In spite of its 20-year-old basic concept, the much-loved VW 10-seater (whether it be Kombi, Microbus or Kamper) remains the top-seller in its class in South Africa and a leader in both performance and specification.

At the end of 1975, VWSA introduced a bigger 2-litre engine in place of the earlier 1800 unit on Microbus models. This is the culmination of a steady growth in engine capacity: the original Kombi models sold in South Africa in the mid-'Fifties were 1200 models; then came increases in engine capacity to 1500, 1600, 1700 and (for 1975) 1800 cm³. The new 2000 models (seven of them!) replace the 1800's, though the 1600 engine is retained in the five commercial vehicles and the basic Kombi.

EXECUTIVE LAYOUT

Our test vehicle this year was the luxury-equipped Microbus Executive model, which has such special equipment features as wall-to-wall carpeting, anti-glare tinted windows, chrome window and waistline trim, chromed bumpers with thick rubber inserts to cushion minor impacts, and a retracting step at the side door.

It is the most cosy-feeling of all the Kombi models, principally because the carpets add a touch of warmth and softness to the large interior space, as well as cushioning both internal and external noise.

The exterior rear-view mirrors (which should be placed further forward for full advantage) are a useful feature, as the interior rear-view mirror is too high-set and does not give long-range rear view: it has to be angled downward and gives no view of the horizon.

One omission: there should be a grab-handle at the driver door, to make it easier to get in and out of the lofty cab.

INCREASE IN TORQUE

The engine capacity is raised from 1795 to 1970 cm³ mainly by increasing the stroke from 66 to 71 mm — although the specifications also show a 1 mm increase in bore diameter. Compression ratio (a low 7,3 to 1, for regular-grade fuel) and carburetion show no major changes, and the bigger engine is said to give a small gain (3 per cent) in power output, but an 8 per cent improvement in torque at output, at lower revs than the 1800 motor.

With its greater reciprocating mass and longer stroke, the 2-litre engine has a more "lomp" feel than the smaller versions, and has a lower revs peak — but the gain in torque is immediately apparent when driving, particularly when it comes to climbs.

STILL BIGGER ENGINE

The final drive ratio is reduced from the 4,86 to 1 of the 1800 model, to 4,57 to 1 on the 2000. With the indirect final drive, this gives an overall ratio of 4,05 to 1 in top, to take advantage of the extra torque and give adequate engine range with lower revs peak. At the same time the gearbox is uprated, we are told, though it retains the well-spaced ratios used in earlier models.

The 2-litre model in its Executive form is the heaviest of the Microbus models, turning the scales at 1 290 kg for a power/mass ratio of 38,0 watts/kg:

a small improvement on that of the 180 (CAR Road Test, April 1975).

It is worth noting, incidentally, tha 2 litres is not the ultimate for this VV engine — we have heard of it bein "stretched" to 2,2 litres experimentall and it might even go further. But w would suggest that VW calls a halt roun about here: going bigger would not be i the best interests of engine willingne and economy!

PERFORMANCE

Like all of the Kombi models i recent years, the Microbus 2000 Execu tive stands nose-high, and tends to li even further at front in a sharp sta from rest. In pure performance tests such as acceleration runs — the bigge engine did not feel all that much stronge than the 1800, and it was necessary t use plenty of revs to counter a tendenc to stall with quick clutch engagemen

Even with two litres of engine and good spread of torque, the big-bodie 10-seater is no performance vehicl though its 0-100 time of 21,4 second is probably the best ever recorded wit the VW Type 2 units. Acceleration the gears — and specially in top —

KEY FIGURES

1 km sprint	41,6 seconds
Terminal speed	116,0 km/h
Fuel tank capacity	56 litres
Litres/100 km at 80	9,7
Fuel range at 80	580 km
Litres/100 km at 90	10,6
Fuel range at 90	527 km
Engine revs per km	2 030
National list price	R5 575

Storage space is provided by a lockable glove box and two mesh parcel trays under the facia. The fuse box is readily accessible.

The stroke of the previous 1 795 cm³ unit was increased by 5 mm 71 mm to raise the capacity of the Microbus engine to 1 970 cm

EXECUTIVE

ACCELERATION

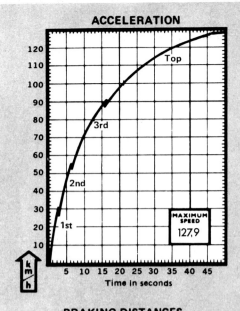

MAXIMUM SPEED
127,9

km/h vs Time in seconds

BRAKING DISTANCES

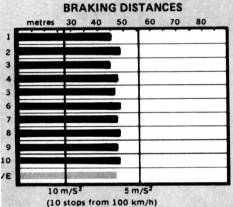

metres
10 m/S²   5 m/S²
(10 stops from 100 km/h)

ENGINE SPEED

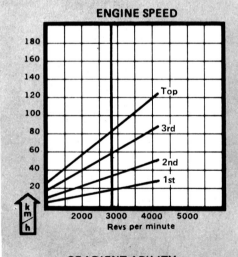

km/h vs Revs per minute

GRADIENT ABILITY

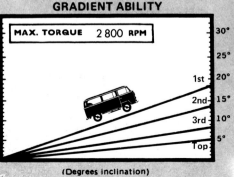

| MAX. TORQUE | 2 800 RPM |

(Degrees inclination)

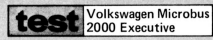
test Volkswagen Microbus 2000 Executive

PERFORMANCE

MAKE AND MODEL:
Make . . . . .Volkswagen
Model. . . .Microbus 2000 Executive

PERFORMANCE FACTORS:
Power/mass (W/kg) net. 38,0
Frontal area (m²) 3,34
km/h per 1 000 r/min (top) . . .29,5

INTERIOR NOISE LEVELS:

	Mech.	Wind	Road
Idling	.56,5	—	—
60	.73,0	—	—
80	.77,5	—	—
100	.82,0	83,0	87,0
Average dBA at 100			84

ACCELERATION FROM REST:
0-60. 7,5
0-80. 12,7
0-100. 21,4
1 km sprint 41,6

IMPERIAL DATA

ACCELERATION FROM REST
(seconds):
0-50. 13,0
0-60. 19,8
MAXIMUM SPEED (m-p-h)
True speed 79,5
FUEL ECONOMY (m-p-g)
40 m-p-h 33,1
50 m-p-h 29,1
60 m-p-h 24,9

OVERTAKING ACCELERATION:

	3rd	Top
40-60	.4,7	.8,2
60-80	.5,2	.8,4
80-100	.8,6	12,7

MAXIMUM SPEED:
True speed 127,9
Speedo reading 135
Calibration:

Indicated:	60	80	100
True speed:	56	76	96

FUEL CONSUMPTION (litres/100 km):
60. 8,2
80. 9,7
100. 11,9

BRAKING TEST:
From 100 km/h:
First stop. 3,6
Tenth stop. 3,9
Average. 3,79
(Measured in sec with stops from true speeds at 30-second intervals on a good bitumenised surface).

CRUISING AT 80

Mech noise level. . . . . . . .77,5 dBA
0-80 through gears . . . . . 12,7 seconds
km/litre at 80 10,4
litres/100 km 9,7
Braking from 80. . . . . . . .3,0 seconds
Maximum gradient (top) . . . 1 in 14,0
Speedometer error . . . . .5% over
Speedo at true 80 . . . . .84 km/h
Engine r/min. 2 720

GRADIENTS IN GEARS:
Low gear. . . . . 1 in 3,0
2nd gear . . . . 1 in 4,3
3rd gear . . . . 1 in 7,2
Top gear . . . . 1 in 11,6
(Tabulated from Tapley (x gravity) readings, car carrying test crew of two and standard test equipment).
GEARED SPEEDS: (km/h)
Low gear 29,1
2nd gear 53,4
3rd gear 87,3
Top gear 123,8
(Calculated at engine peak r/min — 4 200.)

NOISE VALUES

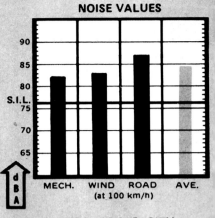

dBA — MECH. WIND ROAD AVE. (at 100 km/h)

LUGGAGE CAPACITY
(dm³)

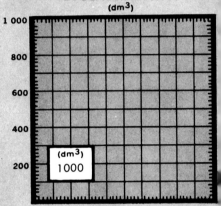

(dm³)
1000

FUEL RANGE
(km)

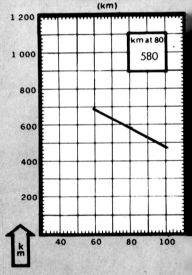

km at 80
580

FUEL CONSUMPTION
(litres/100 km)

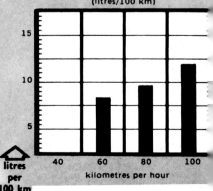

litres per 100 km vs kilometres per hour

SPECIFICATIONS

ENGINE:

Cylinders . . 4, horizontally opposed, rear-mounted
Carburettors . . . . twin Solex
Bore . . . . 94 mm
Stroke . . . . 71 mm
Cubic capacity. . . . . . 1 970 cm^3
Compression ratio. . . . . . 7,3 to 1
Valve gear . . . . ohv, pushrods
Main bearings . . . . four
Aircleaner . . . . . . paper element
Fuel requirement . . 93-octane Coast
87-octane Reef
Cooling. . . . . . air, blower-driven
Electrics . . . . 12-volt AC

ENGINE OUTPUT:

Max power SAE (kW) .58 (78 b-h-p)
Max power net (kW) . . 49 (51 DIN)
Peak r/min 4 200
Max torque (N.m) at r/min . .143 at
2 800

TRANSMISSION:

Forward speeds . . . . four
Synchromesh . . . . all
Gearshift. . . . . floor
Low gear . . . . 3,78 to 1
2nd gear . . . . 2,06 to 1
3rd gear . . . . 1,26 to 1
Top gear . . . . 0,88 to 1
Reverse gear . . . . 3,78 to 1
Final drive . . . . 4,57 to 1
Drive wheels . . . . rear

WHEELS AND TYRES:

Road wheels . . .14 inch pressed steel
discs
Rim width . . . . .5,5 J
Tyre size . . . . . 185 SR 14 radials
Tyre pressures (front) 200 to 220 kPa
Tyre pressures (rear) .210 to 250 kPa

BRAKES:

Front. . . . . .discs
Rear . . . . drums
Pressure regulation . . . . nil
Boosting . . . . .vacuum servo
Handbrake position . fascia pullhandle

STEERING:

Type .Ross worm and roller, damped
Lock to lock. . . . . 2,8 turns
Turning circle . . . 10 metres approx.

MEASUREMENTS:

Length overall . . . . 4,545 m
Width overall . . . . 1,670 m
Height overall . . . . 1,955 m
Wheelbase . . . . .2,400 m
Front track . . . . .1,395 m
Rear track . . . . .1,455 m
Ground clearance . . . . . .0,200 m
Licensing mass. . . . . . . 1 290 kg

SUSPENSION:

Front. . . . . independent
Type . . . . torsion bar and stabiliser
Rear . . . . independent
Type . . . . torsion bar, dual-jointed
half-axles

CAPACITIES:

Seating. 8-10
Fuel tank. . . . . .56 litres
Luggage space . . . .1 000 m^3 gross
Utility space . . . . .5 000 m^3 gross

WARRANTY:

Twelve months, no distance restriction.

TEST CAR FROM:

Volkswagen of South Africa, Uitenhage.

TEST CONDITIONS:

Altitude . . . . At sea level
Weather . . . . . fine and hot, windy
Fuel used. . . . . .93 octane
Test car's odometer . . . . . 4 733 km

greatly enhanced in the new model, and gradient ability shows a marked improvement, as well.

Rather surprisingly, the 2000 showed no gain in maximum speed — probably because the bigger engine is less free-revving and achieves only what it is geared for.

ECONOMY AND BRAKING

The specifications show a drop in fuel tank capacity from 60 on the 1800 to 56 litres on the 2000 model, but the bigger-engined model is lighter on fuel right through the usable range at steady road speeds, such as in cruising.

Its 10,6 litres/100 km (26,6 m-p-g) at 90 km/h is pretty fair for a 10-seater, and promises a cruising range of up to 500 km with a bit of care.

Like all the premium Kombi models, the Microbus Executive is shod with big radials on wide rims, and has quite exceptional stopping power. It pitches sharply in a hard stop, but there is no wheel locking and the g-force is quite spectacular as the big vehicle comes to a quick and clean stop. Full marks for this important safety feature!

NOISE AND HANDLING

There is a small drop in interior noise levels under the influence of the carpeting on the vast floor, though a big-bodied vehicle of this kind could hardly be really quiet-riding. At present-day cruising speeds, engine noise is not offensive, but road noise tends to be high in spite of the cushioning effect of the radials.

The modern-day Kombi models handle well, particularly when they are radial-shod as this one is. The steering is responsive and accurate, the Microbus is surprisingly stable at speed — though prone to wind buffeting. its big wheels and torsion-bar suspension give a most comfortable ride, and the vehicle is fully capable of a one-ton load in people or goods.

SUMMARY

Considering the growth in engine capacity and improvement in gearing, the actual point-to-point performance of the Microbus 2000 may be disappointing to some people. But it scores in ordinary road performance (such as in overtaking, or on hills) and has increased towing ability for caravan or trailer.

At the launch of the 2000 models at the end of 1975, a VW spokesman pointed out that the monthly sales figure for the full Type 2 range regularly exceeded 1000 units — placing it above some of the top-selling car models in South Africa.

The Kombi well deserves that distinction: it is a very honest vehicle, tremendously versatile, and holds a very special place in the family-car field in the Republic. ∎

Heating and ventilation is carried to rear passengers through a channel in each door that connects to a tube behind the front seats

A step automatically emerges from underneath the body as the side door is opened. The end of the foremost rear seat tilts forward to ease access to the back.

The tailgate lifts high to reveal a carpeted luggage area aft of the rearmost seat. The spare wheel is set into a well and is covered.

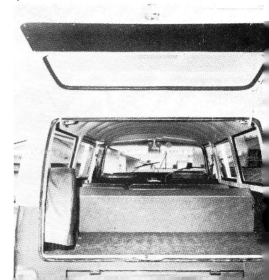

PV4 TEST

HO,HO,HA, ha, hee, hee, heh, heh, heh! Pwhew! Ho, ha, hee, heh! Those are the recorded comments of the loafers at the corner service station when, in 1949, they cast their mirth-teared eyes on the first Volkswagen van (bus, Kombi, Campermobile) to arrive on U. S. shores. It didn't look like a Ford, a Chevy, a Kaiser or a Fraiser. It resembled a rural route mailbox on wheels, and made an exhaust sound much like that of an ailing Model T. The laughter has tapered off a good deal in the intervening 27 years.

The VW van's 27 years on these shores reflect steady engineering development, continued refinement and growth to meet the changing needs of the family/recreation van market. That 1949 VW bus was powered by a flat opposed Four of 69.02-cu-in. (1131-cc) piston displacement and delivered 30 gross horsepower—about what four husky squirrels on a treadmill could produce. In those days, when VW buses went up hill, they did it very slowly.

Through the years, the flat 4-banger was tweaked, prodded and enlarged to produce 36, then 40, then 50, then 53, then 57, then 60 gross horsepower from 96.66 cu in. (1584 cc). In 1971-72, the last years that VW issued gross

horsepower ratings, the bus was powered by a 74-bhp dual-carburetored, 102.5-cu-in. (1679-cc) engine. In 1973, VW started to rate engines in net (not gross) horsepower, so the Four of that year was down 11 bhp to 63 bhp, net, from 102.50 cu in.

In 1974, things were upped slightly to 65 bhp, net, from 109.5 cu in. (1795 cc). A year later, in '75, the 109.5-cu-in. engine was fitted with an electronic fuel injection system, raising its peak power output to 67 bhp, net.

The current, that is 1976, "Type 2" model Volkswagen van/bus/Kombi/ Campermobile series, was given the electronic fuel injected "pancake" engine, a direct relative of the slick Porsche 914's prime mover. This engine produces 67 bhp, net, also, at 4200 rpm, and achieves its peak torque of 101 lb-ft at 3000 rpm. Essentially the effect is identical horsepower production, as compared with the 1975 engine, but at lower rpm, which results in reduced engine wear.

The Volkswagen obtained for this test report is known in the U. S. as the

The mailbox on wheels gets fuel injection, and very little laughter nowadays...

VW Station Wagon, with three long windows per side, curved windshield, and rear door window—glass all-around. Typically flawless VW paint was "Reef Blue" below the window-high beltline and "Pastel White" on top and around window moldings. Bumpers, front and rear also were painted white, not chromed. Interior upholstery for front driver and passenger buckets, the two-passenger mid-bench and the three-passenger rear bench, and door and side panel covering, was in "Alabaster" textured vinyl "Leatherette," and was smooth and taut, and obviously displayed craftsmanship in assembly. Flooring was covered in black neoprene matting.

Instrumentation was in two dials, one a speedometer, calibrated in both mph and kph, with recording odometer, and the other a fuel gauge with a semicircular warning light cluster for oil pressure, alternator, exhaust gas recirculation, catalytic converter temperature, turn flasher and headlamp high beam.

The steering wheel, mounted in the "cabover Kenworth" position, was of large diameter and close to the driver's stomach. The manual shift lever for the automatic transmission, marked front-to-rear "P, R, N. D, 2, 1," appeared stout enough for changing gears in a 7-speed Spicer truck box, or, detached, for a stone axe sort of offensive weapon against intruders.

As with all VW buses, past and pre-

VOLKSWAGEN VAN

VOLKSWAGEN VAN

sent, the '76 features independent suspension all-around. At the front of the unitized body/chassis are transverse torsion bars, trailing arms, a stabilizer bar and telescopic shock absorbers. At the rear are a pair of torsion bars, also transversally mounted, with trailing arms, diagonal locating links and telescopic shocks.

The test VW van was fitted with a set of made-in-Germany Continental Radial 185R x 14C tubeless tires, in Load Range C, and constructed with six rayon tread plies and two rayon sidewall plies, mounted on 14 x 5.5J wheels.

Suspension and tires together gave the VW a 4961-lb Gross Vehicle Weight Rating (GVWR). Gross Axle Weight

shaft maintain the engine's operating temperature.

The heart of the nifty "pancake" engine is its AFC (Air Flow Controlled) Fuel Injection system. Using electronic circuitry, the AFC injection system minimizes variations in fuel charge volume caused by engine rpm-related load changes, variations in fuel charge volume that result from wear, deposits and improper valve settings, and variations in exhaust backpressure that are created by emission control devices, such as the catalytic converter that was installed on the test VW van.

In the AFC system, the volume of fuel injected just ahead of the intake valve, into the incoming air charge, depends on the volume of intake air and specific engine rpm. The injection pulse is triggered by every other opening of igni-

tion contact breaker points. Warm-up, which requires fuel enrichment, is controlled by an intake air volume sensor, and two temperature sensors, one for intake air, the other for the cylinder head. The intake air sensor also controls fuel requirements for acceleration. Fuel enrichment for full load is accommodated by circuitry in the intake air throttle valve. Essentially, the higher the engine's rpm, the more air is drawn into the engine, and greater amounts of fuel are injected into the cylinders.

When the points trigger the fuel system, all four fuel injectors are triggered at the same time. Thus two cylinders receive fuel, while the other two cylinders, in a sense, store the fuel in the intake manifold until their intake cycle begins, and their intake valves open to admit the now mixed fuel/air charge.

ratings (GAWRs) for the vehicle, front and rear, were 2227 lb and 2800 lb, respectively. Maximum load rating of the Continental Radials was 1675 lb at 5 psi, cold inflation pressure.

The '76 VW bus/van series carries disc brakes at the front, drum brakes at the rear, actuated by a pressure-regulated dual hydraulic system.

Most of the refinement, the majority of development, chief evidence of the engineering talent in Wolfsburg, appears in that new 120.2-cu.-in. engine. The powerplant receives the appelation "pancake" because, though past VW engines have been "flat," so to speak, shrouds, carburetors, induction manifolds and electrical hardware have been pyramided on top of the various engines' crankcases. The 120.2 powerplant is really clean on top and flat—flat as, well, a "pancake."

The horizontally opposed 4-cylinder unit features a magnesium alloy block/crankcase, finned cast iron cylinders, and aluminum alloy cylinder heads. Two overhead valves per cylinder are pushrod and rocker arm actuated through a camshaft in-line with and above the crankshaft. An oil cooler and small blower at the rear of the crank-

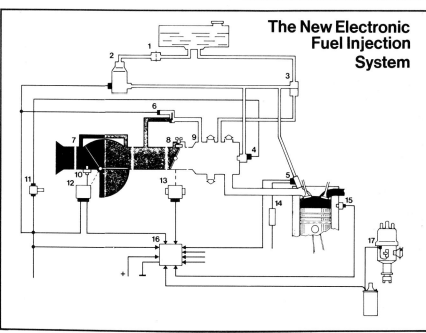

The New Electronic Fuel Injection System

1—FUEL FILTER, 2—FUEL PUMP, 3—PRESSURE REGULATOR, 4—COLD START VALVE, 5—INJECTOR, 6—AUXILIARY AIR REGULATOR, 7—INTAKE AIR SENSOR, 8—THROTTLE VALVE HOUSING, 9—INTAKE AIR DISTRIBUTOR, 10—TEMPERATURE SENSOR I, 11—THERMO-TIME SWITCH, 12—POTENTIOMETER WITH FUEL PUMP SWITCH, 13—THROTTLE VALVE SWITCH, 14—RESISTOR, 15—TEMPERATURE SENSOR II, 16—CONTROL UNIT, AND, 17—IGNITION CONTACT BREAKER POINTS.

1976 VOLKSWAGEN VAN

MPH at RPM, Calculated*

Third Gear Auto. Trans.***		Fourth Gear Manual Trans.	
MPH	RPM	MPH	RPM
70 —	3863	70 —	3810
60 —	3314	60 —	3259
50 —	2760**	50 —	2715**
40 —	2204	40 —	2175
30 —	1657	30 —	1630
20 —	1106	20 —	1087
10 —	552	10 —	543
0 —	0	0 —	0

* Calculated at 810.36 rear tire revolutions per mile at 44 psi full load inflation pressure, not considering torque converter slippage or aerodynamic drag.

** At 55 mph, the automatic's engine is turning 3050 rpm, and the manual's engine is turning 2984 rpm. These figures split the VW powerplant's torque peak rpm, which is 3000.

***See accompanying test data panel for actual speeds in gears.

The control unit for the AFC system is simply a mini computer that receives incoming signals with information on air volume, rpm and throttle position. From these bits of electronic intelligence, the computer calculates the proper injection time for the injectors. The computer accepts voltage signals from the intake air sensor and time intervals from the distributor points in order to calculate the amount of air and fuel required for each cylinder. Start-up, warm-up and full load enrichment requirements influence the duration (time) of the injection pulse.

Fuel pressure is regulated by a diaphragm that senses intake air negative pressure, and maintains the injection system's line pressure at approximately 35 psi. Manifold vacuum influences fuel pressure to the injectors, depending on engine load.

Troubleshooting the system is simply a matter of plugging into a VW computerized engine analyzer, assessing what's wrong and repairing or replacing the offending AFC Electronic Fuel Injection system component.

PICKUP, VAN & 4WD test driver assessment is that the AFC system is very effective—with the possible exception that the engine seems to run very lean during the warm-up period, and thus is balky and tends to die when loaded before minimum operating temperature is reached. In all other respects, the AFC delivered smooth acceleration through the gears and effortless cruise at 55 mph. Passing demands—floorboarded throttle—were instantly met with full-load fuel metering. Together with the fully-automatic 3-speed transmission's kick-down capability, this Volkswagen's passing ability surpassed that of all others in test drivers'

experience.

The automatic transmission was introduced in 1968 on 1600TL and Variant "Squareback" station wagons, replacing a semi-automatic 3-speed. This transmission features a hydrodynamic torque converter, which is coupled to a three-speed epicyclic (planetary) gear train. Similar in design to GM's Turbo Hydra-matic, gear changes are accomplished by bands that clamp-in gears. The bands are actuated by hydraulic valve circuitry sensitive to both engine speed and load.

The automatic transmission's internal ratios are: First, 2.55:1; second, 1.45:1; and third, 1.00:1; with final drive gearing of 4.09:1. As the accompanying table shows, the VW van hits 52.4 mph at the horsepower peak of 4200 rpm in second gear, and 54.4 mph at the torque peak of 3000 rpm in third (top) gear. The second/third-horsepower/torque combination is absolutely perfect in context of the 55-mph national speed limit. What this means is that the VW van, which previously was forced to creep up hills, automatically changes down, under load, exchanging the torque peak for the horsepower peak, with no reduction in road speed.

(The 4-speed manual transmission that's available in VW bus/van vehicles has internal ratios as follows: First, 3.78:1; second, 2.06:1; third, 1.26:1; and fourth, 0.88:1 overdrive; with final drive gearing of 4.57:1. The manual transmission van achieves 54.2 mph in third gear at the horsepower peak of 4200 rpm, and 55.3 mph in fourth (top) gear at the torque peak of 3000 rpm. This means that the manual transmission makes the van just a shade faster than the automatic unit in the top two

gears. The lower (first and second) manual ratios mean that the stick-shifting VW van is a better slow-speed creeper/crawler than the automatic. But the third/fourth-horsepower/torque equation works equally as well for the freeway running, long grade climbing manual transmissioned van, as the second/third split does for the VW bus with the 3-speed automatic.)

With regard to transmission, test drivers agreed that the automatic proved smooth and positive, and effective in 'round-town and freeway driving, but were unanimously regretful that no opportunity presented itself to evaluate, first-hand, the 4-speed manual, and compare it with the 3-speed automatic.

In operation, the automatic's shift points were directly linked to torque/horsepower production of the engine. For example, in attacking a hill in third gear, from a level run, at 56 mph, at just over 3000 engine rpm, when rpm and road speed dropped to approximately 52 mph, the automatic "kicked-down" to maintain road speed, while permitting the engine to achieve horsepower maximum rpm.

Initial driving impressions, that is out on the freeway, were that, first, the VW van is a whole lot quicker than before, but that the boxy body and independent torsion bar suspension remains, as ever, susceptible to gusts, wind wander and a good deal of body roll in cornering. In overtaking an 18-wheel tandem rig, for example, the VW van tended to duck into the big truck's slipstream, stay there, held by aerodynamic pressure, then slingshot away as the passing move was completed. At first, the feeling of that dip to the right and the squirt out to the left were spooky, but as

1976 VOLKSWAGEN VAN

Speeds in Gears,
3000-RPM Torque Peak
And 4200-RPM Horsepower
Peak, Calculated*
Final Drive Ratios:
Automatic 4.09:1   Manual 4.57:1

Trans. Automatic	Ratio	MPH at 3000 RPM	MPH at 4200 RPM	Trans. Manual	Ratio	MPH at 3000 RPM	MPH at 4200 RPM
1	2.55	21.3	29.6	1	3.78	12.9	18.0
2	1.45	37.4	52.4	2	2.06	23.6	33.8
3	1.00	54.4***	76.2	3	1.26	38.7	54.2
				4	0.88**	55.3	77.5
Reverse	2.41	22.7	31.6	Reverse	3.28	14.8	21.2

* Calculated at 810.36 rear tire revolutions per mile at 44 psi full load inflation pressure, no considering torque converter slippage or aerodynamic drag.

** The 0.88:1 transaxle fourth gear and 4.57:1 final drive ratio together create an effectiv 4.02:1 final drive ratio with the manual transmission, somewhat taller than the automati transmission's 4.09:1 final drive ratio.

***See accompanying test data panel for actual speeds in gears.

VOLKSWAGEN VAN

drivers gained experience with the vehicle, the wanders were anticipated and recognized when encountered, simply put down as a peculiar quirk of the vehicle, and nothing to get nervous about.

Initially, the vehicle seemed to exhibit an excessive body lean in the turns. Tire pressure was checked and found to be 30 psi all-around. That 30 psi is the recommended full load pressure for the 185R x 14C tires at the front, but is 14 psi shy of full-load tire pressure at the rear. So, the rear tires were pumped to 44 psi, and some of that body lean disappeared, handling improved greatly, and the ride firmed up a pleasant bit. The rear-engined VW van is very tire pressure sensitive.

Cruising on pavement, at 55 mph, that 3000 happy rpm torque peak could be felt and heard throughout the vehicle. After a time, the engine buzz at cruise became oppressive. Some additional sound proofing is called for here.

Off pavement, the '76 VW wagon was pure delight. Early winter storms had eroded back country trails, leaving tracks cross-cut, boulder strewn and rutted. Moreover, deer hunters' 4wd pickups, Jeeps and Toyota Land Cruisers had chewed the wet tracks, in places, to tacky muck. A Hi-Lift Jack and Snatch-'Em tow straps had been stowed in the VW—just in case. However, in no way did the Volks give any indication that it would become stuck. And in no way did the VW go thundering through. Rather, with the automatic transmission in first gear, the VW tid-

Injected VW engine, right, develops 67 bhp. Interior, below, shows typical VW finish. Below right, van displays seats for seven or cargo capability.

dled and trundled easily down, up, over and through the assorted rough stuff. The vehicle's weight was in the right place, smack over its drive wheels, to produce the best tractive effort. Through use of a very tender accelerator foot, wheelspin was held to a minimum, and the Continental Radials provided sufficient bite to negotiate the tough, loose and wet terrain. Jack and straps weren't necessary

Test drivers agreed that the lower first gear of the manual transmission would have proved a better crawler, but the automatic's low range was adequate. Only the automatic's lack of downhill compression braking was of disadvantage in the off-pavement environment. The 4-speed's first gear and engine compression would have served better

in letting the VW van down steep, rough inclines.

In terms of fuel mileage, the Volks was the best mpg producer of three similar vehicles tested by this publication—though its engine was the largest in piston displacement. Though electronic fuel metering equipment was not used, close pump/mileage readings showed the '76 model delivered 17.56 mpg in normal city driving, 17.34 mpg in the off-road and paved mountain road environment, and 20.74 mpg in 55 mph freeway driving.

On the dragstrip, the VW van proved itself a better accelerator, but less effective in terms of braking than either of the two Volkswagen bus-type vehicles tested previously by PICKUP, VAN & 4WD. The following table shows how the

MODEL YEAR	PISTON DISPLACEMENT CUBIC INCHES	TRANSMISSION	STANDING START ¼-MILE E.T at MPH	0-60 MPH, SEC.	PANIC STOP FT.	PERCENT BRAKE FADE SIX ½-g STOPS
1973	102.5 cu in.	Automatic	23.6 at 58.0	26.8	123.5	nil.
1974	109.5 cu in.	Manual	21.7 at 61.5	20.0	151.0	15%
1976	120.2 cu in.	Automatic	21.6 at 62.0	19.9	172.0	10%

PRICES

Basic list, West Coast POE
VW Kombi $5145
VW 7-pass. Station Wagon $5495
VW 9-pass. Station Wagon $5545

Standard Equipment .... 120.2-cu.-in. horizontally opposed Four engine, 4-spd manual transmission, adjustable driver's seat and backrest, 2-spd electric wiper/washers, electric rear window defogger, heater/defroster, power front disc brakes, 185SR x 14C tires

GENERAL

Curb weight, lb (test model)	2950
Weight distribution, %, front/rear	40/60
GVWR (test model)	4961
Optional GVWRs	none
Wheelbase, in.	94.5
Track, front/rear	54.9/57.3
Overall length	179.0
Overall height	77.0
Overall width	69.3
Over ang, front/rear	46.5/38.0
Approach angle, degrees	24
Departure angle, degrees	25

Ground clearances (test model):

Front axle	11.0*
Rear axle	9.0*
Oil pan	9.5
Fuel tank	19.3
Exhaust system (lowest point)	10.2

*Clearance is 7.8 in. at front steering knuckle and 6.1 in. at rear shock mount

Fuel tank capacity (U.S. gal.)	15.8
Auxiliary	none

ACCOMMODATION

Standard seats	front bucket seats
Optional seats	2 passenger center bench seat, 3 passenger rear bench seat
Headroom, in.	36.4
Accelerator pedal to seatback, max	46.7
Steering wheel to seatback, max	16.8
Seat to ground	39.5
Floor to ground	21.7

Unobstructed load space (length x width x height)

With seats in place	35.7 x 46.8 x 34.1
Rear folded or removed	74 x 60.8 x 55.4
Tailgate (width x height)	48.4 x 28.3

INSTRUMENTATION

Instruments	speedometer, odometer, fuel gauge
Warning lights	oil pressure, alternator, exhaust gas recirculation (EGR), catalytic converter overtemp, hazard warning
Optional	none

ENGINES

Standard	120.2 cu.-in. horizontally opposed Four
Bore x stroke	3.70 x 2.80
Compression ratio	7.3:1
Net horsepower @ rpm	67 @ 4200
Net torque @ rpm, lb-ft	101 @ 3000
Type fuel required	leaded or unleaded*

*For catalytic converter equipped vehicles, unleaded fuel is required

Optional	none

DRIVETRAIN

Standard transmission	4-spd manual
Clutch dia., in.	8.0
Transmission ratios: 4th	0.88:1
3rd	1.26:1
2nd	2.06:1
1st	3.78:1
Synchromesh	all forward gears
Optional: 3-spd automatic	$295
Transmission ratios: 3rd	1.00:1
2nd	1.45:1
1st	2.55:1

Rear axle type	spiral bevel gears and two double-jointed rear axles
Final drive ratios	4.57:1, (4-speed); 4.09:1 (automatic)

CHASSIS & BODY

Body/frame	unitized body, frame plates reinforced with side and cross members
Brakes (std)	front, 11.2-in. dia. disc; rear, 10.1 x 1.6-in. drum
Brake swept area, sq in.	252
Swept area/ton (max load)	101
Power brakes	std
Steering type (std)	worm and roller
Steering ratio	14.7:1
Power steering	none
Turning circle, ft	37.1
Wheel size (std)	14 x 5.5J
Optional wheel sizes	none
Tire size (std)	185SR x 14C
Optional tires sizes	none

SUSPENSION

Front suspension	independent with trailing arms, transverse torsion bars and tube shocks
Front axle capacity, lb	2227
Optional	none
Rear suspension	independent with trailing arms, diagonal links, transverse torsion bars and tube shocks
Rear axle capacity, lb	2867
Optional	none
Additional suspension options	none

TEST MODEL

VW 9-passenger Station Wagon, automatic transmission, AM radio

West Coast list price	$5900

ACCELERATION

Time to speed, sec:

0-30 mph	5.7
0-45 mph	11.1
0-60 mph	19.9
0-70 mph	31.5
Standing start, ¼-mile, sec.	21.6
Speed at end, mph	62

SPEED IN GEARS

High range, 3rd (4000 rpm)	67
2nd (4000 rpm)	46
1st (4000 rpm)	26
Engine rpm @ 55 mph	3300

BRAKE TESTS

Pedal pressure required for ½-g deceleration rate from 60 mph, lb	40
Stopping distance from 60 mph, ft	172
Fade: Percent increase in pedal pressure for 6 stops from 60 mph	10
Overall brake rating	excellent

INTERIOR NOISE

Idle in neutral, dbA	59.0
Maximum during acceleration	86.0
At steady 60 mph cruising speed	82.0

OFF PAVEMENT

Hillclimbing ability	good
Maneuverability	very good
Turnaround capability	very good
Driver visibility	excellent
Handling	very good
Ride	very good

ON PAVEMENT

Handling	very good
Ride	excellent
Driver comfort	very good
Engine response	very good

FUEL CONSUMPTION

City/freeway driving, mpg	20.7
Off pavement	17.3
Range, city/freeway driving, miles	327
Range, off pavement	273

1976 model fared against its 1973 and 1974 model counterparts.

As a footnote to the above braking information, the 1976 VW bus accomplished the all-on panic stop from 60 mph in a straight line, with no protests, no heart-stoppers in changes of direction, and with no hoisting of the engine-heavy rear end. The VW van's brakes, with the soft, flexible Continental radial treads, gave brake testers a warm sense of security.

Mechanically, the VW was an interesting experience. Peoplewise, the vehicle displayed a few negative quirks. The VW van's shoulder/lap restraint belt system, when latched into place, is comfortable and lends feelings of great security. However, adjustment and attachment of the single point belt system are so difficult and time-consuming that use of the belts is discouraged. This publication's tallest test driver, at 6 ft, 4 in., found the VW offered adequate space for shoulders, legs and head, with one exception. In the move to place his right foot on the brake pedal, his right knee would sometimes actuate the operating lever for windshield wipers and washers, located on the right side of the steering column. This lever could be actuated, too, by attempting to insert the ignition key into the column-mounted lock. The alternate key insertion was over the steering wheel center crossmember. Both ways proved awkward. Test drivers agreed that, typically with rear-engined VW vans, the liftover height for the rear cargo compartment was a bit tall for items of any great weight; and the main center cargo bay is neither long enough to sleep in, nor adequate for large cargo, such as motorcycles, for example.

To sum up, the automatic transmissioned VW van, at some $6100, taxes, freight and license included price, may be a bit more expensive than some domestic van products. What it offers is either passenger or cargo (not motorcycles, though) capability, reasonable economy, great all-around visibility definitely improved horsepower and performance, an acceptable degree of off-road performance (with the manual 4-speed gearbox preferred), a very comfortable ride and precise handling

The Volkswagen van has grown up along with surfers, the war protester flower children of the 1960s, and the vanthusiasm of the 1970s. This vehicle for many families, for numerous roamers of the outback, has become the favored friend of the road.

Remember those service station hangers-on of 1949? Well, none of them are laughing now—and a lot of them are driving 1976 Volkswagen Station Wagons without so much as a snicker. In 2 years of development and refinement Volkswagen has had the last laugh.

VW KOMBI 2000 AMBULANCE

A new VW Ambulance, developed locally by Volkswagen of South Africa, entered the South African market last month.

The vehicle is based on the 2-litre VW Microbus — the most powerful model in the Kombi/Microbus range — and its main features are:

A large ambulance compartment, separated from the driver's cabin by a partition panel, with two stretcher beds, arranged side by side on guide rails and kept in position by a locking mechanism designed for fast and easy operation.

● Cupboards with drawers for the storage of medical equipment. The storage areas are easily accessible, yet do not impede access to the patients.

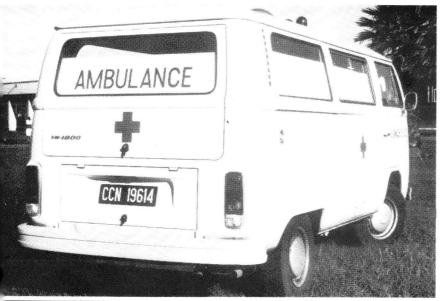

● The ambulance section incorporates a full-width bench seat, right behind the cabin, with seat belts, for patients who do not have to lie down.

● A fluorescent light, hooks for transfusion bottles, and an electric ventilator are built into the roof.

● The panel behind the cabin incorporates a sliding window made of frosted glass. The ambulance section is fitted with two large sliding windows. All windows in the rear section are partially frosted for privacy.

● Like all 2-litre VW buses, the Ambulance is equipped with a large sliding side door which facilitates entrance to the vehicle, specially when it is parked in a confined area.

● When the side door is opened, a step designed for ease of entrance automatically slides into position from underneath the vehicle.

● White formica side panels and worktop surfaces, which are both easy to clean and disinfect, are used. An equally practical floor covering material is used.

● The driver's cabin contains a bench-type seat, and apart from the internal rearview mirror, the vehicle is fitted with two external mirrors.

The VW Ambulance can be fitted with a number of optional items, including a roof mounted, emergency flasher light, a roof-mounted spot light and a three-tone horn. ●

VW's new Ambulance. The windows are partly frosted. There is a rear door and a large sliding door on the left hand side.

VW KOMBI 1600 FOR 1977

A better-equipped and more attractive VW 1600 Kombi was launched on February 9 by Volkswagen of South Africa.

The new model is the 1977 version of Volkswagen's lowest-priced bus model. Last year Volkswagen substantially uprated the vehicle by redesigning the front end to incorporate the cab and one-piece windscreen typical of the German-based Microbus, together with changes to the rear suspension which improved ride and roadholding.

For 1977 the 1600 Kombi has undergone further changes, primarily aimed at creating a more comfortable and attractive vehicle, without sacrificing its relatively low price.

The 1977 Kombi is said to operate more quietly than its predecessor thanks to improved sound insulation materials used in the engine compartment. In addition, thick underfelting and ribbed rubber mats in the luggage compartment and on the floor of the vehicle contribute to better sound deadening.

The interior finish has been redesigned. Seats, doors and side trim panels are upholstered in cognac vinyl, while the spare wheel — mounted behind the front seat — is covered with thick foam padding and vinyl trim matching the interior of the vehicle.

Externally, the new Kombi is distinguished from its predecessor by bright paint colours — including a cool, white upper half, similar to the 2-litre Buses. Bumpers are painted arctic white and hubcaps are finished in metallic silver. A further major improvement is the fitment of 185 SR 14 radial-ply tyres as standard equipment.

The panel van version of the 1600 Kombi has also been improved for 1977. To add to the comfort of the driver, the front seat has been separated from the load area by a partition panel that extends to the roof, thus greatly

eliminating engine noise. The panel contains a window for rearward vision.

The 1977 VW Kombi, Microbus and commercial vehicle range consists of:

VW 1600 Panel Van	R3 945
VW 1600 L Panel Van	R4 395
VW 1600 L Hi-roof Panel Van	R4 720
VW 2000 L Panel Van	R4 820
VW 1600 Kombi	R4 525
VW 1600 L Kombi	R5 130
VW 2000 L Microbus	R5 490
VW 2000 L Microbus a/t	R5 775
VW Executive Bus	R5 808
VW Executive Bus a/t	R6 120
VW 1600 Pickup	R3 845
VW 1600 Double-Cab Pickup	R4 645
VW 2000 L Ambulance	R8 215

The new Kombi 1600 has improved two-tone colour schemes, and better trim and sound-deadening.

DIESEL-POWERED MICROBUS

Initial cost is high, but over the long haul it pays handsomely

BY JIM NORRIS

Oops, there goes another insect-powered box. Wrong! This camper, be it known, has swallowed one large dose of Nissan vitamins, and now burps diesel exhaust. Impossible? No, very possible, under the capable direction of WILCAP's Tony Capanna.

WILCAP owner Capanna has al-ready dropped in several swaps of note, including other 4-cyl. Nissan diesels into various Datsun models, showcased by a turbocharged 6-cyl. example into a Z-car. Capanna will slip a diesel into your small car from a variety of choices, including a 908-cu.-in. monster V-8 that he will install in anything that you care to set before him.

The most popular conversion is a 4-cyl. diesel into a Pinto that will deliver an honest 85 mpg with a 2.79:1 rear end at a steady 55-mph.

These were undoubtedly strong reasons for Charles Mouille's Volkswagen camper, and the 4-cyl. Nissan Diesel that is now securely installed

in the VW's familiar rear-engine configuration. From all reports, it wasn't a bad swap at all. Mouille will know more, however, when he returns from a planned 50,000-mile trip, all around the Western Hemisphere, in his capacity as an electronics field engineer for Bendix.

Mouille, who lives in Jonesboro, Ark., came to Capanna's California firm, after spotting an earlier WILCAP swap in a PPC book—the story of the Nissan diesel into the Z-Car.

Figuring that a high-mileage/reliability diesel was just the ticket for an upcoming business/pleasure assignment to South America, Mouille brought his faithful camper to the

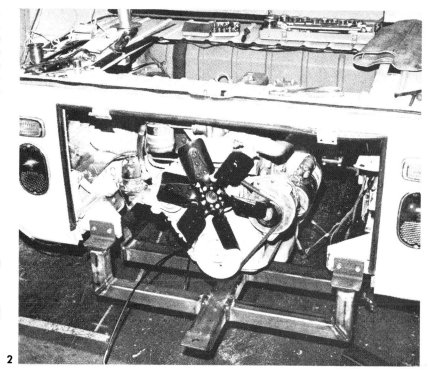

2

3

1. Charles Mouille, a Bendix field engineer from Jonesboro, Arkansas, will take a 50,000-mile trip through Mexico, Central and South America, a jaunt of more than a year-and-a half. His '69 VW Camper has a 4-cyl. Chrysler-Nissan Diesel, mounted in the familiar rear location. The cross-flow radiator utilizes a reversed 6-blade fan that blows air outward from the engine.

2. Tony Capanna's WILCAP of Torrance, California, supervised the engine swap,

and was selected by Mouille from an article in an earlier PPC publication (Complete Datsun Book). Into Mouille's van was cut a larger access. opening. Fan was stock Chrysler gasoline industrial. Alternator was 60-amp Motorola.

3. Engine mounts were extra strong, made of ⅜-in. plate, and using connections of 3 x 2-in.- .120 square wall steel tubing. VW frame members were boxed out to the end.

PHOTOS BY ERIC RICKMAN

good diesel doctor and gave him carte blanche to do whatever was needed. After all, Mouille would have faced Latin American gasoline prices that are anything but cheap, fluctuating nearly with the tides into niceities per gallon like a reported $2.50 in Argentina. That's the dollar equivalent, too. It's easily around a dollar a gallon in most South American Countries, as a minimum. The easiest place south of the border to obtain gas seems to be Mexico, but it can reach around 85¢ per gallon there.

Diesel fuel, on the other hand, because it is cheaper to refine, has become the staple fuel for trucks and rail transport, a big boon to hard-pressed developing countries, hence it is sold more widely than in the U.S. where there is general restriction to normal truck stop areas.

In Mexico, a recent trip there confirmed an absolute rock-bottom cost for the cheaper-to-refine diesel fuel. Since 3.785 liters equals 1 gal. and since diesel fuel recently cost 50 Mexican Centavos per liter, or 4 American Cents, the roughly 4 liter amount per gallon will come to between 15 and 16¢ per gallon!

In Mouille's case, the diesel engine's installation cost (including engine) was $3000, and he gets some 30 mpg—a figure that at 50,000 miles will consume around 1,666.6 gals. of fuel. A few spins of your calculator will show that the cost comparison of using diesel fuel will pay for the installation. Not a bad situation for a guy interested in long-term benefits.

Just how the conversion was made provides all VW camper owners with grist for their think mill. Capanna, of course, is an expert at this, as he has completed enough to know what one should do, what works and what doesn't; what the VW will stand and what it won't.

Capanna made the adaptor, Tom Carter and Mike Capanna were able and experienced assistants, especially son Mike, and Ross Reynolds installed the engine; the latter is a particularly good installation man.

The adaptor was huge, and especially beefy, with 356 T-6 cast aluminum, specially machined to clear the diesel's starter splines on the big flywheel. But the diesel flywheel was cut down a tad, and the VW's flywheel was machined to match. Of particular interest was the fact the VW's gutsy but sometimes overstressed flywheel gland nut was completely machined out. This is an excellent procedure on the single attaching point, when the VW's flywheel is suddenly saddled with oodles of extra torque. The new modification included 6 bolts, where once there had been just the single gland nut.

The flywheels were now a single unit, and Mouille used a heavy-duty 200mm pressure plate—the kind used in hot dune buggies and other competition VW activities.

The 4-cyl. Diesel was mounted via late-model Plymouth rubber pads. On the stock VW's there's the yoke with the rubber mount on the transaxle, and a standard metal-to-metal two mount set-up. The same setup was used with the diesel, that now added

4. Working with WILCAP, Ron Reynolds did the sano engine mounts, which used late model Plymouth rubber pads. The same configuration as the two-mount-plus transaxle stock setup was used, except that the diesel's CG was positioned over these center mounts in order to relieve the V-Dub's aluminum 4-bolt transaxle housing. WILCAP has had a lot of experience doing these things.

5. Top view of the 4-cyl. Chrysler-Nissan diesel, peeking out from under the larger access hole under the camper's floor. Note aluminum adaptor to the intake manifold so they could reposition stock VW air cleaner, used because it's a good unit.

4

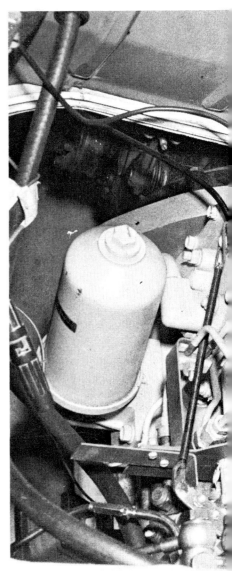

5.

about 300 lbs. more to the balancing points, except that Mouille wanted less weight over the transaxle, which is what they came up with. The two main bolts that attach the 3x2-in. .120-wall square wall steel tubing, has supported much heavier installations that a 4-cyl. diesel into a V-Dub, and is considered a nice and tidy way to go.

A trailer hitch is incorporated into the engine mounting framework, and Mouille added a pair of access doors at each side in order to reach the dual-battery setup that he uses to start the engine and power the camper accessories. A 60-amp. Motorola heavy-duty alternator was used to charge the batteries through a dual switching system.

The fuel tank was stock: 60 liters or 15.6 gals. There is also a large BX conduit used to route additional wiring and controls under the floor pan, while a Honda cycle cable is used to control the fuel shut-off valve.

As was mentioned, it was felt necessary to keep the bulk of the engine weight off the aluminum 4-bolt transaxle housing, with the mounts installed at approximately the engine's center of gravity point. An extra feature was the fact that Mouille had the VW frame members boxed on out to the end, and the new motor mounts were bolted to the frame, as opposed to the stock system of spot welding the mounts to the frame. That's why WILCAP was selected. Many VW owners come to grief when not understanding a few basics to bigger engine swaps.

Cooling was obviously a major hurdle, but Capanna again showed his experience. Working with Mouille, he came up with the workable system of a rear-mounted cross-flow radiator, set on its side atop the back end of the square steel tubing frame, which consisted of three hex stainless steel bars, one in the center, and one on each end. The radiator was bigger that normally used with the rugged 4-cyl. Nissan diesel, and now had a special four-row tube core. Biggest news was that the fan was mounted backwards, so as to push the air outwards from the engine, rather than sucking it through. The VW camper provides enough of a negative area under the engine, so free-flowing air is in plentiful supply. In order to do this, Mouille used a stock Chrysler gasoline industrial fan with six blades, reversed the blades, and doctored up the assembly. In operation,

his system has performed perfectly. There are several reasons for this.

One is the fact that there is plenty of air circulation around the exposed radiator, and under the engine from the point of a relatively high ground clearance. The other is in the engine operating characteristics:

The Nissan Diesel's C.A.V. injector assembly uses a spring operated governor on its injector pump which cuts maximum rpm to 3200, rather than the available 4000 rpm. The torque curve, which is amazingly flat anyway is extremely content at the heat-saving lower rpm figure. After all, the diesel is putting out some 94 lbs.-ft. at 2000 rpm, yet still pulls 80 lbs.-ft. at 4000 rpm, with its total diameter 27-in. wheels and V-Dub's standard 4.40:1 transaxle gears.

You've got to remember that a diesel's 22:1 compression is not aimed at the high rpm set anyway. It's a different concept. Also, the property of diesel fuel is such that it will vaporize at much, much higher temperatures than gasoline, which removes almost entirely the threat of vapor lock, but the point is that the lower you can keep your rpm the better everything will be, other things considered, especially.

While Mouille's '69 camper's stock flat-4 put out a breathless 78 lbs.-ft. of torque at 2600 rpm, and 53 gross horsepower at 4200 rpm, the 132-cu.-in. 4-cyl. diesel is much better in all categories, as can be understood.

Dyno tests show the Nissan powerplant to produce 61 hp @ 4000 rpm; 48 hp @ 3200 rpm, and 36 hp @ 2600 rpm, which are continuous

load and net figures by the way.

To be exact, with the governor's limit, it was reported that the engine will be turning 3286 rpm at 60 mph. On a recent postcard returned to WILCAP from Mouille in Arkansas, the diesel-powered camper averaged over 25 mpg all the way from California, and ran flawlessly. The camper was burdened with 5000 lbs. of gear, yet still racked up this impressive result. The only thing that might concern Mouille, as refected in the card he sent was the fact that the Michelin radials, as good as

they are, might need a bigger substitute. When you're planning a 50,000-miler, over the Pan-American Highway, through vast stretches of primitive, rock-strewn jumping-off places, you had better understand your burst pressure of what's under foot. Mouille is currently looking at several tire alternatives, all of which involve going to bigger wheel configurations. For the present, at least, everything still works fine.

Also, Mouille is looking around for an extra high camper top, something

6. Excellent view of the diesel connected to the VW's transaxle before installation. Mouille had the rugged transaxle carefully inspected. Note the huge aluminum 356 T-6 adaptor. Big C.A.V. can on engine's top right is a fuel filter, while critical injector assembly shows off its spidery plumbing in perfect detail. Bolt holes behind the crankshaft pulley are for mounts.

7. Good view of transaxle's interior U-joints. Mouille reports no signs of fatigue with sturdy unit. Also note the downward sweep of the exhaust pipes. Exhausting was put straight down and over to muffler connections with special attention not to disrupt critical airflow which is needed for cooling.

a little more solid that the dropped canvas setup. But again, that's strictly a personal preference—to bring a little more satisfaction to Mouille, his wife, and some 5000 lbs. of gear (total camper weight) as they slog through the South American boonies.

Mouille will install a gasoline heater for camping if a diesel burning heater can't be found. He will use hot water while underway.

He will torque up the rear torsion bars a tad, but to start things off on the right note, and has installed a set of Delco air shocks in order to adjust the camper's level.

The large access opening in the rear deck lid over the engine compartment has been enlarged for easy access, and has been covered with a sheetmetal cover that is secured with Dzus fasteners.

Mouille is using a stock VW air-cleaner, too, which is just one more example, that a VW is about as adaptable a machine is about as adaptable a machine has ever challenged the great back-road areas of the world. ♣

VW Microbus 2000 Automatic

Strong and easy-driving— but this Executive model with A/T is getting away from the old Kombi concept.

The well-loved Kombi holds a special place in family motoring in South Africa — though in its modern form it seems to be getting beyond the means of the ordinary salaried man: the price of the 1978 top model (the Executive Automatic) is nearing R9 000!

But while this aristocratic model has grown out of the ranks of popular transport, it is an attractive and comfortable 9/10-seater, with a relaxed driving style which comes from a high-torque 2-litre engine and automatic transmission.

Like the manual-shift Executive 2000 model tested in August, 1976 (soon after the original 2-litre models were announced), the Executive 2000 Automatic has wall-to-wall carpeting to give it a soft and habitable appearance, plus anti-glare tinted windows, rubber-cushioned bumpers, retracting side step and chrome trim.

IMPROVED PERFORMANCE

It is just over 5 years ago that VWSA made history by announcing a Microbus (in those days, a 1700) with automatic transmission. Then came an 1800 model, followed by the 2-litre, at short intervals, to provide more power and performance. The gain has been principally in acceleration and overtaking ability, as a short table (based on earlier tests of A/T models) shows:

	1700	1800	2000
0-80	16,7	13,9	13,7
60-80	7,4	6,2	6,0

There has also been a small gain in fuel economy with the 2000 model, owing to improved torque and gearing. But the 2-litre engine has not been an unqualified success: with its big pistons and long stroke, it feels more "lomp" than earlier motors, and maximum speed has actually dropped.

Although the 2000 Executive Automatic is a shade better than the 1800 Executive Automatic tested in June 1975, in fuel consumption at the upper end of the usable speed range, it still burns a lot of gas by family car standards: we registered 12,3 litres/100 km at 80, and 13,5 at 90 — in the region of 21-23 m-p-g.

In overall running over a distance of about 1000 km, we logged 14,0 litres/100 km (20,1 m-p-g), and found effective tank range to be between 350 and 400 km in urban use.

SUMMARY

Riding smoothly on big radials, this Microbus 2000 Executive Automatic showed up at its best as a town car for many passengers, and its ideal use would seem to be as a staff bus or lift-club vehicle. It is not as noisy as earlier Kombi models, and is easy-driving with its extra power and responsive transmission. ∎

SPECIFICATIONS

ENGINE:
Cylinders . . .4 horizontally opposed, rear mounted
Fuel supply . twin Solex carburettors
Bore/stroke . . . . 94 x 71 mm
Cubic capacity . . . . . . 1 970 cm³
Compression ratio. . . . . . 7,3 to 1
Valve gear . . . . . . .o-h-v, pushrods
Ignition. . . . . coil and distributor
Main bearings . . . . four
Fuel requirement . .93-octane Coast, 88-octane Reef
Cooling. . . . . . air, blower-driven

ENGINE OUTPUT:
Max power I.S.O. (kW) 51
Power peak (r/min) 4 200
Max permissible r/min 4 400
Max torque (N.m). 143
Torque peak (r/min) 2 800

TRANSMISSION:
Forward speeds . . . . . .three — VW Automatic
Selector . . . . .floor
Low gear . . . . 2,55 to 1
2nd gear . . . . 1,45 to 1
Top gear . . . . Direct
Reverse gear . . . . 2,46 to 1
Final drive . . . . 4,1 to 1
Drive wheels . . . . rear

CAPACITIES:
Seating 9-10
Fuel tank. . . . . .56 litres
Luggage trunk . . . . . 990 dm³ gross
Utility space . up to 5 000 dm³ gross

TEST CAR FROM:
Volkswagen of South Africa, Uitenhage.

ACCELERATION

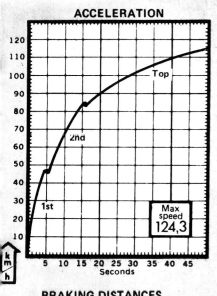

Max speed 124,3

BRAKING DISTANCES

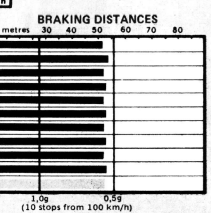

1,0g   0,5g
(10 stops from 100 km/h)

NOISE VALUES

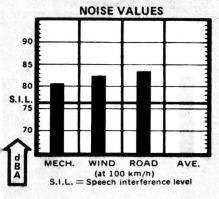

S.I.L. = Speech interference level

CALCULATED FUEL RANGE
(km)

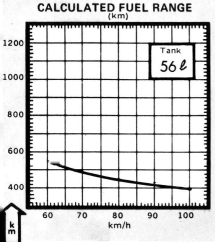

Tank 56 ℓ

test VW Microbus 2000 Executive Automatic

PERFORMANCE FACTORS:
Power/mass (W/kg) net 39,3
Frontal area (m²) 33,4
km/h per 1 000 r/min (top) . . 28,8

INTERIOR NOISE LEVELS:

	Mech	Wind	Road
Idling	55,0	—	—
60	72,5	—	—
80	76,5	79,0	80,0
100	80,5	83,0	84,0
Average dBA at 100			82,5

ACCELERATION (seconds):
0-60 8,2
0-80 13,7
0-100 28,8
1 km sprint 42,8

KEY FIGURES

Maximum speed . . . . .124,3 km/h
1 km sprint . . . . . . .42,8 seconds
Terminal speed . . . . .111,0 km/h
Fuel tank capacity . . . . .56 litres
Litres/100 km at 80 12,3
Optimum fuel range at 80 . 453 km
Engine revs per km 2 080
National list price R8 610

OVERTAKING ACCELERATION (A/T):
40-60 . . . . .3I9
60-80 6,0
80-100 14,1

MAXIMUM SPEED (km/h):
True speed 124,3
Speedometer reading 134
Calibration:

Indicated:	60	70	80	90	100
True speed:	58	67	76	85	94

FUEL CONSUMPTION (litres/100 km):
60 10,2
70 11,3
80 12,3
90 13,5
100 14,5

BRAKING TEST:
From 100 km/h.
First stop 4,1
Tenth stop 4,2
Average 4,16

GRADIENTS IN GEARS:
Low gear . . . . 1 in 3,4
2nd gear . . . . 1 in 6,5
Top gear . . . . 1 in 11,5

GEARED SPEEDS: (km/h)
Low gear 47,8
2nd gear 84,2
Top gear 122,0
(Calculated at engine peak r/min 4 200.)

ENGINE SPEED

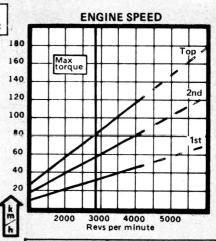

Max torque

IMPERIAL DATA

ACCELERATION (seconds):
0-60 26,6
MAXIMUM SPEED (m-p-h):
True speed 77,4
FUEL ECONOMY (m-p-g):
50 m-p-h 22,7
60 m-p-h 19,8

GRADIENT ABILITY

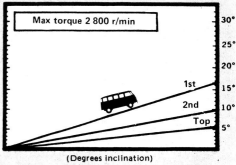

Max torque 2 800 r/min

(Degrees inclination)

CRUISING AT 90

Mech noise level . . . . 75,8 dBA
0-90 through gears . . 20 seconds approx
litres/100 km at 90 13,5
Calculated fuel range at 90 . . . 414 km
Braking from 90 . . . . 3,6 seconds
Maximum gradient (top) . . . 1 in 17,3
Speedometer error . . . . 6% over
Speedo at true 90 . . . . . . .95 km/h
Engine r/min at 90 . . . . 3 120

STEADY-SPEED FUEL CONSUMPTION
(litres/100 km at true speeds)

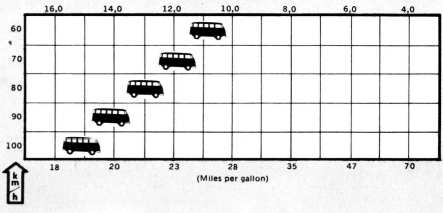

(Miles per gallon)

Volkswagen 2000 pick-up range

Volkswagen of South Africa's 1978 r pickups consists of two brand-new r single and double-cabin VW pickups equipped with VW's powerful 2-litre

Both vehicles are of German origin (w a Brazilian-sourced pick-up was pre used), which means that apart from t engine, there are also other major changes:

● The new pickups feature the all-inder torsion bar/hydraulic shock absorber sus made popular by the VW Bus range.

● A double-jointed rear axle with c velocity joints identical to that of the Bus range is used (whereas the previou up used a swing axle layout with u joints and reduction gears).

● A 56-litre fuel tank replaces the tank of the previous model.

Engine output of 51 kW/4200 r/mir is 40 per cent more than with the 16(motor used in the superseded range.

"With this high power output, and good torque figure of 143 N.m/2800 the new 2-litre pick-ups are in a class own, and ahead of any other 1-tonne spect of loadspace. The two-litre engine ecutive Bus suspension add an all-new sion to the pick-up range," a Volk spokesman said.

Reverting to German model styling, th pick-ups also have a two-litre engine an sophisticated suspension.

VW KOMBI AND TRANSPORTER

Volkswagen's 1979 range of buses and transporters consists of nine revised models; as follows:

1600 L Panel Van
2000 L Panel Van
1600 L Kombi
2000 L Microbus
2000 L Microbus automatic
1600 L Pick-up

2000 L Pick-up
2000 L Double Cab Pick-up
2000 L Ambulance

Among detailed modifications and improvements for the new model year, are:

● A folding bench rear seat on the 2-litre Bus. When folded forward, the seat forms a spacious double bed reaching from the rear door to the central bench seat.

● The floor and luggage compartment of th 2-litre Bus is lined with loop pile colour-keye carpeting.

● Three-point seat belts are fitted to a models in the range.

● The 2-litre automatic Bus is fitted wit tinted glass all round.

● An improved aircleaner is used on all mode in the range.

A folding rear bench seat — which makes a double bed — is a new feature on the 2-litre Microbus models.

View through the tailgate of the double bed facility in the 2-litre Microbu

The VW Bus Lives:
VOLKSWAGEN LANDMARK VAN
But the question is, is it past its prime?

V4 TEST

The Volkswagen van/bus has endured through the years almost as well as the legendary VW Beetle. Like the Beetle, the van has undergone many changes and is no doubt a much superior vehicle than it was when first introduced; however, the basic shape and design is very similar to the first one bought in from Germany in 1949.

The Volkswagen obtained for this test started life as a Kombi, a combination passenger vehicle/van with two bucket seats up front and an open cargo area in the rear. The Volks is also available as a Station Wagon with full passenger seating or as a Campmobile complete with a pop top and facilities for self-contained camping.

Volkswagen of America recently entered into an agreement with the National Coach Corporation of Carson, California to transform the Kombi into an Americanized van conversion similar to the customized domestic vans that have gained popularity all across the U.S. in recent years. Volkswagen plans to produce 300 of these units for the Southern California dealer network to test the marketplace and if the test proves successful, the conversion will be distributed nationally.

National Coach takes a rather spartan Kombi and transforms it into a luxuriously appointed touring vehicle. The interior decor group consists of four aircraft-style swivel bucket seats, convertible sofa, wet bar with icebox and storage cabinet, removable dining/game table, carpeting on all floor areas, wood-grained paneling and padded headlining, plus other decorator items. National has also given the exterior a going over with a stylish paint scheme and aluminum alloy turbo-type wheels.

Volkswagen believes the VW/Landmark van fills a need between the family-oriented VW Station Wagon and customized domestic vans. The thought behind this would be the fuel economy advantage of the VW vs. the appetites of full-sized American vans. Unfortunately, this advantage did not fully materialize in our test. More on this later.

The venerable VW is still powered by a horizontally opposed four-cylinder engine, although this engine is considerably different from the original 72.7-cid (1192 cc) powerplant, which was hard pressed to propel the van up hills of any degree of steepness. The offering for model year '78—'79 VW availability remained months away at press time—is an electronic fuel-injected engine rated at 67 net horsepower from 120.2 cubic inches. The 49-state engine can burn leaded or unleaded fuel, whereas the California version must use the unleaded variety only. The horsepower rating has not changed since 1975, so it seems as if VW has squeezed the ultimate out of the current engine without major modifications or a new design altogether.

The Landmark conversion weighed approximately 200 pounds more than the 1976 VW Station Wagon tested by PV4 in January '77. This extra weight may also account for the decrease in gas mileage and poorer performance of the '78. The '76 achieved 20.7 mpg in the city/freeway driving cycle, which isn't too shabby for a van with an automatic transmission; however, the '78 could manage only 15.9 mpg, a drop of almost five mpg. So the one advantage that a VW would normally have over a domestic van, fuel economy, is missing in the '78 model. Performance of the '78 was also considerably below that of the '76, with a zero-to-60 elapsed time of 23.4 seconds, compared to 19.9 sec-

onds for the '76. The engine was performing normally with no apparent problems, so the loss in performance is probably due to the additional weight with some loss also attributable to exhaust emission laws much stricter in '78 than they were in '76. Everyday driving of the VW/Landmark, however, shows acceptable performance; keeping pace with freeway traffic is no problem. Engine rpm at 55 mph is 3200, which is just above the peak torque rating. This translates to effortless cruise and reasonable passing ability.

The VW van is similar to most vans in that this type vehicle is more sensitive to side winds and passing 18-wheelers than a pickup or passenger car, except that the VW is even more sensitive than most. The rather soft, independent suspension, combined with the driver sitting on top of the front wheels, accentuates the feeling and falsely gives one the impression that the VW is squirrelly. Not so. A day behind the wheel and all concern is gone. Once the behavior is noted, the handling becomes predictable and twisty mountain roads are negotiated at legal speeds with ease.

Quality control on the base VW Kombi is excellent, as is the quality of the Landmark conversion. There is one glaring fault, however. For anyone over 5 feet, 8 inches in height, there is just not enough head room with the aftermarket seats and headliner. Test crewmen taller than 5 feet, 8 inches simply had to scrunch down in the seat or lean their heads to one side to prevent being wedged between the roof and seat bottom. So if you're taller than the average person, better check this accommodation out carefully before purchasing the VW/Landmark.

The Landmark Special Equipment package has as standard four pillow-back swivel bucket seats, a convertible sofa that makes into a full 78-inch dou-

The taller staffers were unable to drive the Landmark VW because of a paucity of head room (above). Otherwise (top right), the van's driver was treated to all the usual VW features. Back bench and intermediate bucket seats boosted the van's passenger capacity (near right). A cooler and sink are part of the Landmark package (far right).

LANDMARK

ble bed with full-length foam mattress, cut-loop nylon carpeting with one-inch foam pad, wood-paneled walls, padded vinyl headliner and door panels, wet bar with a top-fill icebox, stainless steel sink and beverage center, magazine rack, battery indicator, suede cloth curtains and drapes, high-intensity interior lighting, two rear speakers, spare tire carrier and cover, chrome roof rack and ladder, chrome front and rear bumpers, and Quest designer paint scheme. This special package carries a price tag of $2627. Other optional equipment is also offered.

The test VW was fitted with a 3-speed automatic transmission controlled by a tall T-handled shift lever in the center of the driver's compartment. The steering wheel is almost flat and combined with the uncommon driver's-seat-over-the-front-wheels position, the VW offers the driver a feeling of being at the control of a city bus. But the feeling ends right there. The VW is very nimble in urban traffic and requires only a light touch to maneuver in and out of tight parking spots.

Coupled to the optional automatic transmission is a 4.09:1 rear axle ratio. The standard 4-speed manual gearbox comes with a lower 4:57 gear. Fourth gear in the manual is an overdrive which brings the effective rear axle ratio close to that of the automatic.

The VW van has independent suspension at all four wheels, a feature which puts this vehicle right up there at the top as far as ride is concerned, especially when rough terrain of either the asphalt or dirt variety is encountered. This particular vehicle did have a suspension-related problem that was not common with previously tested VW vans. Perhaps due to the Landmark seats and interior trim plus the rear-mounted spare tire, the VW's weight was too heavily biased towards the rear, so much so that when at rest, the van's front suspension was almost fully extended, whereas the rear sagged several inches from level. What this rear weight bias does is cause the front suspension to top out when rebounding from hitting a dip in the road. If the dip is hit hard enough, the front wheels will completely leave the pavement. This is very unnerving the first time or two it happens, but what's even more unsettling is when the inside front wheel lifts during a hard turn at speed. A possible cure for this might be to mount the rear tire on the front of the vehicle instead of the rear. Even though the tire and wheel aren't all that heavy, transferring the tire and wheel from behind the rear axle to a position ahead of the front axle should result in a sizable weight transfer that should improve the weight bias. Of course, the tire at the front of the van will not look nearly as nice as it does at

the rear, but test crewmen feel strongl¦ that good handling takes precedenc¦ over cosmetics.

This rearward weight bias also cre¦ ated an unusual feeling during th¦ panic-stop-from-60-mph braking tes¦ Hitting the brakes caused the nose o¦ the van to dip considerably because o¦ the extended wheel travel afforded b¦ the suspension being at the top of it¦ travel. Other than the test driver bein¦ surprised at the amount of nose dive¦ the VW stopped in a creditable 168 fee¦ with no side sway, loss of directiona¦ control or wheel lockup. In fact, th¦ brakes were rated excellent in al¦ phases of the braking test and in nor¦ mal driving conditions.

From a base price of $6135 for th¦ VW Kombi, the VW/Landmark as teste¦ goes out the door at $9782, which in¦ cludes $124 freight but does not in¦ clude local taxes or vehicle license. S¦ a prospective buyer has to be serious t¦ consider this vehicle at a price of mor¦ than $10,000 ready to roll without¦ radio or air conditioning. The VW¦ Landmark is a good looking vehicle¦ handles well with the exception of th¦ weight bias, is comfortable to drive ex¦ cept for taller people, possesses rea¦ sonable performance, but is down o¦ fuel economy from past years. What a¦ this adds up to is an expensive vehicl¦ that has a few shortcomings, which ma¦ take the VW/Landmark out of the Goo¦ Buy category.

VOLKSWAGEN/LANDMARK
SPECIFICATIONS AND PERFORMANCE

PRICES

Basic list, Port of Entry
VW Kombi $6135

Standard Equipment 120.2-cid
horizontally opposed Four, 4-spd manual
transmission, adjustable driver's seat and
backrest, passenger bucket seat, 2-spd electric wiper/washers, electric rear window defogger, heater/defroster, power front disc
brakes, 185R x 14C tires

GENERAL

Curb weight, lb (test model) 3175
Weight distribution, %, front/rear 41/59
GVWR (test model) 4960
Optional GVWRs ....none

Wheelbase, in. 94.5
Track, front/rear 54.9/57.3
Overall length 179.0
Overall height 77.0
Overall width 69.3
Overhang, front/rear 46.5/38.0

Approach angle, degrees 26
Departure angle, degrees 24

Ground clearances (test model):
Front axle 11.1*
Rear axle 8.8*
Oil pan 9.4
Fuel tank 19.0
Exhaust system (lowest point) 10.4
*Clearance is 8.0 in. at front steering knuckle
and 6.0 in. at rear shock mount

Fuel tank capacity (U.S. gal.) 15.8
Auxiliary ....none

ACCOMMODATION

Standard seats ....front bucket seats
Optional seats 2-passenger
center bench seat, 3-passenger rear bench
seat
Headroom, in. 34.1
Accelerator pedal to seatback, max 44.9
Steering wheel to seatback, max 15.1
Seat to ground 41.3
Floor to ground 21.9

Unobstructed load space (length x
width x height)
With seats in place ......36 x 46.8 x 34.0
Rear folded or removed ......74 x 60.8 x 55.0
Tailgate (width x height) ....48.5 x 28.0

INSTRUMENTATION

Instruments ....speedometer, odometer, fuel
gauge
Warning lights ....oil pressure, alternator,
hazard warning, catalytic converter, over-
temp indicator
Optional ....none

ENGINES

Standard 120.2-cid horizontally opposed Four
Bore x stroke, in. ....3.70 x 2.80
Compression ratio 7.3:1
Net horsepower @ rpm ....67 @ 4200
Net torque @ rpm, lb-ft ....101 @ 3000
Type fuel required..........leaded or unleaded*
*Unleaded only in Calif.

Optional ....none

DRIVETRAIN

Standard transmission ....4-spd manual
Transmission ratios: 4th 0.88:1
3rd 1.26:1
2nd 2.06:1

1st 3.78:1
Synchromesh ....all forward gears

Optional ....3-spd automatic $295
Transmission ratios: 3rd 1.00:1
2nd..1.45:1
1st 2.55:1

Rear axle type ....spiral bevel gears
and two double-jointed rear axles
Final drive ratios ....4.09:1 (auto),
4.57:1 (4-spd)
Overdrive ....4th gear is overdrive with
manual transmission

CHASSIS & BODY

Body/frame....................unitized with
box-shaped side and crossmembers
Brakes (std)................front, 11.2-in. dia. disc;
rear, 10.1 x 1.6-in. drum
Brake swept area, sq in. 252
Swept area/ton (max load)..................101
Power brakes ....std

Steering type (std) ....worm and roller
Steering ratio 17.8:1
Power steering ....none
Turning circle, ft 37.1

Wheel size (std) ....14 x 5.5J
Optional wheel sizes ....none
Tire size (std) ....185R x 14C
Optional tire sizes ....none

SUSPENSION

Front suspension ....independent with
transverse torsion bars, trailing arms, sta-
bilizer bar and tube shocks
Front axle capacity, lb 2227
Optional ....none
Rear suspension ....independent with
transverse torsion bars, diagonal links and
tube shocks
Rear axle capacity, lb 2867
Optional....................................none

Additional suspension options ....none

TEST MODEL

VW Kombi, automatic transmission, sliding
passenger windows, sunroof, California emission certification, Landmark Special Equipment Package, aluminum alloy wheels
West Coast list price ....(includes $124
freight) $9782

ACCELERATION

Time to speed, sec:
0–30 mph 5.9
0–45 mph 12.7
0–60 mph 23.4
0–70 mph 38.8
Standing start, ¼-mile, sec. 23.4
Speed at end, mph 60

SPEED IN GEARS

High range, 3rd (4000 rpm) 70
2nd (5500 rpm) 60
1st (5500 rpm) 38
Engine rpm @ 55 mph 3200

BRAKE TESTS

Pedal pressure required for ½-g deceleration
rate from 60 mph, lb 38
Stopping distance from 60 mph, ft 168
Fade: Percent increase in pedal pressure for
6 stops from 60 mph 18
Overall brake rating ....excellent

INTERIOR NOISE

Idle in neutral, dbA 58.1
Maximum during acceleration 84.2
At steady 60 mph cruising speed 80.8

ON PAVEMENT

Handling ....very good
Ride ....excellent
Driver comfort ....fair/very good*
Engine response ....good
*Tall drivers had inadequate head room

FUEL CONSUMPTION

City/freeway driving, mpg 15.9
Range, city/freeway driving, miles............251

Trimmed of some 'fat cat' items, this improved family bus gets bac to an easier price category

Volkswagen 2000L Microbus

CAR test

South Africa's long-standing love affair with the VW Kombi should get new impetus this year: VW has trimmed some of the frills off the top-ranking 2000L Microbus models, and something like R1 000 off the price. They are no longer "Executive" — but they are back at the R7 000 to R7 500 level where the family motorist can just reach them.

In the past few years, the so-called "Executive" models had been gaining in luxury to the stage where they became "fat cats" costing more than R8 000. VWSA has countered on the 1979 models by cutting out some of the tinted glass and exterior chrome, taking away the retracting side step and a few fittings which will hardly be missed, and calling them "2000L" instead of "Executive".

PLAIN BUMPERS

The bumpers are painted now instead of chromed, and the rubber facings have been dropped (a pity, because these did serve a useful purpose). The full carpets are not quite as plushy as before — but the big-engined Kombi has suddenly become competitive again in the important family-bus market.

A bonus this year is that the rear seats fold flat with the engine cover to form a useful double bed inside the tailgate for camping — and this also makes a long and shallow utility space for loads or children, if necessary.

There are no major mechanical changes: the low-compression, twin-carb, 2-litre engine has been going strong for just over three years now. One improvement is a new high-capacity aircleaner on the new model, but power output, transmission and a fairly long-legged ride on big 185 radials are as for the earlier "Executive".

PERFORMANCE

The test car had all the zest of the 2-litre Kombi, but had to have workshop attention for jamming gearshift linkages before we could complete performance tests. It proved to be the fastest of the 2-litre Kombi models we have tested, topping 130 on a level road and sprinting to 90 in 16,7 seconds. With a big-bodied vehicle the gearshift has to be used more than with a five-seat car, but the Microbus is pleasing to drive.

It also achieves fair economy in rela-

tion to seating and load capacity, loggir 11,5 litres/100 km (24,6 m-p-g) at 90 fc a 480 km cruising range potential. braked exceptionally-well for its siz with no wheel locking in spite of a co siderable pitching action.

SUMMARY

The Microbus differs from its compet tors in having the rear engine and wall through facility from the front seats t the rear. This is convenient — particular for families with young children though it reduces seating capacity by on while the rear engine cuts load space bit and has a small effect on direction stability in crosswinds.

But this is still the versatile Kom that families love, in a comfortabl equipped form — and much more bu able without that "Executive" tag!

SPECIFICATIONS

ENGINE:

Cylinders	4 horizontally opposed, rear-mounted
Fuel supply	twin Solex carburettors
Bore/stroke	94 x 71 mm
Cubic capacity	1 970 cm^3
Compression ratio	7,3 to 1
Valve gear	o-h-v, pushrods
Ignition	coil and distributor
Main bearings	four
Fuel requirement	93-octane Coast, 88-octane Reef
Cooling	air, blower-driven

ENGINE OUTPUT:

Max power I.S.O. (kW)	51
Power peak (r/min)	4 200
Max permissible r/min	4 400
Max torque (N.m)	143
Torque peak (r/min)	2 800

TRANSMISSION:

Forward speeds	four
Gearshift	floor
Low gear	3,78 to 1
2nd gear	2,06 to 1
3rd gear	1,26 to 1
Top gear	0,88 to 1
Reverse gear	3,78 to 1
Final drive	4,57 to 1 (4,02 overall)
Drive wheels	rear

WHEELS AND TYRES:

Road wheels	5,5J x 14 steel discs
Tyres	185 SR 14 radials

CAPACITIES:

Seating	8-10
Fuel tank	56 litres
Luggage space	780 dm^3
Utility space	2 070-4 020 dm^3

ACCELERATION

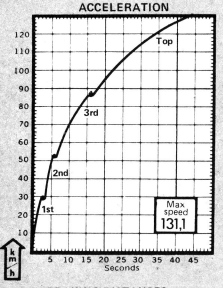

Max speed **131,1**

BRAKING DISTANCES

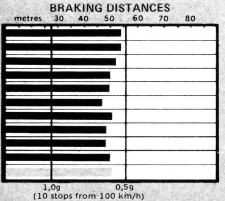

1,0g   0,5g
(10 stops from 100 km/h)

NOISE VALUES

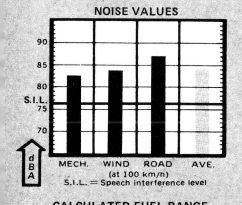

(at 100 km/h)
S.I.L. = Speech interference level

CALCULATED FUEL RANGE
(km)

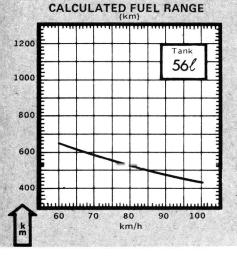

Tank **56ℓ**

---

test Volkswagen 2000L Microbus

PERFORMANCE

PERFORMANCE FACTORS:
Power/mass (W/kg) net 39,5
Frontal area (m^2) 3,34
km/h per 1 000 r/min (top) . . 30,1

INTERIOR NOISE LEVELS:

	Mech	Wind	Road
Idling	61,0	—	—
60	73,5	—	—
80	78,0	79,5	83,0
100	82,5	84,0	87,0
Average dBA at 100			84,5

ACCELERATION (seconds):
0-60 7,8
0-80 13,1
0-100 22,2
1 km sprint 41,3

OVERTAKING ACCELERATION:

	3rd	Top
40-60	4,9	8,3
60-80	5,7	8,6
80-100	9,3	13,2

KEY FIGURES

Maximum speed . . . . .131,1 km/h
1 km sprint . . . . . . 41,3 seconds
Terminal speed . . . . .117,5 km/h
Fuel tank capacity . . . . . 56 litres
Litres/100 km at 80 10,4
Optimum fuel range at 80 . 538 km
Engine revs per km 1 995
National list price R7 430

MAXIMUM SPEED (km/h):
True speed 131,1
Speedometer reading 142
Calibration:

Indicated	60	70	80	90	100
True speed	58	67	76	85	94

FUEL CONSUMPTION
(litres/100 km):
60 8,7
70 9,6
80 10,4
90 11,5
100 12,5

BRAKING TEST:
From 100 km/h:
Best stop 3,9
Worst stop 4,3
Average 4,08

GRADIENTS IN GEARS:
Low gear . . . . 1 in 2,9
2nd gear . . . . 1 in 4,5
3rd gear . . . . 1 in 7,4
Top gear . . . . 1 in 13,2

GEARED SPEEDS (km/h):
Low gear 29,4
2nd gear 53,9
3rd gear 88,2
Top gear 126,3
(Calculated at engine peak r/min —
4 200.)

ENGINE SPEED

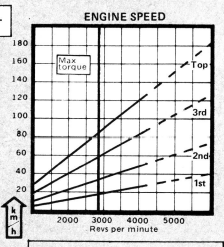

Max torque

IMPERIAL DATA

ACCELERATION (seconds):
0-60 20,7
MAXIMUM SPEED (m-p-h):
True speed 81,5
FUEL ECONOMY (m-p-g):
50 m-p-h 26,9
60 m-p-h 23,2

GRADIENT ABILITY

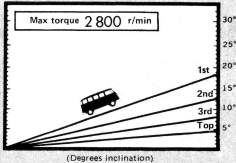

Max torque **2 800** r/min

(Degrees inclination)

CRUISING AT 90

Mech noise level . . . . 80,5 dBA
0-90 through gears . . . . . 16,7 seconds
Litres/100 km at 90 11,5
Optimum fuel range at 90 . . . . 487 km
Braking from 90 . . . . . .3,6 seconds
Maximum gradient (top) . . . 1 in 15,6
Speedometer error . . . . . . 5,5% over
Speedo at true 90 95
Odometer error . . . . . .2,4% under
Engine r/min at 90 . . . . 2 990

STEADY-SPEED FUEL CONSUMPTION
(litres/100 km at true speeds)

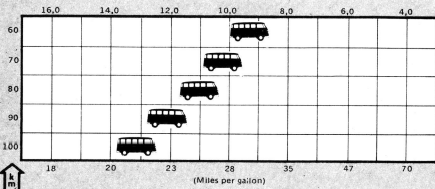

(Miles per gallon)

WHY A **KOMBI** IS THE ONLY WAY TO GO

By Tony Curtis

WHEN THE ALL-ENGULFING 4WD tide ebbs — as it eventually must — many of us will breathe a collective sigh of relief. And in that pleasant downtime before the next Big Fad comes flooding in, we should be able to gather our senses and consider the realities of horses-for-courses and trucks-for-tracks.

As a lawyer friend once remarked: "CB radio is like pornography. You can't stamp it out because it attracts so many self-righteous fanatics." To CB/ pornography I would add 4WDs. The idea of all-round traction gathers more nuts than a certain American preacher named Oral Roberts did years ago in Sydney. But at least they ran him out of town.

For those who aren't entirely bedazzled by the mystique of low-speed torque, the average 4WD is suspected of being an expensive waste of time and money for all except cockeys grinding livings out of flood plains and mountain goat strongholds. And many of these folk I've encountered have expressed grave doubts about the wisdom of these cutely engineered tax-depreciated purchases.

What I'm getting to, ever so slowly, is that 99 percent of rough road driving can be achieved more comfortably, economically and successfully with the correct two-wheel-drive vehicle. Take, for example, the VW Kombi.

Without trying to be definitive, I'd like to list some of the Kombi's pluses:

o Low revving engine developing high torque in low gear.

o Compact design, without excessive overhang front and rear.

o Spaciousness for a wide variety of creature-comfort configurations.

o Previous popularity that has spawned a far-flung service network.

o Air-cooled flat four engine that's not disabled by a punctured radiator.

Sure, the Kombi has some disadvantages, particularly its height and long wheelbase. But in many years of owning one I found that the two metre height proved a nuisance only in that it excluded me from automatic car washers and city parking stations. In the bush I've never had a problem picking a track around low level branches, although I suppose a low-profile Suzuki or Daihatsu would enable a closer approach to timbered river banks in the duck season. Big deal. Why not park nearby and dodge the mosquitoes? You have to use Shank's pony sometimes!

The long wheelbase, of course, is a trade-off for space and comfort. But the trade is a practical one when you consider the alternative — the cramped, bone-shaking ride, short range and limited storage capacity of the SWB 4WD. Again, Kombi drivers can always hedge their bets by installing a winch up front.

Go-anywhere vehicle?

The effective use of any vehicle depends mostly on the confidence and experience of the driver, and for this reason I believe most 4WD salesmen pander to the mental uncertainties of the buyers. There are, too, the fashion buyers who will spend $7000 or more on a 4WD in which to do the shopping. But we're not concerned here with the sucker end of the industry.

Now for the big statement: The experienced and confident Kombi driver can go almost anywhere a 4WD-er can go — except the beach below the high water mark. One Kombi owner I know took his 1600 cm³ vehicle up a 40⁰ plus slope near the Wombeyan Caves (NSW) in competition with a Nissan Patrol and made the top after the Patrol driver had given up. In fairness, it should be noted that the Kombi driver's girlfriend didn't share his confidence and jumped out halfway.

Given the Kombi's torque and power-weight ratio with the engine over the rear wheels, the achievement was not so surprising.

Performance aside, the Kombi's box-like spaciousness, once fully exploited with camping and living facilities, provides not just a handy vehicle, but a way of life. There are a lot of fringe benefits, too.

During one period of penury I took advantage of my campervan to park in loading zones and enjoy a cheap, hot lunch in the street outside the office. I'd just pop the top, grab a cold tinnie from the fridge and sit back while the sausages sizzled and the toast browned on the gas stove. It saved me at least $1.50 a day on current counter lunch prices, not to mention saving on beer.

It wasn't unsociable, either. The "school" from the pub around the corner simply shifted to the Kombi. The bar price was right and there was no waiting.

Curious passers-by didn't really annoy us, but if they had done so the problem would have been solved by drawing the curtains.

Like a holiday house, the Kombi camper also proved to be an income producing asset, although the "mortgage" was less than you would pay for a beach cottage. I would rent it to friends for $200 a week flat. There was no mileage charge, but they would pay the short-term insurance, or take out a cover note, which was free. They would pay for all the petrol and LPG for the stove/fridge, and were expected to look after the vehicle, which they always did. Needless to say, the rental was on a cash basis. Renting it for five weeks of the year meant I wasn't really inconvenienced by a prolonged lack of wheels and earned me $1000 cash without my having to work for it.

Profits of ownership

I must admit I often thought about putting the profits towards another campervan and starting a business. One fellow I knew did this with his caravan and ended up with a dozen caravans parked in his driveway, outside his house and at various spots around the block. But he ran foul of complaining neighbours and, eventually, the taxman. Too much of a hassle.

Without doubt the campervan market has waned, and I think this has been for two reasons. Kombi, Toyota and Nissan campers no longer receive the massive promotion they once did and as a result have slipped out of sight of prospective buyers. The second reason is cost. A fully fitted campervan (cost: around $10,000) is a very expensive vehicle indeed.

But, as the sages say, there is always a way. My campervan, bought five years ago, cost $4000, and the conversion a further $1,800. If the price has changed, the tricks of purchase haven't. My 1600 cm³ base vehicle was the "delivery van" model and therefore hundreds of dollars cheaper than the Microbus with its windows and bright shiny door and body strips. It was also, naturally, much cheaper than the bigger engined 1800 cm³ version.

But what were the real differences? The delivery van version had panels that came out easily to be replaced by windows at lower cost than the factory delivered higher-in-the-range model. I chose the 1600 cm³ version because I considered it to be a simpler, more reliable engine than the 1800. There wasn't of course any argument about getting manual instead of automatic, particularly as some automatics I have seen had trouble getting over footpath kerbing. The 1600 cm³ engine didn't rate with the 1800 for quickness, but when I went into the market for a campervan I neither expected nor wanted a quick vehicle. One other campervan aficionado beefed up his 1600 cm³ powered vehicle with bolt-on equipment from an auto engineer which lengthened the stroke and gave him 1800 cm³ performance with 1600 cm³ economy and reliability. It cost him less than $200.

Bringing in a new model with a bigger engine is a fairly standard marketing ploy and, being tried and true, it gets 'em in. When the two litre Kombi came in with a big promotional push, the 1800 cm³ version faded into the background and the 1600 all but disappeared.

For those who tried to sell at a handsome profit, the superseding of the 1600 and 1800 cm³ Kombis was a big disappointment. But in my experience most campervan people are more interested in the game than they are in the profit, and so long as they don't get their fingers burnt financially they're quite happy to come out at par. You can now pick up a 1600 cm³ camper in good condition for $3500, which is top value when you consider the ravages of inflation and the inherent long life of the vehicle.

The best news of all for campervanners is that the vehicle they covet is no longer fashionable. That means the price is right. But now is the time to get one. When the 4WDs have run their course, the smarties in the industry may decide it's time once again to inspire another campervan craze, probably under a different name — how about "mini-mobile homes"? And prices — once again — will sky-rocket. ☀

VW BUS Continued from page 27

misleading as it's not spongy and control is good, thanks in part to double acting shock absorbers and the constant spring rate inherent in the torsion bar system used fore and aft.

The detail finish is exceptionally good, even by Volkswagen's traditionally excellent standards and here, of course, is the visible evidence that the VW bus is not just a van outfitted with seats and windows. Its vices are the traditional ones associated with the products of Wolfsburg (or rather Hanover in this instance) and include perhaps the most inaccessible of all the inaccessible batteries in the family and susceptibility to wind wander. It's not just a matter of lifting a seat cushion with this battery; you have to remove it (first removing the air cleaner) from its hiding place in the engine compartment to even check the water level. The wind wander is to be expected from any van shape but obviously it's aggravated by the machinery being concentrated at the rear. At least the steering is not as precise as that of the squareback or beetle so there is less danger of overcorrecting.

This vehicle is easy to summarize. If you like the practicality offered by the van configuration and are more concerned with exceptional resale value and 22-mpg economy than you are with performance, buy the VW bus in preference to domestic offerings. Remember, though, to drive defensively as there is no power whatever in reserve to bail you out of an error in judgement at today's highway speeds. Also, there's precious little structure in front of you and yours should you ever have to pay the piper. ●

VW
MICROTEST

BY RAY BARKER

For years, the idea of purchasing a VW van had circulated through my mind. But that's all it did — circulate — for, in that time, I had purchased many vehicles, including some of the more popular 4 x 4's. Something always held me back from putting money down on a Volkswagen. Maybe it was just a little too utilitarian and unconventional for my psyche which had been conditioned to having unquestioned faith in straight sixes and vee-eights.

However, on paper, the VW Kombi/Camper/Bus or Type 2 seemed to have plenty going for it. For starters, it must be the most popular long-distance touring vehicle in the world. Pick up any magazine on travel, outdoors, discovery, or whatever, and chances are that someone, somewhere will be seen wafting along in a "Kombi". And the number of advantages it appeared to have over more conventional cars were many — things like the air-cooled engine, walk-through cabin, flat floor, excellent ground clearance, and almost timeless design combined with proven reliability, availability of spares and good economy on standard grade fuel. They all add up to a pretty convincing statement for the marque — so convincing, in fact, that over 20,000 kilometres ago I purchased my first ever VW, or, as my motorised friends call it, "Hitler's revenge on the world".

Of the three most popular Type 2 models, I chose the Microbus. It wasn't absolutely perfect for my requirements but I didn't have the time or the inclination to outfit a basic van shell, and I couldn't see the sense in purchasing a fully decked-out Campmobile when I already had a garage full of regular camping equipment. Besides, the VW would have to double as a weekday, business vehicle, and the thought of chugging around in the front of a small house didn't appeal either.

The day after I took delivery, the vehicle was booked into the local windscreen fitter and the screen was re-placed with a laminated one that also featured a blue tint across the top. Apart from improving the vehicle's appearance, I believe the laminated screen is absolutely essential: how Volkswagen Australia can justify the cheaper version as standard is beyond me. All four-wheel-drives sold in Australia now have laminated screens — it's about time VW followed their example.

During the next few months I discovered a few other things that were in need of improvement. The first and most serious was the ever-increasing evidence of rust in the door seams, window frames, back door edges and engine air-scoops. A quaint situation regarding warrantable rust complaints is that VW Australia will not take the dealer's word for the claim — the vehicle must be inspected by a staff member of VW Australia (who was away in the country for a few weeks!). Finally, I took the vehicle to VWA's head office and they gave the dealer the go-ahead to fix it. However, the dealer then admitted that the job would be sub-contracted out to a spray-painter, and when questioned closely, agreed that the painter might just spray over all the rust that was showing.

The spray painting scene was given a big miss, and the vehicle ended up at Ziebart for rectification at my own expense. I must admit that VW did replace the side window frames under warranty even if it took a couple of months to get the parts from Germany.

The other things that needed improvement were the heating system and the seats. There is just no way you can get the heater fan to blow out a good gust of warm air on to the front passenger's feet. Sure the vehicle's interior does eventually get quite warm, but the heat just trickles in and, on a freezing, cold morning, that can be annoying. The original seats always made me feel as if I was sliding forward towards the screen. They're obviously designed for bread-carters, etc. who have to jump in and out every sixty seconds. I don't know how long-distance travellers tolerate them.

A pair of Scheel 201S seats fixed the comfort problem, and the rear seats were upholstered to match at the same time. This not only gives the replacement seats a more co-ordinated look, it also solves the necessity of rear passengers sitting on burning black vinyl if the vehicle has been sitting in the summer sun.

Escaping the effects of summer heat and dust led to the installation of an air-conditioner, and this proved to be a most frustrating experience. The job was undertaken by one of Sydney's leading air-conditioning companies and, after assurances that the job could be done (it was their first on a Microbus), they were given the go-ahead to fit an American DPD overhead console unit.

The predicted installation time of four days turned into two weeks, during the last of which I occasionally called in to see if work was under way. Each time, there were at least two employees working on it, and always with worried expressions! Finally, it was finished and I handed over the quite substantial cheque, but even at this stage, I calculated that they had lost money. It was the middle of summer and cold air tumbled down from the adjustable vents like a waterfall from heaven — for two miles, that is! The compressor belt snapped. Back she went the next day for rectification. It was to be the first of approximately six such trips during the summer months — 95 per cent of the time the air just didn't work. According to the fitters, the distributors had supplied an early model fitting kit that wasn't suitable for a two litre engine (I knew from the bits that were hacked about), plus the fact that the unit had been sitting on a warehouse shelf for some years and apparently the corroded electrical contacts were causing many of the hassles. Now that the problems have all been sorted out the unit works beautifully and, surprisingly, does not have much effect on engine power or economy.

Anyone contemplating fitting DPD air-conditioning should steer clear of the general automotive air-conditioning agents and go to a VW specialist like Trakka Van in Sydney.

On the highway, the VW's performance is a mixture of brilliant and doubtful. Anyone who has driven a 2 litre model with emission equipment will know how infuriating the waste fuel burning system can be. It is like driving with a combination of a sticking throttle and a slipping clutch. Owners may like to know that the problem can be rectified with a spanner in about sixty seconds. Of course, I only mention this in case you are taking your vehicle to a country that doesn't require fuel wasting emission systems.

The 2 litre motor will propel the bus along at very respectable speeds. The top speed of 128 kph also happens to be the recommended cruising speed. I have found that on long, open, outback roads the VW will sit quite contentedly on 140 kph. In fact, it tends to creep up to that speed even if you endeavour to stay around 130 kph. General cornering and braking are excellent, and have never given me any cause for alarm — even when pushing the vehicle along perhaps a little harder than it was meant to be. A word of warning, though: unexpected sidewinds can be super dangerous to an unladen VW van travelling at high speed. It pays to be especially careful of freeways that cut through hilly terrain. A good blast of wind can tilt the vehicle slightly, altering its steering geometry and sending you off course — perhaps into another traffic lane, and maybe into oblivion.

Rough roads highlight the suppleness of the suspension. The VW will soak up mile after mile of sub-standard road without discomfort to the occupants — and in a way that puts most other vehicles to shame. We have followed stiffly sprung four-wheel-drives that have been doing the Charleston over corrugated roads where the VW has hardly even needed a wheel correction. However, contrary to some published articles of VW fanatics, the Type 2 is no match for a four-wheel-drive in off-road situations. We have been "stuck" on wet grass, firm but slippery clay, and the VW wouldn't have a hope in hell of tackling any of our favourite fire trails to secluded campsites.

In 20,000 very varied kilometres, the vehicle has only broken down once. Naturally, it was when we were fully laden, miles from anywhere, and it was raining. It was then that I cursed that so unobtrusive engine. To get over the top of it the cargo over the motor has to be removed, then the top engine hatch comes off, but to get daylight in there, the rear hatch must be opened, and then where can you stand so that you can see into the top of the motor? As it turned out, it was a loose high tension lead caused by the shortness of the lead from the body mounted coil to the distributor.

Except for the rust problem, the standard of service from two VW dealers I have encountered has been absolutely first-class and, in fact, the fellow who told me about the spray-painter was doing me a favour, anyway.

On reflection, the Microbus has been a fairly pleasant experience. It is a multi-purpose vehicle in the true sense of the word. Just try and name one other vehicle that can carry eight people and a lot of gear; cruises at 130 kph; rides like a car; is shorter than the average Holden, Falcon or Valiant sedan; has numerous hidden storage areas; never needs a drink of water, and returns around 25 mpg on a run and even 20 mpg fully laden and flat out.

If they made a 4 x 4 version, there would be a queue from Sydney to Melbourne.

COMPARATIVE CAR test HI-ACE SUPER T

Anyone who buys one of these two-litre buses without studying the other is acting rashly . . .

ONCE YOUR family swings past three children, the family car becomes cramped. It's dangerous to pile them into a station wagon's load space and only one saloon offers twin-bench seats for six. But when you switch to a minibus, the perspectives change; you now have enough seats to take some friends along, combined with generous luggage space...

Moreover, as you can no longer buy performance (though you may still pay for

it), why not go for space and convenience — the freedom to throw it all in the back for that trip to the beach or the holiday cottage, including the dog? For braais, Brownie trips, lift clubs, monthly shopping sprees or furniture removal you can't beat the family bus, which can be run for about the same cost as a medium sized car.

Nor is the modern minibus awkward to drive. It's a compact, light-handling package

with exceptional visibility (subject to minor reservations that will appear in the course of our report). So the busy housewife often gets to prefer driving it anyway...

All of which sets the scene for our confrontation between two of the market leaders. In the one corner, the Volkswagen Microbus 2000 L — the latest optimum-value derivative of a line stretching back a full 21 years. In the other, the Toyota Hi-Ace

Super Ten — a young Japane challenger with the power, t looks and the functional ef ciency to force any buy to think at least twice befo he makes his choice.

Two-litre power

They both come into t top "performance" catego of the growing minibus mark being equipped with two-li motors that enable them hold their own, quite effo lessly, at today's cruisi speeds, regardless of the t

n. And they demonstrate w much space is "lost" thin the *overall* dimensions the ordinary car.

Take the Super Ten, for example: it has the same overall gth, to a millimetre, as the rtina saloon, and it's 10 mm rrower. And while VW's Mibus/Kombi body is 205 mm ger, its only 20 mm wider an the Cortina.

So they're both more comt than you thought. They share forward control,

a carpeted interior, a surprisingly modest turning circle and easy, "four-corner visibility" to simplify parking. Both designers opted for a sliding door, to give easy access to the middle and rear rows of seats, and decided on disc/drum, boosted brakes. But the parallel progress stops right there: although they are priced within R65 of each other (and once cost exactly the same) they are radically different vehicles, backed by

contrasting pros and cons. And the man who buys one of them, without studying the other, is acting rashly.

The basic problem facing the two design teams was, of course, the same: how to transport nine/ten people (or six, plus a mountain of luggage), within the approximate dimensions of a family car, incurring only marginally higher running costs. But the formulae chosen by the German and Japanese factories

were about as divergent as they could be.

In developing the Kombi, which in various forms has dominated the world's minibus markets for two decades, the Germans experimented initially with a Beetle chassis. And to this day, the Microbus retains the same wheelbase (2 400 mm) and has a flat-four air-cooled motor tucked into its tail, driving the rear wheels through swinging half-axles. Like the Super Beetle (which never

CCN 16931

came to South Africa) the vehicle's handling and road-holding were vastly uprated by the adoption of double-jointed rear axles, some years ago, and the off/rough road capabilities of the deep-travel torsion bar suspension have become legendary.

When the Japanese entered the minibus fray, much later, they adopted an even shorter wheelbase (2 340 mm) and, as VW had done, they used it to tuck the front wheel arches away beneath the front row of seats, with another row in front of the rear axle and a third row in between.

Predictably, they used a four-in-line water-cooled engine; and by mounting it (and a four-speed transmission) between and behind the front wheels, they achieved two useful objectives: they utilised space that would otherwise be wasted and they obtained good mass distribution, with a low centre of gravity to improve both handling and stability.

Tucking the power train away into "dead" space produced a valuable gain at the rear, where the area behind the back seat was left completely free for luggage, with a floor-level loading sill. This gives the Hi-Ace a larger loading bay at a much lower level than can be done with the VW layout, which necessitates placing the luggage on top of the engine bay, where it raises the c of g and increases the vehicle's tail-heavy characteristics.

The Toyota suspension is conventional, with coils, wishbones and anti-roll bar in front and a leaf-sprung rear axle. In the current Series 2 version, the body has been mounted lower on the chassis, to improve roadholding, performance and access. The spare wheel has been mounted beneath the back of the body (where it can bottom quite easily, even on "unusual" suburban roads), whereas VW recess their's into the side of the loading bay.

Contrasting engines

While VW developed a range of specialised pushrod "boxer" motors for their Type 2 Transporter vehicles (of which the smooth, torquey and fuss-free two-litre unit is certainly the finest), Toyota "dropped in" the low compression ver-

Both the Super Ten (left) and the Microbus (right) provide fairly easy access to the front seats. But the squab level is just 10 mm higher in the Volkswagen and unlike its competitor, there are no overhead grab handles.

Both vehicles' rear seating converts into double bed but VW's (right) is only partly sprung. Both vehicles use wide sliding doors to provide easy access to the main passenger space but this particular Microbus lacks a slide-out step. The Toyota's step is built-in.

Front seat layout differs radically. The Toyota (left) provides three front seats, while the Microbus has two seats and a walk-through gangway. Neither engine bay (below) is easily accessible for Do-it-yourself maintenance.

sion of their 1 968 cm³ 18R engine, which is also used in several cars. It has a chain-driven single overhead cam and a twin-choke Aisan carburettor and in this form, it develops a hefty 71 kW at 5 000 r/min, with 160 N.m of torque at 3 600 r/min.

While the 18R is moderately over-square (88,5 x 80 mm) the 1 970 cm³ VW unit is more so, using a 94 mm bore with a 71 mm stroke. It is designed to perform at much lower revs, producing its 51 kW at only 4 200 r/min and delivering its peak torque of 143 N.m at 2 800 r/min.

On the face of it, you might expect the 39 per cent nominal power advantage enjoyed by the Japanese vehicle to be decisive, enabling it to walk away from the opposition in both acceleration and top speed — especially since its frontal area is 0,1m² smaller and its roof is 35 mm closer to the tarmac. But in fact, the torque "gap" is much narrower — 11,8% — and there are many other factors involved, among them vehicle mass, gearing and power train efficiency. The Microbus is 100 kg lighter than the Hi-Ace and in conjunction with the low speed, flat-curve torque of its boxer motor (which puts its power straight onto the road, through those swinging axles) this enables it to pull significantly longer overall gearing — 30,1 km/h/ 1 000 r/min in top, compared to a figure of 27,6 for the Toyota.

Both vehicles use 14 x 5,5 J wheels, shod with 185 radial tyres. But while the Hi-Ace employs a 4,375:1 final drive, the Microbus uses a 4,57:1 ratio in conjunction with an 0,88:1 overdrive top gear.

In a 0-100 km/h sprint match, the VW actually pips the Hi-Ace by a fraction over two seconds to record a time of 22,2 secs. But in a 1 km drag, the Japanese vehicle would come only one second behind and its top speed is the faster, as our tables show.

Fuel consumption

In top-gear overtaking or hill-climbing there's nothing much in it. But when it comes to fuel consumption, the Hi-Ace's more efficient engine and lower profile contribute to a clear advantage, though both models do remarkably well, for their load capacities. The Super Ten uses 5,7 per cent less fuel at a steady 60 km/h, an advantage that falls to 2,4 per cent at 90 km/h. And over two laps of a 52 km varied road circuit, with the vehicles running closely together and one midpoint driver change, the Toyota recorded 9,7 litres/100 km — 0,9 litre or 8,4 per cent below the figure for the Microbus.

Now let's look at the seating, luggage and access arrangements. If you accept that a vehicle of this width can seat no more than three abreast, then the Volkswagen can carry up to eight and the Toyota, nine — for the latest model lacks the little fold-down seat in the rear luggage compartment that was a feature of the Series One Super Ten.

But while some owners would value the "walk through" access to the front seats of the VW, others would

TESTER'S COMMENTS

Body styling design and finish	Both modern, airy designs with lots of glass and sliding doors. On test vehicles, paintwork, chrome and panel fit were exemplary.
Minor collision protection	Both equipped with heavy gauge steel bumpers — chrome on Hi-Ace and white-enamelled on Microbus. But the Toyota's rear bumper is virtually in line with its bulbous rear door. Only the Toyota has protective side trims.
Boot design and size	Hi-Ace luggage area is at floor level with no intervening sill. With all seats occupied, it provides slightly more volume than VW, increasing to 750 dm³ advantage with rear seats folded. Microbus's luggage area located relatively high, above engine bay.
Seating, upholstery and access	Eight seats in Microbus, nine in Super Ten, arranged in three rows (VW has "walk through" access to front seats). Vinyl upholstery in both but Toyota has higher-backed seats which provide more support. Main sliding door access involves one 500 mm step in the VW, two (340 + 200 mm) steps in Hi-Ace.
Dashboard design	Both have cubbyholes without lock and VW provides full width "net" parcel shelf, while Toyota has steel tray on left hand side. Microbus's finely finished "wood panelled" dash has fuel gauge plus a combined indicator light and warning lights for charge, main beam, oil pressure and handbrake. Hi-Ace has these, plus separate indicator light and a temperature gauge in vinyl-trimmed dash. It also has a cigarette lighter — a conspicuous absentee in the VW.
Heating and ventilation	VW scores in cold weather with copious ducted hot air flow, whereas Toyota relies on central heater ducted only to windscreen. But powerful fan and eyeball vents give Hi-Ace bigger cooling air flow, unless VW's big quarter lights are used as scoops. Hi-Ace has seven sliding windows in passenger compartment, VW only four.
Under-bonnet accessibility	Poor in both vehicles, due to power train and body design. Requires methodical approach and practice.
Control layout	Pendant pedals, in conjunction with organ throttle on the VW, which uses higher geared steering ratio with larger wheel. Both use two stalks — one for indicators, flasher and dip, the other for wash and/or wipe.
Gearchange	Microbus has 0,5m long floor-mounted gear lever that gives notchy, rather vague change. Super Ten uses precise column-mounted selector.
Handling	Excellent in both, for vehicles of this type. But while Toyota's characteristics are sustained in gusty weather, Microbus handling deteriorates, especially in strong side winds.
Ride quality	On the move, noise levels are on a par and quite acceptable. Super Ten is smoother over bumpy roads, when Microbus is more prone to pitching.
Braking	Disc/drum combinations give both vehicles excellent stable stopping power and vacuum servos keep pedal effort low, while retaining good feel. Both under-dash handbrakes work well.
Fuel tank and cap	Super Ten has 58-litre tank and locking flap over cap. Microbus has 56-litre tank and ordinary twist-off cap.
Lights/signals	Both equipped with one pair of round headlamps and signal lights which are reasonably visible from side.
Horn(s)	Button in steering wheel boss works single "poop" hooter on VW. Super Ten has more strident single hooter, operated by two buttons inset into steering wheel spokes.
Guarantees and service intervals	Microbus is backed by "12 months or 12 000 km" warranty. Super Ten has "six months or 10 000 km" warranty. Both require servicing every 10 000 km, with lubrication/safety check every 5 000 km.

much prefer the extra seat — and a barrier that can be used to confine small children to the middle-and-rear of the vehicle.

The Hi-Ace has much deeper-backed, rather more comfortable seats and the back one can be folded forwards, in seconds, to create a truly cavernous luggage space. Moreover, its middle seat reclines to form, (in conjunction with the rear one) a comfortably sprung double bed. Although the Microbus has a comparable facility, it requires an empty luggage space and forms a "bed" which is only partly sprung.

Luggage spaces compared

When all seats are in use, the Toyota provides about 5 per cent more luggage space: although the VW's "boot" is much shallower in terms of height, it extends further into the body. But when maximum goods capacity is utilised (short of removing all the seats) the Super Ten's volume rises to 4 770 dm³, which is 750 dm³ or 18,6 per cent more than its competitor's figure. Its rear door opening measures 1 300 (w) x 1 225 mm (H), compared to 1 235 x 720 mm for the VW.

Access is easier for both driver and passengers in the Hi-Ace, which has a built-in two-step entry at its main side door involving 340 mm and 200 mm risers from ground level. This particular Microbus comes without a slide-out side step, so demands one 500 mm "step" to gain entry; and although its front squabs are 10 mm higher from the ground than those in the Toyota, there are no overhead grab handles to help you climb aboard — a useful feature in the Japanese bus.

While the VW's sliding door seemed altogether more ruggedly mounted than the one in the Toyota, it was also much harder to slam shut, and this operation had to be repeated several times in the course of the test. In contrast, the Toyota required a gentle, two-finger push.

On the road, both vehicles started readily and warmed-up quickly, the Hi-Ace using a manual choke and the Microbus, an automatic arrangment which proved to be a model of efficiency. Idling noise levels were higher in the German bus, but soon evened-out as road speed rose towards

The Microbus (left) is wider, taller and longer than the Super Ten.

Contrasting rear access in the VW (above) and the Toyota (below).

100 km/h, when both vehicles recorded 82 decibels — just four higher than what you would expect, for example of a middle market "six" — and slightly quieter than one Continental-sourced FWD minicar. Ride was surprisingly good in both cases, but more prone to pitching in the Microbus.

The Microbus' long, floor-mounted gear lever produced a notchy, somewhat vague change which demanded gentle movement for optimum results. Because of its baulky character, it did not give the time-saving advantage you would expect over the column-mounted change used in the Hi-Ace, which was sweet and precise.

Both engines pulled smoothly and responded well to the throttle, though with a sharp difference in character: while the low-revving VW unit felt much the stronger initially, being matched to beautifully-spaced ratios to make driving a pleasure, the Hi-Ace unit came into its own, as you would expect, when the revs climbed past 3 000 r/min; it invited the driver to use its full 5 500 r/min potential.

Handling variations

Handling comparisons varied with the conditions, for while the Toyota could be driven

with the smooth assurance of a modern car in virtually any conditions, the Microbus proved sensitive to wind — something that had been improved but not eradicated by the suspension refinements previously referred to.

In calm conditions, the Microbus was sweet-handling and predictable. But in lively sidewinds, it demanded constant "driving" to keep to an acceptable line and on two occasions when it was struck by strong gusts streaming through openings in a screen of tall trees, it required quick and appropriate reactions to maintain full control.

While both vehicles are generally well equipped and fully carpeted, the VW gives an impression of long-lasting interior quality which is quite outstanding. It is spoilt only by such irritations as the lack of a cigarette lighter (in a R7 000-plus vehicle!) and the irritations associated with having two keys which had to be inserted the right way round, every time you used them. It also suffers on visibility, for while there are two mountings for external mirrors, only one is provided and the result is a left-side blind spot that we considered dangerous. The interior mirror, too, is too narrow and too

Sliding doors provide easy access to the rear passenger space.

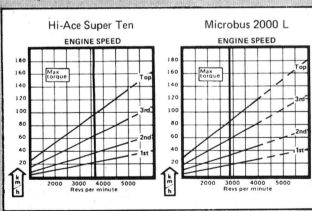

Hi-Ace Super Ten	Microbus 2000 L
ENGINE SPEED	ENGINE SPEED

high to provide an optimum view. The Hi-Ace, on the other hand, scores with three large, well-located mirrors.

Powerful, disc/drum braking systems bring both buses to a stop stably from 100 km/h in around four-second averages — a performance that would have seemed unattainable, in a vehicle of this type, only a few years ago. And both employ vacuum servos to bring pedal effort within the range where the average housewife can cope quite comfortably. While dash-mounted handbrakes are never the nicest or the most efficient to use,

in both Hi-Ace and Microbus they work well enough, holding securely on a steepish incline and forming a useful emergency brake, should the main system fail.

One area of significant difference is the arrangements for heating and ventilation. In cold conditions, the VW scores with its copious supply of heat, distributed throughout the passenger space by ingenious and effective ducting. In contrast, the Toyota has a centrally-mounted heater which looks a little crude, is ducted only to the windscreen, but has plenty of power.

However, when the weather is hot you must open the Microbus' large quarter lights to obtain sufficient air flow, whereas the Toyota provides a powerful fan and eyeball vents to supplement the (smaller) quarter vents. And while the Toyota has seven sliding windows in the passenger space, the VW has only four.

Maintenance snag

There has to be a catch, somewhere, in the ingenious designs that pack so much into so little, in these buses. And it emerges when you come to service them. Neither is easy to work on, from

a D-I-Y viewpoint, though the Toyota's engine is probably more accessible once you have the covers up. In the market place, the Kombi/Microbus has become so strongly entrenched, and so loved by so many families for its toughness and practicability, that despite its weaker points, any serious challenger just *has* to be good.

The Toyota certainly is — and the 3 533 sales notched up by the Hi-Ace range last year, compared to the 5 356 by the VW Type 2s, shows that the minibus battle is very much "on". ●

Performance and Specifications

Microbus 2000L   R7 430
Hi-Ace Super Ten   R7 495

MAKE AND MODEL:

	Toyota	Volkswagen
Make	Toyota	Volkswagen
Model	Hi-Ace Super Ten	Microbus 2000 L

INTERIOR NOISE LEVELS:

Idling	49	61
60	74	73
80	78	78
100	82	82

(Measured in decibels, "A" weighting, averaging runs both ways on a level road with car closed.)

ACCELERATION FROM REST:

0-60	7,4	7,8
0-80	14,1	13,1
0-100	24,3	22,2
1 km sprint	42,2	41,3

OVERTAKING ACCELERATION:

	3rd	Top	3rd	Top
40-60	4,7	8,6	4,9	8,3
60-80	5,6	9,5	5,7	8,6
80-100	—	11,5	9,3	13,2

(Measured in seconds, to true speeds, averaging runs both ways on a level road, car carrying test crew of two and standard test equipment.)

MAXIMUM SPEED: (km/h)

True speed	136	131

Calibration:

Indicated:	60	80	100		60	80	100
True speed:	57	75	93		58	76	94

FUEL CONSUMPTION (litres/100 km):

60	8,2	8,7
80	10,1	10,4
100	12,2	12,5

(Stated in litres per 100 kilometres, based on fuel economy figures recorded at true speeds.)

FUEL CONSUMPTION (OVERALL):

	9,7 litres/100 km	10,6 litres/100 km

(Recorded over two laps of a 52 km varied road circuit including suburban traffic and parkways, with the vehicles travelling closely together and with one mid-point driver change.)

BRAKING TEST:

Ten stops from 100 km/h:

Best stop	3,6	3,9
Worst stop	4,1	4,3
Average	3,86	4,1

(Measured in sec with stops from true speeds at 30-second intervals on a good bituminised surface.)

GRADIENTS IN GEARS:

Low gear	1 in 3,7	1 in 2,9
2nd gear	1 in 5,0	1 in 4,5
3rd gear	1 in 7,7	1 in 7,4
Top gear	1 in 15,9	1 in 13,2

(Tabulated from Tapley (x gravity) readings, car carrying test crew of two and standard test equipment.)

GEARED SPEEDS: (km/h)

Low gear	34	29
2nd gear	55	54
3rd gear	90	88
Top gear	138	126

(Calculated at engine peak power r/min: 5 000 for the Hi-Ace and 4 200 for the Microbus.)

ENGINE:

Cylinders	4 in line	4 horizontally opposed; rear-mounted
Carburettors	Aisan t/choke	twin Solex
Bore	88,5 mm	94 mm
Stroke	80 mm	71 mm
Cubic capacity	1 968 cm³	1 970 cm³
Compression ratio	8,5:1	7,3:1
Valve gear	ohv, sohc	ohv, pushrods
Main bearings	five	four
Fuel requirement	93-octane (Coast) 88-octane (Reef)	93-octane (Coast) 88-octane (Reef)
Cooling	water	air

ENGINE OUTPUT:

Max power SAE (kW) (I.S.O.)	71	51
Peak power r/min	5 000	4 200
Max torque (N.m)	160	143
Torque peak (r/min)	3 600	2 800

TRANSMISSION:

Forward speeds	four	four
Gearshift	steering column	floor
Low gear	4,016 to 1	3,78 to 1
2nd gear	2,510 to 1	2,06 to 1
3rd gear	1,534 to 1	1,26 to 1
Top gear	Direct	0,88 to 1
Reverse gear	4,571 to 1	3,78 to 1
Final drive	4,375 to 1	4,57 to 1
Drive wheels	rear	rear

WHEELS AND TYRES:

Road wheels	5,5J x 14 steel	5,5J x 14 steel
Tyre size/type	185 SR 14	185 SR 14

BRAKES:

Front	discs	discs
Rear	drums	drums
Pressure regulation	on rear circuit	nil
Boosting	vacuum servo	vacuum servo
Handbrake position	under dash	under dash

STEERING:

Type	recirculating ball	worm and roller
Lock to lock	4,3 turns	2,8 turns
Turning circle	10,6 m	10 m (approx)

MEASUREMENTS:

Length overall	4 340 mm	4 545 mm
Width overall	1 690 mm	1 720 mm
Height overall	1 920 mm	1 955 mm
Wheelbase	2 340 mm	2 400 mm
Front track	1 430 mm	1 395 mm
Rear track	1 400 mm	1 455 mm
Ground clearance	195 mm	200 mm
Licensing mass	1 350 kg	1 250 kg

SUSPENSION:

Front	independent	independent
Type	coils, anti-roll bar	torsion bar, stabiliser
Rear	live axle	independent
Type	leaf springs	torsion bar, dual-jointed half axles

CAPACITIES:

Seating	9	8
Fuel tank	58 litres	56 litres
Luggage trunk	820 dm³	780 dm³
Utility space	2 430-4 770 dm³	2 070-4 020 dm³

THE VW KOMBI

A hefty price-tag for new Kombi vans hasn't lifted the price of second-hand units out of the reach of Everyman.

Only rich men can afford to buy a new Kombi in 1979. The $10,000 price tag is more than $2000 above comparable Japanese one-tonne vans.

Yet, for around $4500 to $5500, you can pick up a good used Kombi, spend a few painstaking, PVC-covered hours armed with a pop-rivet gun and sponge, fabric and plywood, and a round-Australia vehicle is yours.

Mechanically, the Kombi is straight-forward and with a good workshop manual in one hand, and spare parts, spanners and screwdrivers in the other, even bush mechanicking is possible.

The most attractive feature of the Kombi is its high ground clearance; as well, most of its weight is concentrated over the driving wheels, and its all-independent suspension is superior to that of most 2WD cars.

The Kombi has been around for 30 years. It is one of the few vehicles which can tolerate climatic and terrain extremes varying from the Arctic tundra to the Sahara sand.

The models

From an overlander's viewpoint, concentrate on 1969 and later models. Anything earlier is getting too long in the tooth for reliable long-distance touring.

There are five basic models: the single and double cab pick-ups; the panel van; the Kombi (factory fitted side windows); the Microbus (seats, head lining, skylights and so on). Variations on the theme include high-toppers and double sliding doors.

The easiest way to determine the year model is to look at the chassis number. The third number always indicates the model year, whether it was assembled in Australia (up to 1977) or imported from Europe. For example: 224215326 means that the vehicle was built in 1974 (certainly, it could indicate 1964 (but one look at the body and its condition should tell

Top: 1955/67 Kombi had split 'screen, pointed front. Above: 1968 range included Microbus, twin cab, ute, panel van, and true Kombi with factory fitted side windows.

you if the vehicle is ten years older than the salesman tells you).

Distinguishing model features are:—

1965-66: V-front, 1500cm^3 engine, 6V electrics; split windscreen; 14-in wheels on European models, 15-in wheels on Australian versions; axle reduction gears.

1967: 12V electrics on European models; European panel vans had an optional sliding side door.

1968: one-piece curved windscreen, wind-up front door windows, walk-through bulkhead; 1600cm^3 engine; 14-in wheels (all models), higher rear air intakes.

1969: bigger front axle mounting flange.

1970: front dash painted matt black.

1971: front disc brakes; perforated wheel rims; relocated oil cooler; regulator to stop rear brakes locking in emergency; rear wheel track widened.

1972: European models had optional

Top: 1977/78 Kombi with factory Sopru camper conversion. Centre: 1968 models had one-piece screen, parking lights above bumper. Above: parking lights were lifted in 1973.

1700cm^3, twin-carburettor engine; larger tail-lights; through-flow ventilation in front doors; gearbox chassis-mounted.

1973: larger front disc brake pads; front indicator lights mounted higher; 1700cm^3 engine option in Australia; paper air filter; square bumper bar; engine bay hatch.

1974: 1800cm^3 engine; petrol filler flap removed; one-piece headlight reflector and lens.

1975: uprated front seats and headrests.

1976: 2000cm^3 engine; fuel injection; 1600cm^3 engine discontinued.

1977: all Australian models fully imported; front door quarter vents; chrome bumper bars on Microbuses.

What to look for

Dust is the Kombi's biggest demon, especially on later models fitted with paper air filters. Check the condition of the carburettor if the engine is fitted with a paper element. While inspecting the engine, compression test all four cylinders (they should be at least 750kPa) and check for oil leaks, which indicate a hard-worked motor. Inspect the oil cooler: if it leaks, the engine must be removed for repair.

On a test drive, listen for excessive gearbox whine; it can mean the crown wheel and pinion or pinion bearings are worn (again, expensive to repair).

Rust is not really a problem except in the battery compartment and in the bodywork around the gutter rails.

Check that the front suspension has not sagged; there should be plenty of clearance between the front wheels and wheel arches.

Although later model Kombis can withstand an 80km/h collision (if the passengers are restrained by seat belts), examine the front door/windscreen pillars for damage or rewelding.

Front suspension ball joints are expensive to replace, so check around the rubber boots.

Left: Kombi is excellent touring vehicle but not immune to bogs. Below: check engine carefully, especially later models fitted with paper element air filters — dust is biggest enemy.

Excessive wear on the inside of a rear tyre can indicate a bent rear control arm.

If the vehicle you are considering is already converted to a campervan, inspect how well the conversion has stood up to wear and tear. Expecially check around sink tops and door hinges — any swelling here or patch-up jobs indicate the wood (especially if particle board) has warped.

Pop-top roofs should be raised and the sleeve checked for damage. Flush water through the pump (if fitted) and note any rust or foreign matter — it could mean a new water tank is needed.

Operate the folding bed mechanism; check underneath near the wheel arches for rust or dust — excessive amounts indicate poor care and hard work.

Press up the headlining and feel for any protruding screws (most likely found in Sopru conversions). Several vehicles were recalled to have screws adjusted so that they didn't puncture the driver's head on impact.

Fridges and stoves should be checked (if fitted). Inspect wiring for both 12V and 240V power systems.

If a low-pressure stove is fitted, ensure that a separate gas compartment, ventilated to the outside and stamped with a gas-installer's licence plate, is also included. Turn on any gas appliances and check for leaks.

How much to pay

Price naturally is determined by age and quality and whether the vehicle is camper converted.

Obviously, larger engined models are going to give better highway performance than early-model 1600cm³ versions. Bear this in mind, as the premium may well be worth paying.

Partially-converted vans are generally around $1000 less than a fully converted camper; they usually do not have pop-top roofs but do feature seat/beds, stoves and fridges. Extras such as 'roo bars, radio/cassette decks and automatic transmission will also boost used vehicle prices. ☀

SECOND-HAND PRICES

Price*	Vans	Semi-campers	Campers
Up to $2000	-1970	-1969	-1969
$2000-$2500	1970-71	1970	1969-70
$2500-$3000	1971-72	1970-71	1970
$3000-$3500	1972-73	1971-72	1970-71
$3500-$4000	1973-74	1972-73	1971-72
$4000-$4500	1974-75	1973-74	1972-73
$4500-$5000	1975	1974-75	1973
$5000-$5500	1975-76	1974-75	1973-74
$5500-$6000	1976	1974-75	1974-75
$6000-$6500	1976-77	1975-76	1975
$6500-$7000	1977	1976-77	1975-76
$7000-$7500	1977-78	1977	1976
$7500-$8000	1978	1977-78	1976-77
$8000-$9000	1978	1978	1977-78
$9000-	1978-79	1978-79	1978

*Prices are based on classified advertisements for private sales and dealers' yard quotations for vehicles in good condition.

CONTINUED FROM PAGE 16

ability, greater comfort and increased convenience.

Most noticeable change in the Campmobile for 1968 is its sleek new design which includes a one-piece wraparound windshield, large "picture windows," a 41-inch-wide sliding door on the right side and rounded corners both front and rear. Still shorter than a conventional sedan, the Campmobile's 174-inch length permits it to maneuver around hairpin turns which could be troublesome for larger vehicles.

Two major options are available for the 1968 VW Campmobile. One is a "pop-top" which literally raises the roof, providing more standing space inside as well as a luggage rack and child's "upper berth" on top. The other major option is a free-standing tent which quickly can add a fully-enclosed 9'8" by 6'6" room alongside the vehicle. Polyvinyl "flooring" is standard with the tent.

The inside of the standard Campmobile makes up quickly into a bedroom complete with a 76-inch-long double bed and sleeping space for two children. The "pop-top" option provides sleeping space for a third child.

Birch-grained plywood walls and ceiling are fully insulated with fiber glass and the wall-to-wall polyvinyl flooring is backed with felt sound-proofing. Cabinets built in the compact home-on-wheels include three utility storage closets, a linen closet, full-length clothes closet with door-mounted mirror and a three-shelf food locker. Also included is a 2.7-cubic-foot insulated icebox and a 4¼-gallon water tank with pump and faucet.

Center windows on either side of the Campmobile are louvered for rain-proof ventilation and are screened on the inside to keep out insects. The four-foot-wide door over the rear engine compartment also is equipped with a snap-on screen. All windows are equipped with curtains for privacy.

A utility table folds upward from the side of the icebox to provide kitchen counter space and a kitchen sink is recessed into the top of the icebox cabinet. The dinette table, hinge-mounted to the left side of the main living compartment, swings up into place and seats four persons.

A passageway between the driver's and front passenger's seats provides ready access to the rear compartment, even when the vehicle is moving. There are seats for four in the rear, two facing forward and two to the rear. All are covered with wipe-clean leatherette.

The optional "pop-top" is made of fiber glass and canvas and has screens on three sides. Hinged to the roof at the front end of the vehicle it raises at the rear to provide sleeping space for a child and also provides access to the roof luggage rack from inside the Campmobile.

Electrical equipment includes three-way overhead lamp operated off the vehicle's 12-volt battery and both a 110-volt electrical inlet and outlet.

Compression ratio of the vehicle flat-four 96.66-cubic-inch engine has been raised for 1968—to 7.7 to from last year's 7.5—and a thermostatically-controlled preheater has been added to the engine to help control intake air temperature. The 57-horsepower engine still operates on standard grades of gasoline.

Fuel tank capacity in the 1968 models is 16 gallons compared 10.6 last year, enough fuel now give each vehicle in the line a range of more than 300 miles under normal driving conditions. Maximum and cruising speed is about 65 mph.

Markedly improved riding and handling qualities were achieved the new vehicles through development of a double-jointed rear axle which has two joints on each half shaft, one on each side of the transmission case and one at each wheel. Diagonal trailing links keep both rear wheels nearly parallel under all road and load conditions, providing exceptional roadability.

Starcraft-VW Bus

The Luxolook for a familiar face.

• The word "venerable" could well have been created to describe VW's bus. It is certainly worthy of respect for its age—it's in its 29th season—and for the success that has let it attain that age. Venerable, indeed. And simple, and strong, and all those other good Volkswagen traits. But in this age of commodious and powerful Ford and Chevy and Dodge and Plymouth and GMC vans, VW's tiny entry has been a touch ignored. It hasn't been a serious part of the van scene since the last flower children packed their macramé pot hangers and their tooled leather stash pouches and left the Haight for the ultimate trip back into mainstream America.

So the VW bus is and isn't a lot of things. However, give it the double-throw-down travelin'-in-style interior treatment and it suddenly becomes as much a van for today as anything built on or around a Detroit piece.

VW campers have been around for years in just about every guise from the official factory version to the one from Sam's Plywood City and Propane Stove Store. But few buses have gotten the luxo station-wagon-with-a-plus treatment. Ours came from Starcraft RV in Topeka, Indiana. Starcraft RV is the recreational-vehicle (surprise) branch of a company that is best known for its aluminum boats. RV-division president Don Cuzzocrea, who had seen a piece we'd done on a GMC van conversion in the March issue, called one day last spring to say, in effect, that if we liked the GMC conversion, wait until we see what they had done to a VW.

Hah, we thought, memories flooding back. Like memories of a friend's father who used to lay a brick on the accelerator pedal of his bus when he rocked onto the freeway for the hour's run to St. Louis. He had invented the world's simplest cruise control to keep the world's simplest, and slowest, bus up to speed. Not exactly the stuff great vehicles are made of. Starcraft's pet project sounded a lot like the classic sow's ear/silk purse routine.

Wrong. First of all, VW was making a few improvements as that venerability built up. For one thing, the bus now has enough power and torque to actually move right along with the traffic, and that automatically makes the thing much more appealing; no longer does the VW-bus driver feel as well equipped as Willie Shoemaker trying to guard Bill Walton when it comes to facing everyday traffic. And hills.

And then, of course, there's the stuff Starcraft has spread around on the inside of the bus. Nothing revolutionary or even particularly innovative. The standard front seats have been reupholstered in a soft, pseudo-velvet fabric; two captains' chairs have been added in the traditional spots directly aft of the front seats; and a bench stretches across the far end of the box. And of course there is

Vehicle type: rear-engine, rear-wheel-drive, 7-passenger, 4-door van
Price as tested: $11,000 (estimated)
Engine type: flat-4, air-cooled, fuel injection
Displacement . . . . 120.2 cu in, 1970cc
Power (SAE net) . . . . 67 bhp @ 4200 rpm
Transmission 4-speed
Wheelbase . . . . 94.5 in
Length . . . . 177.4 in
Curb weight. . . . . 3200 lbs
EPA estimated fuel economy . . . . 17 mpg, city driving

carpeting everywhere. If something wasn't already covered with seat upholstery, Starcraft covered it with carpet. But unlike those conversions that go in for deep-pile shag or the high-low patterns so popular down at the discount carpet store, Starcraft selected a tight, low-pile carpeting very reminiscent of the quality carpeting found in BMWs. Very classy. In the don't-ask-why, it's-just-there department, there are real teak boards running front to rear along the tops of the windows. There are map pockets in strategic locations, overhead swiveling lights, a console, and a storage area with its own ice chest under the couch. All in all, definitely one of your better luxotouring buses.

But the real plus in this equation is the size of the package. The VW bus is small. It's easy to see out of, easy to maneuver, easy to park, and simply fun to drive. Combine that with a very luxurious and efficient custom interior and you have a van that's hard to beat.

By late summer, Starcraft said, its conversions should be available through VW dealers. The package is sold to the dealer for $2700 to $3200, depending on radios, wheels, and other oddments. Figure a dealer is going to tack on his 20 percent. That means you should be able to own the most luxurious small van on the block for around $11,000. That's a lot for a Volkswagen. But it's a lot of Volkswagen. —*Mike Knepper*

Although Volkswagen have announced a new and restyled Type 2 range it is unlikely to be available in right-hand-drive form until the end of the year, and it will be some time after that before caravan conversions can be produced.

There is, therefore, still a considerable market for motor caravans based on the VW Type 2 as we know it, and I have just spent a most enjoyable week testing the 1979 model **Devon** *Moonraker*.

With several new features, including the new Devon 'Double Top' elevating roof, the 1979 Moonraker is proving to be a best seller.

Comprehensively and luxuriously equipped, extremely well made, and with the optional 2-litre engine that was fitted to the test vehicle offering lively powerful road performance, the Moonraker is a most impressive multi-purpose caravan.

Starting at the top, the new elevating roof runs the full length of the vehicle. It is fitted with two solid base foam mattress bed sections which slide together forming a 6 ft. x 3 ft. 9 in. double bed.

The Moonraker is a genuine four-berth caravan, the upper bed offering the same standard of comfort and dimensions as the lower bed.

If you slide the two upper bed sections to opposite ends you have twin single beds for children, and in this configuration you have maximum headroom over the cooking/dining area.

To raise the top you simply release a couple of catches and push — it then swings up effortlessly on gas-filled struts.

The top is made of fibre-glass with a striped vinyl skirt coloured to match the van's paintwork, and the interior is fully lined with a carpet-type material. Ventilators are incorporated at each end of the elevating roof.

The lower bed is formed by pulling the rear bench seat out flat so that it joins up with the mattress cushion on top of the engine compartment.

If I had the money I would buy one !

Unique feature of the Devon Double Top is the solid base upper bed in the roof.

Plenty of storage space is provided. There is a wardrobe immediately behind the front passenger seat, storage cupboards along the offside of the vehicle, a roof locker, shelves, drawers, and space beneath the rear seat.

I particularly liked the action of the catches on the cupboards and drawers which are easy to operate — but secure enough to stop them flying open when cornering quickly.

The kitchen unit on the offside of the vehicle comprises a double burner gas cooker with grille, a stainless steel sink with electric water pump connected to a built-in 7-gallon water tank under the floor, and (as an extra cost option) an **Electrolux** 'fridge which works off gas or the vehicle's own 12-volt battery.

The refrigerator costs £177 extra (fitted) in place of the basic 'cool box', but it is well worth having for the serious camper.

It uses about 85 watts when running off the battery and it is useful to switch it to this mode when travelling so as to conserve gas.

The changeover is quite simple and when powered by gas the temperature setting is controllable.

The gas bottle is housed in a separate cupboard, vented to the outside.

Adjacent to the kitchen unit there is a louvred window for ventilation.

The table is stored beneath the roof locker and when in use is fixed on a single column leg which locates in a socket in the centre of the floor.

In addition to the rear bench seat there is a rear facing folding seat attached to the wardrobe, plus a single folding stool/seat which hooks on the side of the latter to provide seating for four around the table.

This folding side seat has no backrest so it is not ideal for use when travelling, and as a passenger carrier the Moonraker is limited to five (including the driver) facing forwards plus one facing rearwards.

Passengers found the rear bench seat to be very comfortable, and the cushioned area behind the seat (above the engine) proved to

be an ideal location for small children to sleep during a late night motorway journey.

The Moonraker has an external spare wheel mounting on the rear of the vehicle, which provides more interior space for the bed.

Attractive curtains in beige/orange pattern to match the cushions run smoothly on a continuous curtain track, and ha neat straps to fasten them when not in use.

There is a fluorescent interi light as well as the standard courtesy light in the cab.

Devon have added a de-luxe touch to the normal Kombi cab trim by providing seat covers in brown brushed nylon material, head restraints, and matching carpet throughout.

The carpet is removable; underneath there is a patterne vinyl floor covering over a polystyrene insulation layer which makes the caravan extra quiet and warm.

It all adds up to an extreme pleasing and practical mobile

ome, cleverly designed to make good use of the space, and built to particularly high standard of quality in all the fittings and furniture.

On the road the 2-litre Moonraker is equally impressive. The twin carb Type 4 engine delivers 70 bhp, offering performance which makes it much more enjoyable to drive than the 1500 cc version.

It will out-accelerate many cars and easily cruise at the legal limit on motorways, regardless of headwinds or hills.

The 0–60 mph time is 21 seconds, top speed is about 80 mph, and the 30–50 mph acceleration in top gear takes only 13.2 seconds. From 50 to 70 mph in top requires just over 20 seconds.

Performance generally is as good as that of a Polo, and indeed the 2-litre caravan is nippier than quite a few saloons up to 1100 cc.

Overtaking presents no problems

The Kombi cab is made more luxurious by the addition of carpet and brushed nylon seat covers.

Behind the passenger's seat is a wardrobe (fitted with doors both sides) and a rear facing folding seat.

and I found it just as easy to drive as a car, and capable of averaging practically the same speeds on a typical journey.

I have always found the 1600 cc Type 2 a little more tiring on long journeys because you have to think about headwind and gradient before overtaking.

With 40% more power the 2-litre has a much greater reserve to deal with such situations and you can make quite rapid progress without having to keep your foot hard on the floor.

According to the Government figures the 2-litre engine is also more economical at a steady speed. My overall average fuel consumption was 22 mpg including a lot of 70 mph motorway travelling with five adults and two children on board.

This is excellent for a motor caravan, but with the present fuel supply difficulties the tank capacity of only 12 gallons rather limits the range.

The 2-litre engine is an extra cost option. If you choose the low-powered 1600 engine you save £423, but included with the bigger engine are radial ply tyres

and a brake servo so that I think the package is well worth having.

Braking and roadholding are pretty good, the **Phoenix 185 SR 14** (reinforced) radials on the test vehicle gave reassuring grip in the wet and although cross winds were noticeable I was happy to maintain maximum cruising speed in gusty conditions.

The padded rim steering wheel helps to reduce the impression of driving a van, and the driving position really is comfortable.

Heating and ventilation are up to saloon car standards, the massive 'glove box' is useful for storing maps and everything else you might need in the cab, and visibility is excellent.

Reversing lights and mud-flaps are fitted, but there is no demister for the rear window. Twin door mirrors are, of course, standard.

As tested, the Moonraker with Double Top elevating roof, refrigerator, 2-litre engine, radial tyres and brake servo, costs nearly £7,300.

The flat roof 1600 Moonraker price starts at £6,225.

Devon Conversions Ltd supply various other optional extras such as a drive-away tent, hammock bunks for the cab, fire extinguisher (which in my opinion ought to be standard), side step for the sliding door entrance, and melamine crockery set.

Everyone who travelled in the Moonraker was astonished at how much equipment and furniture there is, yet at the same time it remains roomy and spacious inside.

We were also amazed at how effortlessly it covered the ground from A to B.

Notwithstanding the fact that the Type 2 will be replaced next year, Devon have done an excellent job with the '79 Moonraker and if I had the money to spend I would have absolutely no hesitation in buying one !

The Electrolux refrigerator can be switched from gas to electric and has adjustable shelves and an ice-box.

The Fellows gas cooker has two burners (with simmer control) plus a grille, and folding stainless steel splash guard.

PERFORMANCE

Load of two people plus ½ tank petrol. Mean of two runs, corrected speedo, fine conditions.

Acceleration:

0–40 mph	8.7 sec.	
0–50 mph	14.3 sec.	
0–60 mph	21.0 sec.	
0–70 mph	32.0 sec.	
30–50 mph	(3rd gear)	8.9 sec.
30–50 mph	(4th gear)	13.2 sec.
50–70 mph	(4th gear)	20.8 sec.

Maximum speeds:

1st gear	25 mph.
2nd gear	40 mph.
3rd gear	61 mph.
4th gear	80 mph.

Dimensions:

Overall length	15 ft. 3 in.
Width	5 ft. 8 in.
Height	6 ft. 11½ in. (roof lowered).
Weight	9 ft. 7½ in. (roof raised)

The dining table is supported by a single column leg which fits in a socket in the floor.

The rear bench seat can be pulled out to make a 6ft. long double bed

Extra storage compartments along the offside of the vehicle and in the roof.

External spare wheel mounting. The installation includes a fitted vinyl cover and relocated number plate.

Based on the versatile VW Microbus 2000, this mobile home is attractive and driveable

Jurgens Auto

Motorised caravans are a highly-specialised category of vehicle — and one of the best was conceived and designed right here in South Africa, using the faithful VW Kombi as a base.

Jurgens Caravans, of Kempton Park, Transvaal, initiated and built the first Auto-Villa in 1973, and since then more than 1 000 units have been built and sold.

Not only that, but this attractive mobile home is also built under licence in Germany and Brazil by the famous Karmann Organisation, designer and builder of many specialised vehicles of international repute. Herr Wilhelm Karmann saw the Auto-Villa on a visit to South Africa a few years ago, and was so impressed that he asked for the right to build it overseas, Jurgens reports.

FOUR-BERTH MODEL

The current Auto-Villa falls in the "Brilliant Series" of Jurgens caravans, and features a Luton extension over the cab roof which houses a double bed. It is a four-berth caravan built on the VW Kombi chassis, with 2000L Microbus cab, controls and machinery.

The caravan body itself is a remarkable achievement. It is patterned on the traditional Jurgens designs, yet blends with the Kombi to form an attractive and homologous vehicle.

LIVING FACILITIES

One of its endearing features is a walk-through ability from the cab to the caravan area — entering into another world as you do so. The design is magnificent, making the fullest use of every centimetre of space to create a comfortable and self-contained living area, complete with kitchenette and cloakroom compartment.

Continued overleaf

KEY FIGURES

Maximum speed	111,5 km/h
1 km sprint	46,7 seconds
Terminal speed	97,0 km/h
Fuel tank capacity	112 litres
	(2 tanks, 56 litres each)
Litres/100 km at 80	12,8
Optimum fuel range at 80	874 km
Engine revs per km	2 020
National list price	R9 200

Villa motorised caravan

The rear-end dinette set up for daytime use (above), and converted as a couch or double bed (below) with the table folded down.

The cab and controls are pure Microbus, with walk-through to the living space at rear. (Below): The kitchen area behind the passenger seat, with stove and wash-up opened for use.

(Below): Looking into the cloakroom from the aisle.

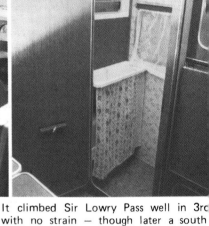

test — Jurgens Auto-Villa motorised caravan

Walking rearward from the cab one can stand at full height in the 1,9 metre-high interior. First on the left is the door of the cloakroom, equipped with mirror, cabinet, washbasin and footbath, and with room enough to hold a chemical toilet unit, if required. Aft of the cloakroom is the 85-litre gas/electric (12 Volt) refrigerator.

At right is the kitchenette, with sink unit and two-burner stove with griller, plus overhead cupboards, and aft of this the side door, which is insect-screened and has a slide-down window.

SPECIAL EQUIPMENT

In the rear end of the vehicle is the dinette, with seating for four to six persons and a removable table. This dinette converts into sleeping berths — either a transverse double or two long-itudinal singles. The other double berth above the cab is reached by a removable step ladder. There are plenty of cup-boards, storage lockers and shelves, and twin gas bottles are housed in a ventilated floor-level cupboard.

Special equipment includes 12-volt electric pump drawing water for wash-basin and sink from four 10-litre storage bottles, roller blinds in all the windows, three 12-volt fluorescent lights, and a crested Jurgens crockery set for six people.

Removable Van Dyck carpets are fitted, and an external sun canopy is provided. A free-standing side tent is available as an option. The refriger-ator can be operated by gas or 12-volt DC.

The whole caravan section is con-structed of light and strong extruded aluminium frames with aluminium ex-ternal cladding, polystyrene insulation, and the interior is trimmed with imported Taiwan hardwood veneer — chosen because of its resistance to warping.

RESIDENTIAL TEST

A young CAR staff family (two chil-dren) lived in the test vehicle during a week-end tour through the Western Cape, and found it a delightful holiday facility.

The housewife member of the family reports: "We found the Auto-Villa very pleasant to drive — even the average woman can manage it quite well in traffic.

It climbed Sir Lowry Pass well in 3rd with no strain — though later a south east headwind forced us to change down to 2nd and the high-sided vehicle took a buffeting from the gusty wind when it came from the side.

"The interior is spacious and comfort able, and with the roof and side vents there is plenty of on-site ventilation in hot weather.

"Sleeping was snug and trouble-free even though it turned pretty cool one night."

Only snag — the vehicle's battery went flat with the frequent use of taps and lights, and jump leads had to be used to start it at the end of the stay!

PERFORMANCE

Mechanically, the Auto-Villa is a Micro bus 2000L, with 2-litre motor, four speed manual transmission and big radials on 14-inch wheels. At one time an automatic transmission version was offered as well but current production is manual-shift only. The vehicle is higher and heavier than the Kombi, with nearly 5 m² of gross frontal area and 1 570 kg of body mass.

ACCELERATION

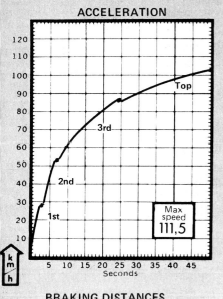

PERFORMANCE

PERFORMANCE FACTORS:
Power/mass (W/kg) net 32,5
Frontal area (m^2) 4,94
Km/h per 1 000 r/min (top) . . . 29,7

INTERIOR NOISE LEVELS:

	Mech.	Wind	Road
Idling	.56,0	—	—
60	.75,0	—	—
80	.79,5	80,5	84,0
100	—	—	—
Average dBA at 80 81,0			

ACCELERATION (seconds):
0—60 9,6
0—80 19,1
0—100 . . . . —
1 km sprint 46,7

OVERTAKING ACCELERATION:

	3rd	Top
40—60	.6,7	11,9
60—80	.8,8	17,7
80—100	—	—

(Measured in seconds, to true speeds, averaging runs both ways on a level road, car carrying test crew of two and standard test equipment)

MAXIMUM SPEED (km/h):
True speed 111,5
Speedometer reading 119
Calibration:

Indicated:	60	70	80	90	100
True speed:	54	63,5	73	82,5	92

FUEL CONSUMPTION (litres/100 km):
60 9,8
70 11,1
80 12,8
90 14,5
100 16,4

(Stated in litres per 100 kilometres, based on fuel economy figures recorded at true speeds)

BRAKING TEST:
From 90 km/h
Best stop 3,8
Worst stop 4,3
Average 4,02

(Measured in seconds with stops from true speeds at 30—second intervals on a good bitumenised surface)

GRADIENTS IN GEARS:
Low gear . . . . 1 in 3,3
2nd gear . . . . 1 in 5,3
3rd gear . . . . .1 in 9,7
Top gear . . . . 1 in 18,9

(Tabulated from Tapley (x gravity) readings, car carrying test crew of two and standard test equipment)

GEARED SPEEDS (km/h):
Low gear 29,0
2nd gear 53,3
3rd gear 87,1
Top gear 124,7

(Calculated at engine peak r/min — 4 200)

ENGINE SPEED

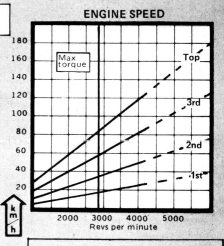

IMPERIAL DATA

ACCELERATION (seconds):
0—60 . . . . —
MAXIMUM SPEED (m-p-h):
True Speed 69,3
FUEL ECONOMY (m-p-g):
50 m-p-h 22,1
60 m-p-h 18,0

GRADIENT ABILITY

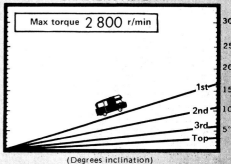

Max torque 2 800 r/min

(Degrees inclination)

CRUISING AT 90

Mech noise level . . . . .81,5 dBA
0—90 through gears . . . . . 29,6 seconds
Litres/100 km at 90 14,5
Optimum fuel range at 90 . . . . 773 km
Braking from 90 . . . . 4,0 seconds
Maximum gradient (top) . . . . 1 in 31,2
Speedometer error . . . . 8% over
Speedo at true 90 97,5
Odometer error . . . . .2 % under
Engine r/min at 90 . . . . 3 030

BRAKING DISTANCES

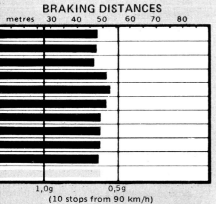

1,0g   0,5g
(10 stops from 90 km/h)

NOISE VALUES

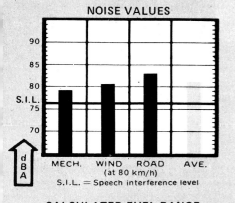

MECH. WIND ROAD AVE.
(at 80 km/h)
S.I.L. = Speech interference level

CALCULATED FUEL RANGE
(km)

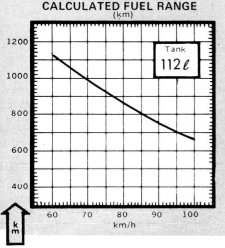

Tank 112 ℓ

STEADY-SPEED FUEL CONSUMPTION
(litres/100 km at true speeds)

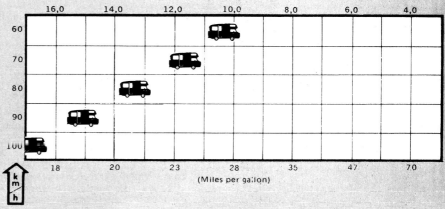

(Miles per gallon)

In performance tests it showed Kombi-style character, leaping forward from rest with the nose rising. It reached 80 in 19,1 seconds and 90 inside 30 seconds, going on to a level-road maximum of 111,5 km/h. Because it does not reach 100 easily, we were unable to do tests up to that figure, and braking, for instance, was tested from 90.

In maximum-effort test runs there was much vibration from doors, crockery and equipment, but everything is properly packed and fastened and there were no breakages, even in full-scale braking tests.

ECONOMY AND RANGE

In spite of its bulk, the Auto-Villa is a pretty steady top-gear cruiser, running easily and with fair directional stability at 80 to 85 km/h. At this cruising speed it returns between 12 and 13 litres/100 km, according to our steady-speed tests, though we would expect this to be somewhat higher if climbing and gearshifting are taken into account. On a long open-road run, Caravan Magazine recorded 13,3 litres/100 km with a similar model.

To give it the necessary cruising range, the Auto-Villa is equipped with twin 56-litre tanks on either side of the engine compartment, giving it a total of 112 litres. This gives it impressive range — up to 900 km on a tankful, depending on speed and terrain. At todays prices it would cost something over R60 to fill those two tanks with regular-grade fuel, but this is a fair cost for a journey of that length, by caravan standards.

BRAKING AND NOISE

The boosted disc/drum braking system of the Microbus is well able to cope with the bulk of the motorised caravan: it stopped consistently and well from 90 km/h in a series of 10 stops, averaging just over 4 seconds per stop. No skids, no overheating. This promises well for touring in mountain country, though we would recommend using the gearbox in long descents to ease the strain on the brakes.

Interior noise levels are Kombi-style, exaggerated a bit by the open body, but not offensive. Even road rumble is within permissible limits.

HANDLING AND RIDE

The capable torsion-bar suspension of the Kombi is well suited to the Auto-Villa, and copes magnificently with the big

Rear view of the Autovilla, showing twin fuel fillers above the engine hatch.

caravan body. It rides well over bad surfaces, without being sloppy or clumsy.

Handling generally is surprisingly light and manageable — far better than we expected — under low-speed conditions. The driver has ample vision by way of outside mirrors and see-through at rear, and the vehicle itself is a little longer than a VW Beetle.

It has high sides, however, and we found it would develop a rocking tendency in sidewinds at cruising speeds, though it cornered surprisingly cleanly and with no alarming degree of body roll.

PROFESSIONAL FINISH

A thorough inspection and trial of the Auto-Villa leaves one filled with admiration for the high professional standards of the designers and manufacturers. It is a magnificent vehicle, in both concept and execution. It even has special and attractive full wheel trims with the Jurgens crest.

We would recommend that the access hatch between the living quarters and the engine be made of steel instead of wood — particularly as the big fuel tanks are in the engine compartment — and that a fire extinguisher be fitted in the cab as a practical safety feature.

Also, an extra battery could be fitted in the engine compartment (there is plenty of space for it) to cope with the electrical load of on-site domestic use.

SUMMARY

This is South Africa's most unusual vehicle: a combination of car and caravan, and a touring vehicle par excellence.

It is not everyone's idea of motoring — particularly as it costs more than R9 000 — but as a specialised vehicle in a specialised field it is a world-beater, and pretty fair value.

SPECIFICATIONS

ENGINE:
Cylinders . . .4 horizontally opposed, rear mounted
Fuel supply . twin Solex carburettors
Bore/stroke . . . . . 94,0/71,0 mm
Cubic capacity. . . . . . 1 970 cm³
Compression ratio. . . . . . . 7,3 to 1
Valve gear . . . . .o-h-v, pushrods
Ignition. . . . . coil and distributor
Main bearings . . . . four
Fuel requirement . 93 -octane Coast, 87 -octane Reef
Cooling. . . . . . air, blower-driven

ENGINE OUTPUT:
Max power I.S.O. (kW) 51
Power peak (r/min) 4 200
Max permissible r/min 4 400
Max torque (N.m.) 143
Torque peak (r/min) 2 800

TRANSMISSION:
Forward speeds . . . . four
Gearshift . . . . .floor
Low gear . . . . 3,78 to 1
2nd gear . . . . 2,06 to 1
3rd gear . . . . 1,26 to 1
Top gear . . . . 0,88 to 1
Reverse gear . . . . 3,78 to 1
Final drive . 4,57 to 1 (4,02 overall)
Drive wheels . . . . rear

WHEELS AND TYRES:
Road wheels . . . . pressed steel discs
Rim width 5,5J
Tyres . . . . 185 SR 14 radials

BRAKES:
Front . . . . .discs
Rear . . . . .drums
Pressure regulation . . . dual circuits
Boosting . . . . .vacuum servo
Handbrake position . . . . . in fascia

STEERING:
Type . . . . worm and roller
Lock to lock . . . . 3,0 turns
Turning circle . . . 10 metres approx

MEASUREMENTS:
Length overall . . . . .4,810 m
Width overall . . . . .2,050 m
Height overall . . . . .2,410 m
Wheelbase . . . . .2,400 m
Front track . . . . .1,395 m
Rear track . . . . .1,455 m
Ground clearance . . . . . .0,200 m
Licensing mass . . . . . . 1 570 kg

SUSPENSION:
Front . . . . independent
Type . . . .torsion bars, stabiliser bar
Rear . . . . independent
Type . torsion bars, dual-jointed half axles.

CAPACITIES:
Seating . . . . 2—6
Fuel tank. . .2 x 56 litres (112 litres)
Utility space . . unrestricted caravan-style lockers and cupboards.

TEST CAR FROM:
Jurgens Caravans and Trailers, Kempton Park, Transvaal.

CARAVAN SPECIFICATIONS

ACCOMMODATION:
Child-sized double berth in overcab extension, dinette, converting to one double or two single berths. Storage space in cupboards and lockers. Walk-through to cab.

KITCHENETTE:
Defy twin-burner stove with griller, Single-bowl stainless steel sink with electric water pump. Wall-mounted crockery cabinet with six-person Jurgens crockery set. Electrolux 85-litre gas/12 volt electric refrigerator.

CLOAKROOM:
Wash handbasin with electric water pump, vanity compartment, fluorescent light, shower head, recessed floor with drain plug for shower.

LIGHTING:
Two fluorescent 12-volt lights in caravan, and one in cloakroom.

SPECIAL FITTINGS:
Roller blinds in all caravan windows. Curtain screen between cab and caravan. Removable Van Dyck carpets. Canvas sun porch. Four 10-litre water storage bottles. Two 4,5 kg gas cylinders.

WARRANTIES:
Caravan warranties by Jurgens Caravans. Mechanical features subject to normal VW warranty, and servicing by VW dealerships world-wide.